R

ok

Peasant and Proletarian

Peasant and Proletarian

The Working Class of Moscow in the Late Nineteenth Century

Robert Eugene Johnson

Leicester University Press 1979

First published in Great Britain in 1979
by Leicester University Press

ISBN 0 7185 1185 9

First published in the USA in 1979
by Rutgers University Press

To L. Z. C. J.
faithful friend and critic

Contents

List of Figures

List of Tables

Acknowledgments

I am deeply indebted to a number of friends and colleagues for the advice, criticism, and encouragement they have provided during the preparation of this book. In the earlier stages of the project, several of these individuals raised new questions, drew my attention to significant sources, and helped me to clarify my objectives. Later, as I labored through successive drafts and revisions, I came to realize how easily an author can become blind to his shortcomings. Once again, a number of friends and colleagues came forward to offer suggestions and criticism, aiding me in sharpening my argument and simplifying its presentation. I am especially grateful to Harvey Dyck, Nancy Howell, Martin Klein, Claire LaVigna, William Rosenberg, Jeremiah Schneiderman, Ronald Suny, and Reginald Zelnik, all of whom offered valuable advice at different stages of my work. I owe a particular debt of gratitude to Walter Pintner, who supervised the dissertation from which this book grew, for his patience and encouragement.

My research in the libraries and archives of the Soviet Union was carried out under the auspices of the International Research Exchanges Board, whose support I gratefully acknowledge; I am grateful, too, to the many Soviet historians, archivists, and librarians who helped to make my stay productive, and to Valerii Ivanovich Bovykin of Moscow State University, who was an extremely cooperative and supportive advisor. I am also indebted to the Foreign Area Fellowship Program, which enabled me to spend six months working in the splendid Helsinki University Library; to Erindale College of the University of Toronto, which provided a sabbatical leave during which I was able to complete the manuscript; and to the Humanities and Social Sciences Research Committee and the Centre for Russian and East European Studies, both of the University of Toronto, for their support of this project. I have been greatly assisted by the library staffs of the University of Toronto, the University of Illinois, Cornell University, and Helsinki University.

I wish to thank the editors of the *Slavic Review*, *Russian History*, and the University of Illinois Press for allowing me to include, in revised form, portions of my articles: "Peasant Migration and the Russian Working Class," *Slavic Review* 35 (1976); "Strikes in Moscow, 1880–1900," *Russian History* 5 (1978); and "Family Relations and the Rural-Urban Nexus," in David Ransel, editor, *The Family in Imperial Russia* (Urbana: University of Illinois Press, 1978). I am also extremely grateful to the editorial staff of Rutgers University Press for the efficient and considerate treatment accorded to my manuscript at every stage.

Having thanked these individuals and institutions for the suggestions, criticism, and material support I have received, I must acknowledge a very different debt to my wife, Laura. She too offered specific suggestions and material support, but her greatest contribution was on another level altogether. When I was confused, she offered good sense; when I was discouraged, she gave me reassurance; when I was impossible, she answered me with patience and encouragement. I have been fortunate indeed.

Peasant and Proletarian

Map 1. Counts of Moscow province.

Introduction

Think of historical evidence as pieces of a jigsaw puzzle. Imagine that half of a puzzle's pieces have been lost and that the remaining ones are mixed together with parts of several other puzzles. Into this jumbled mass a determined problem solver can probably introduce a degree of order. Some of the pieces will fit together; some may be rejected as part of a different set; some may forever tantalize the imagination. The main task, however, is to assemble the bits and pieces to produce a coherent picture, and this requires imagination, creative inference, and some unifying idea or hypothesis. This metaphor illustrates many of the challenges and difficulties of the historian's craft: hypotheses, definitions, and a focused imagination are needed to give structure and direction to the fragmented evidence of the past.

For almost one hundred years, Russian labor historians have sought structure and direction in Marx's definition of a proletariat. This is not to suggest that all labor historians have been followers of Marx but rather that his terminology and conceptual schema have provided guidance for many varieties of historical study. Even authors who disputed the relevance of Marxism to Russian experience have often phrased their objections in the terms Marx himself used: *means of production, alienation, class-consciousness.* Their search for relevant evidence and the ways in which they assembled such evidence have been in large measure defined by writings whose conclusions they dispute.

The basic outlines of the Marxian thesis are so familiar that they need not be repeated. Their application to Russian conditions, however, has been the subject of violent disputes and polemics for over a century. Russia one hundred years ago was a peasant society ruled by an autocratic monarchy. It was entering a period of widespread economic changes. The fetters of serfdom had been loosened (though not entirely abolished), so that a small but increasing proportion of the population was finding its livelihood in mining, manufacturing, and commerce, which together

3

Map. 2.   Districts of Moscow city, 1897.

4

made up a rapidly increasing proportion of the national economy. The social implications of this development were a source of great concern to contemporaries, and they prompted the first application of the Marxian schema to Russia.

Orthodox Marxists pointed to fundamental changes in the peasant economy in the years after the Emancipation of 1861. Rural society, as Lenin argued in *The Development of Capitalism in Russia*, was in a process of polarization in which land and livestock came to be concentrated in the hands of a prosperous minority. The majority was gradually stripped of its assets and became dependent for its living on the sale of its own labor. Wage labor took many forms, but all were exploitative. Eventually peasants were left with no means of survival other than their labor. The conditions of wage labor, more than the fact of impoverishment, decisively altered the peasants' outlook. Alienated from the means of production, they were transformed into a new social class that was defined by the material conditions of their existence: a proletariat. The final step in the abandonment of the village and its traditions was factory work, which freed the individual from patriarchal dependency and instilled in him a new sense both of his own worth and of the interests he shared with other workers. This class-conscious proletariat, once united, became a social force that would overthrow its oppressors.[1]

This view of the Russian working class was endorsed with varying degrees of conviction by Social Democrats at the turn of the century. Many who were convinced that capitalism must come to Russia emphasized nonetheless the backwardness of the mass of workers and the isolation of the skilled, class-conscious minority. Various Marxist authors disagreed over the extent of Russia's capitalist transformation, over the relative strength of the democratic bourgeoisie and the semifeudal landowning class, and over the tactics that revolutionary socialists should follow.

To all of these authors, rural society constituted a yoke of outmoded customs and restrictions from which peasants were struggling to free themselves. If some factory workers retained land allotments or other ties to the village, Marxists regarded this as a relic of the past, a transitory stage in the process of proletarianization. They emphasized the emergence of a hereditary proletariat (especially in mechanized industry) and the higher level of education and sophistication characteristic of skilled workers. Workers in such fields as metallurgy and machine building were described by these authors as the most hardened proletarian cadres.

Other observers, however, disputed even the Marxists' long-term prognosis and drew opposite conclusions about the nature of the Russian working class. The populists of the 1880s and 1890s insisted that Russian social and economic formations were distinctly different from those that Marx had described in England and Western Europe and that they presaged a very different future. In this view, both the Russian worker's retention of agricultural ties and the survival of the village land commune were evidence of Russia's uniqueness; there was by the 1890s no true proletariat and, given the right combination of circumstances, there might never be one. Some saw the primitive socialism of the commune as a potential starting point for the creation of a just and equitable new society through which Russia could avoid the pitfalls of capitalist development.

The revolutions of 1917, far from ending this debate, provided more fuel for the fire. Lenin's party, having achieved power, could claim with some justification that its analysis had been vindicated. Its rivals and critics, however, have consistently challenged this claim. Yes, they acknowledged, power had been attained, but was it really proletarian power, or was the Bolshevik victory rather a fruit of Russia's backwardness? Were the party's followers a disciplined, class-conscious force or a turbulent half-peasant mass susceptible to demagogic appeals? If the Marxian view was sound, why did "proletarian" revolution occur in Russia, the most backward of the European powers, rather than in England or Germany? In attempting to answer questions such as these, Soviet and non-Soviet historians have returned repeatedly to the prerevolutionary decades and to the composition, experience, and outlook of the Russian working class.

Soviet historians have refined but not fundamentally altered the arguments put forward by Lenin at the turn of the century. They point to the rapid growth of Russian industry in the 1890s, to the exceptionally high degree of concentration of industry in enormous enterprises, to the participation of second- and third-generation seasoned worker cadres in the labor movement and in revolutionary struggles.[2] Many non-Soviet authors have found these arguments unconvincing and countered with the claim that worker militancy was an outgrowth of inexperience. Russia's rapid industrialization, by this argument, uprooted peasants from familiar surroundings and left them confused and disoriented. Isolated from the rest of society and unable to formulate a coherent solution to their discontents, they reverted to traditional patterns of violent, localized upheavals. In times of general crisis, they were receptive to the most extreme appeals, which were not necessarily those of the Bolsheviks.[3]

Throughout this debate, there has been a tendency to depict city and countryside as polar opposites and to use the notions of a pure proletarian or a pure peasant as a yardstick to measure empirical reality. Most observers have recognized that many flesh-and-blood individuals fell somewhere between the two ideal types, but they have, nonetheless, usually seen the existence of these mixed types as unstable and transitory—one author even having used the word *schizophrenic*. Any individual, it seemed, would naturally be drawn to one extreme or the other.[4] Soviet historians characteristically describe this process in dialectical terms: quantitative changes in the socioeconomic order intensify its contradictions until qualitative changes occur, and new social formations (classes) are the result.[5] Non-Soviet writers, on the other hand, have often tried to delineate stages of development whereby peasants were transformed into permanent factory workers,[6] reasoning that, if only a minority of workers had gone the whole route, many more had started out and could be expected to complete the transition at some point in the future. They have, for example, described those who still carried agrarian attitudes and grievances as new recruits recently uprooted from the countryside.[7]

Implicitly, Marxists and non-Marxists have been comparing the Russian workers to those of England or Western Europe, where the road from village to factory was usually a one-way street. Can such a comparison adequately reflect the peculiarities of Russian development? To answer this question, one must return to the jigsaw puzzle and test the hypothesis against the available pieces of evidence.

When I began doing research for this study, one of my first steps was to compare the evidence various authors had marshaled in support of "pro" or "anti" proletarian interpretations of the Russian labor movement. I was struck by the number of apparent anomalies and contradictions that turned up on both sides of the debate. A Soviet historian, writing of the 1870s, could disparage the backward, "elemental" qualities of textile workers and extol the more mature or "conscious" metal workers yet also admit that the former group was the leading force in labor unrest of the period.[8] A critic of the proletarianization thesis could describe Saint Petersburg textile workers of the 1890s as isolated, suspicious, and prone to "peasantlike destructive rebellions which lacked clear purpose" yet on the very next page insist that the massive, peaceful, highly coordinated textile strike of May–June 1896, which brought together thirty thousand workers from more than twenty factories, was organized solely by rank-and-file workers.[9]

These examples could be multiplied many times over. Many of the landmarks of the Russian labor movement, such as the famous Morozov strike in Orekhovo (Vladimir province) in 1885, occurred deep in the countryside among workers who were still closely bound to peasant traditions. It seems that the consciousness and discipline of prerevolutionary workers was often highly developed in the darkest, most backward corners of Russia, but neither the proponents nor the critics of proletarianization have explained why this should have been so.

In this study, I have tried to explain this anomaly by examining conditions in Moscow city and province, the center of Russia's oldest and most populous industrial region. I have sought to determine whether Moscow's workers retained significant connections to peasant society, whether such ties had discernible effects on specific aspects of their lives (e.g., migration patterns, family composition), how industrialization influenced traditional peasant culture and was influenced by it, and how these influences affected the course of Moscow's and Russia's development.

I chose to study Moscow not just because of its significance in the national economy but because of the many conditions and problems it shared with neighboring provinces. In particular, Moscow epitomizes a distinctively Russian pattern of economic development in which the forces of industrialization constantly interacted with a surrounding peasant environment. The same interaction occurred in almost every other Russian industrial center, but the process stands out more sharply in Moscow as a result of several distinctive local features. The coming of modern industry to Moscow in the late nineteenth century was the culmination of almost two centuries of more or less steady development during which factory workers were continuously recruited from an essentially homogeneous peasantry drawn from within a narrow radius. These factors make Moscow an ideal locale for studying the impact of industrial experience on Russian peasants and for examining some of the peculiarities of the Russian factory system.

I have limited the study to the years 1880–1900, a period which has often been described as a watershed in Moscow's, and Russia's, development. My choice of these particular dates was partly arbitrary, partly pragmatic. Two essential features of the period were the industrial boom of the mid-1890s (roughly 1894–1900) and the emergence of a large-scale strike movement in two main waves (1885–87 and 1895–98). The first attempts at systematic Marxist propaganda and agitation among workers occurred in this period, especially in the years 1894–97. None of these trends, it may be noted, coincides precisely with the years 1880–1900, but none can be properly understood unless it is compared with conditions and developments of previous years. The economic boom of the nineties is all the more impressive alongside the sluggish or stagnant economy of the early eighties; the militancy of Moscow's workers during the two waves of strikes can best be measured against the quiescence of previous years.

As a starting point for the study, 1880 marks the beginning of an industrial depression that lasted for almost six years. The first large-scale, systematic compilation of information about Moscow's factory workers—the provincial *zemstvo's* multivolume survey of sanitary conditions at every major factory in the province—began in 1879/80. In the political realm, the assassination of Emperor Alexander II in March 1881 marked the end of an era: his assassins lost the hope of revolution through conspiracy; his successors saw a trend toward conservative and repressive policies as the surest way to restore a shaken monarchy.

The year 1900 also marks a turning point in the national economy, the beginning, once again, of a decisive downward trend. For the labor movement, too, rates of activity dropped off sharply from previous years as strikes took on a more defensive character. For the radical intelligentsia, the movement of agitation and propaganda had reached its nadir by 1900–1901. New hopes were raised by student demonstrations in March 1901 and by the preparations for publication of the newspaper *Iskra*, whose goal was to unify the forces of Social Democracy throughout the Russian empire. Here too it seems evident that one era was ending and another beginning. At the very same time, the Moscow police were about to embark on the new and dangerous experiment of *police socialism*, which would be later described as Zubatovshchina (from the name of the Moscow Okhranka chief, Sergei Zubatov). All of these developments were to have serious consequences for the lives and behavior of Moscow's working class, for their net effect was to disrupt many of the patterns and trends of the 1880s and 1890s. For this reason, the post-1900 period belongs to a future study, but I do not adhere rigidly to the dividing line of 1900. When important evidence such as the Moscow municipal census of 1902 crosses the stated boundary, I have usually included it in my investigation.

Of the seven principal chapters of this study, only one is directly concerned with the pattern of strikes or collective unrest. Throughout the study, however, an underlying theme is the workers' ability (or inability) to act together for common ends. In considering the characteristic traits of the working class, its organizational forms, and its relations with the rest of Russian society, the study indirectly examines the workers' outlook on the world and seeks explanations for the patterns of worker collective behavior.

Chapter One

The Pattern of Moscow's Industrialization

At the end of the nineteenth century, Moscow was the greatest manufacturing center in the Russian empire. Nonetheless, the pace of industrial growth and innovation was somewhat slower there than in other parts of the Russian empire. In the geographic distribution of its industries, the use of technology, the patterns of entrepreneurship and management, and the balance between light and heavy industry, Moscow had a heritage that continued to shape, and in some ways retard, its development. This was a heritage of peasant custom but also of autocratic initiative. Other regions of Russia shared in this same legacy that helped to make the nation's economic development distinct from Western patterns; yet the forces of tradition and historical continuity varied in strength from region to region. In Moscow they were especially pronounced, for industry expanded through slow accretion and agglomeration. Elsewhere in the empire, industrialization was (more abrupt and discontinuous, influenced by external forces (e.g., government initiatives, foreign investment). Despite mechanization, diversification of output, and concentration of production in large enterprises, much of Moscow's industrial growth took place at old, established factories, in areas where textile and other manufacturing had been carried on for almost two hundred years.

Industrial Moscow in the Era of Serfdom

The earliest Russian factories were created at the command of the tsar. In the eighteenth and nineteenth centuries, rulers and

11

officials tried repeatedly to impose new tasks or otherwise to control the course of industrial development. They were limited, however, by the habits and propensities of the Russian people and by the legacy of earlier rulers: a centralized state apparatus accustomed to close regulation of almost every facet of national life, an entrepreneurial class whose outlook and habits were predominantly conservative and passive, and a peasantry still bound to the soil and the village commune. Despite numerous attempts to imitate Western models, the industrial society that was created was sui generis Russian. Moscow's industries epitomized this trend.

Moscow's importance as an industrial center dates from the beginning of the eighteenth century. Commerce and artisan activities had, of course, flourished there in previous centuries, but in the reign of Peter I, large-scale manufactories were built to serve the needs of the state. Moscow city became a center of light manufacturing, with the woolen and linen industries playing an especially prominent role. Although the techniques of production were primitive, some enterprises employed as many as a thousand workers.[1]

Some of the early "factories" operated under direct state supervision, whereas others were granted loans, monopolies, and other incentives. Although such close governmental involvement was common to many European states in the era of mercantilism, Moscow's enterprises, from the moment of their creation, bore a distinctly Russian stamp. In Western Europe, factories relied on the wage labor of individuals who had severed (or were in the process of severing) ties with agriculture, but in Russia the predominant pattern was compulsory labor by peasants who remained legally bonded to the soil of their native villages. When the difficulties of recruiting and retaining wage laborers proved intractable, Peter I's government began to "assign" (*pripisyvat'*) serf labor to industry. Later, in the 1730s and 1740s, previously free categories of wage workers (artisans, vagabonds, retired soldiers) were permanently bound to their place of employment and assimilated to the status of serfs.[2]

In the later decades of the eighteenth century, two more types of serf labor became prominent in the Moscow region. One was the "votchinal" factory (from *votchina*, literally "patrimony," a landed estate belonging to a member of the nobility) at which manorial serfs were required to perform nonagricultural labor service for their owners.[3] The second was the system known as *otkhodnichestvo* ("going away"), in which peasants temporarily departed from their native villages in search of employment. To do so, they needed the permission of their lord (or of the village authorities in the case of state peasants). They were required to return home at regular intervals and to turn over a substantial portion of their earnings as quitrent (*obrok*). Some of these migrants engaged in trade or itinerant crafts; some became barge haulers or carters; and some were hired to work in "factories" or artisan establishments; but this in no way altered their legal status as serfs.[4]

Thus, whether or not they received a wage, the industrial laborers of the eighteenth century were enmeshed in a system of noneconomic sanctions and permanently tied to the peasant economy. In some cases a wage contract was negotiated directly between a serf owner and an employer, with wages paid not to the workers but to their lord. Even when the workers arranged their own contracts, the employer's authority was overshadowed by the power of the serf owner, who could arbitrarily recall his peasants to the countryside. Employers and serf owners both relied on the power of the state to enforce their demands on the workers: through a system of internal passports the police were able to control movement through the country, and anyone who departed from a factory without permission could be forcibly returned. The industrial system was fused with the institutions, habits, and traditions of an enserfed peasantry, and even those who departed (*otkhodniki*) normally left their families behind on the land to live a life no different from that of other peasants.[5]

The votchinal system was especially widespread in the woolen industry, while wage-paying peasant workshops predominated in silk manufacturing. In both of these industries, Moscow province was Russia's greatest center of production in the eighteenth century.

Toward the beginning of the nineteenth century, the older factories began to encounter competition from cottage industry (*kustar'*), in which peasants worked at home, often for piecework wages. This form of production was especially prominent in the cotton industry, which was just beginning to flourish in Russia at this time. Soviet historians have correctly emphasized the capitalistic nature of the *kustar'* industries: the producers' dependence on middlemen; the specialization of production and division of labor among producing units.[6] This form of production, which was concentrated in Moscow and a few adjacent provinces of central Russia, made industrial or semi-industrial labor a familiar feature of peasant life. Nonetheless, the small scale of the indi-

vidual units and their location in the countryside meant that
Moscow's industrial development remained fixed in a peasant
milieu.

The unique character of Moscow's industrialization was accentuated by the fact that many entrepreneurs of the early nineteenth
century were themselves serfs. Their unfree status did not prevent
a minority of peasants from enriching themselves and exploiting
others. Some, such as the famous Savva Morozov, amassed huge
fortunes and eventually had thousands of individuals working
for them throughout large areas of the countryside. Morozov and
a handful of others laid the foundations for most of the great
textile enterprises of later decades.[7] Although in time these entrepreneurs purchased their freedom from serfdom and entered the
merchant class, traces of their serf heritage could long afterward
be discerned: narrowness of outlook, xenophobia, political passiv-
ity, and isolation from other strata of Russian society.*

The fusion of peasant traditions and industrial development was
not unique to Moscow, but there it found its fullest expression.
Russia's other industrial centers drew their workers from the
peasantry, as did Moscow, but elsewhere the organization of
factory life and the balance between tradition and innovation
were somewhat different. In the Urals, for example, mining and
metallurgical industries relied mainly on the compulsory labor of
serfs who were permanently "assigned" to particular enterprises;
peasant entrepreneurship and independent initiative were almost
unknown, and there was less diversity in peasants' industrial
experience. In Saint Petersburg, on the other hand, diversity and
initiative were more apparent than in Moscow; factories bore more
resemblance to Western European ones and had higher levels of

---

*Many of the same attitudes were found among Old Believer entrepre-
neurs, a group that largely overlapped with the peasant entrepreneurs. These
sectarians have sometimes been compared to Calvinists and other groups
whose Protestant ethic is thought by some authors to have aided the rise of
Western capitalism. Unlike the Calvinists and many other Protestant denomi-
nations, however, the Old Believers did not emphasize individualistic striving
for worldly success. Their religious tenets set sharp limits to the secular
ideas and economic practices they could accept. The "spirit of capitalism"
as Max Weber defined it found its clearest expression in the rational organization of free wage labor, but among the Russian sects wage relations were
overshadowed by communitarian, noneconomic obligations. On this subject,
see William Blackwell, *The Beginnings of Russian Industrialization 1800–
1861*, pp. 210-23; cf. Alexander Gerschenkron, *Europe in the Russian Mirror*,
chaps. 1-2.

efficiency and mechanization, a more heterogeneous labor force, and a Westernized (often foreign-born) entrepreneurial class.[8] Unlike the Urals, Moscow experienced more or less continuous, often rapid, industrial growth throughout the nineteenth century. More than Saint Petersburg, Moscow confined its growth to the well-worn channels of peasant custom.

In the mid-nineteenth century, Moscow city and province remained Russia's largest manufacturing center. Textile production predominated, accounting for roughly 65 percent of all enterprises and 90 percent of all workers. In general, industries that used wage labor (principally by *obrok*-paying serfs) were developing more rapidly than those whose workers were permanently bound to the factory. Modern machinery, imported from the West, had begun to appear in the 1840s, but for the most part Muscovites were slow to adopt it; thus the cotton-spinning industry, where such innovation was especially important, developed slowly in Moscow while flourishing in Saint Petersburg.[9] A few large cotton mills were built in Moscow city, but even these employed hundreds if not thousands of cottage weavers in the hinterland.[10] Meanwhile the city itself was growing rapidly, owing almost entirely to the influx of peasant *otkhodniki*; these individuals often stayed for only a year or two, but each year thousands more arrived to take their places.[11]

These patterns were not significantly altered by the emancipation of the serfs in 1861. As Chapter Two shows, the reform removed some, but by no means all, of the obstacles to peasant mobility, thereby opening the way to further capitalist development. In the decades that followed, production was mechanized; new branches of industry were introduced; and the number of factories and workers increased considerably. Nonetheless, the trends of the previous century and a half could not easily be reversed, and industrial Moscow retained its distinctive contours.

Innovation in the Postemancipation Era

For Russia as a whole, and Moscow specifically, the postemancipation decades were a time of moderate economic growth punctuated by periodic crises. Between 1860 and 1890 the overall rate of growth was unimpressive, but important qualitative or structural changes were occurring: railroad construction; expansion of heavy industry, especially machine building; mechanization of light industry; expansion of large-scale enterprises and decline—

relative and sometimes absolute—of small and medium-sized ones; growth of foreign investment and trade; and the growth of a national and international grain market. These changes provided a foundation for later, more rapid growth. In the 1890s, with the increasingly active participation of the Russian government, the economy entered what some observers have described as a "take-off" stage of development. Advances in any one sector now stimulated chain reactions throughout the economy, resulting in extremely rapid overall growth.[12]

Moscow was a major beneficiary of these changes. Located in the geographic center of Russia and already a major center of commerce, the city of Moscow became the natural hub of the new rail network. Lines were opened from Moscow to Nizhnii-Novgorod (1862), Riazan' (1864), Kursk (1868), and Smolensk and Iaroslavl' (both 1870), facilitating the movement of people and goods and boosting Moscow's role in the national economy.[13] The development of the railroad system in turn stimulated other changes, especially in the machine-building and metallurgical industries, which expanded to meet the demand for rails and rolling stock.

The railroads' most dramatic effect was in the South, where the iron and coal resources of the Donets and Krivoi Rog areas were brought together to create a whole new industrial region. This in turn stimulated further development in the Moscow region. As internal communications improved, domestically produced locomotives, rolling stock, and rails began to replace imported materials, and the center of Russian machine production began to shift from the port city of Saint Petersburg to the central provinces.* Machine works grew up in Moscow city, as well as in Kolomna (Moscow province), Sormovo (Nizhnii-Novgorod province), and Briansk (Orel province).[14]

Heavy industry was further stimulated by the growth and mechanization of the textile industry. In the cotton industry the number of power looms in Russia is estimated to have grown

---

*Moscow's location proved advantageous in the cotton industry as well, as later rail lines to central Asia and the Far East opened up new sources of raw cotton and new markets for finished cloth; a system of preferential rail tariffs adopted in 1889/90 enhanced the central provinces' position by making their competitors (Saint Petersburg, Russian Poland, and the Baltic provinces) pay higher rates for shipments to and from Asia. (K. A. Pazhitnov, *Ocherki istorii tekstil'noi promyshlennosti dorevoliutsionnoi Rossii: Khlopchatobumazhnaia, l'no-pen'kovaia i shelkovaia promyshlennost'*, pp. 100-101; R. S. Livshits, *Razmeshchenie promyshlennosti v dorevoliutsionnoi Rossii*, p. 191).

from 11,000 in 1860 to 87,000 in 1890.[15] The cotton-spinning industry, mechanized from the very outset, grew even faster than weaving; its output was 1.4 million *puds* (22 million kilograms) in 1858, 4.4 million *puds* (72 million kilograms) in 1879, and 14.9 million *puds* (244 million kilograms) in 1900.[16] Cotton dyeing and dye printing also experienced significant technological improvements and increased their output accordingly. For the most part these developments were concentrated in the older centers of textile manufacturing, especially Moscow and Vladimir provinces.

Expansion and mechanization led to a basic reorganization of the textile industry. The cottage looms and peasant workshops of earlier years were increasingly overshadowed by large mills that combined all phases of production. In 1866, under 50 percent of all factory workers in cotton production worked in mills with 1,000 or more hands; by 1879, the figure had risen to 60 percent, and by 1894 it was 74 percent.[17] The very largest cotton mills were located in Moscow and Vladimir provinces, which by the end of the century not only maintained their earlier preeminence in weaving but also surpassed Saint Petersburg in spinning. By 1900, Moscow province had four mills with 5,000 or more workers, and their combined work force of 32,000 included 30 percent of the province's cotton workers.[18]

The silk and woolen industries grew much more slowly than cotton manufacturing in the postemancipation decades, but they too showed a tendency toward mechanization and concentration of production. In both industries, as in cotton textiles, the Moscow region continued to be Russia's leading center of production. The silk industry was the least mechanized, but by the end of the century new factories were operating with steam-powered equipment, and Moscow city's two largest firms each employed more than two thousand workers. In the woolen industry, progress was uneven. Large-scale enterprises had predominated since the time of Peter I, but many were antiquated and unproductive. This was particularly true of the mills that wove woolen broadcloth (*sukno*). Many of these had originally been possessional or votchinal establishments, supplying cloth to the state on fixed quotas, and they had great difficulty competing in the freer market conditions of the postemancipation era. Toward the middle of the nineteenth century, a few woolen mills had gone through a period of rapid growth and mechanization, but in later decades they too encountered serious competition from other, cheaper textiles. In the last decades of the century, this industry's growth and

Table 1.1. Growth of Factory Production, 1880–1900, Moscow City and Province Combined

Branch of industry	Number of enterprises[a]			Number of workers			Value of output (1,000s of rubles)		
	1879	1900	1900 as percentage of 1879	1879	1900	1900 as percentage of 1879	1879	1900	1900 as percentage of 1879
Cotton	156	210	135	64,485	114,369	177	63,652	169,943	267
Wool	60	73	122	7,872	18,279	232	13,510	27,543	203
Woolen broad-cloth	56	19	34	22,298	8,175	37	24,032	10,492	44
Silk	35	112	348	3,903	20,906	532	4,058	23,441	578
Other fibres	45	13	29	5,088	975	19	5,060	664	13
Combined and unspecified fibers	187	138	74	26,612	26,733	100	22,564	32,810	145
Total textile	539	565	105	130,258	189,437	145	131,972	264,893	201
Machine	27	42	156	5,833	11,880	204	8,414	18,287	217
Metal	50	178	356	2,637	21,586	819	3,526	32,845	931
Leather	38	71	187	2,881	6,081	211	5,264	17,752	337
Clothing	12	9	75	476	564	118	552	793	144
Food and beverages	48	58	121	4,078	12,067	296	26,252	68,588	261

Table 1.1. (*Continued*)

Branch of industry	Number of enterprises[a]			Number of workers			Value of output (1,000s of rubles)		
	1879	1900	1900 as percentage of 1879	1879	1900	1900 as percentage of 1879	1879	1900	1900 as percentage of 1879
Paper and printing	14	111	793	1,318	12,504	949	814	10,325	1,268
Wood	21	55	262	1,360	3,197	235	689	2,826	410
Brick	21	83	395	3,729	9,347	251	1,142	6,877	602
Glass and China	11	23	209	1,091	3,504	321	425	2,074	488
Chemical	24	33	136	1,208	3,471	287	2,692	13,548	503
Miscellaneous	66	42	64	4,183	6,383	153	9,532	8,726	92
Total	871	1,270	146	159,182	280,021	176	191,283	447,534	234
Total for all Russia[b]	32,618	38,141	117	711,097	2,373,400	333	1,102,900	3,005,900	273

Sources: P. A. Orlov, *Ukazatel' fabrik i zavodov Europeiskoi Rossii s Tsarstvom Pol'skim i Vel. kn. Finliandskim*; Ministerstvo Finansov, *Spisok fabrik i zavodov Europeiskoi Rossii za 1900–1903* (my computations).
[a]Includes all enterprises with 16 or more workers.
[b]Includes all enterprises regardless of size of work force. In 1879, roughly three-fourths of all enterprises had fewer than 16 workers.

innovation were confined to a few dynamic enterprises; the majority stagnated.[19]

Outside the metal and textile industries, mechanization and concentration of production were less conspicuous before 1900. Important advances were made in the food and beverage industry, especially in such fields as sugar refining and distillation of spirits, but the scale of production and innovation was smaller than in metalworking or textile manufacturing. Moscow city became the nation's leading center for the manufacture of sweets, conserves, and tobacco products, and individual enterprises such as the Abrikosov and Einem confectionery factories, the Smirnov distillery, or the Bostanzhoglo tobacco factory employed many hundreds of workers.

By the end of the century, important advances were also under way in the chemical and petroleum industries. Although these had an indirect effect on the development of Moscow's industries (e.g., through the improvement of dyes used in textile manufacturing), their development was concentrated in other regions of Russia.

The quantitative effects of all these changes can be seen in Table 1.1, which traces the development of individual industries in Moscow (city and province combined) from 1879 to 1900. Although these statistics are incomplete, they provide the fullest available picture of Moscow's growth in this period.

Moscow Remains Distinctive

Overall statistics on Russian manufacturing industries indicate that in these years Moscow was growing more slowly than other regions. The figures at the bottom of Table 1.1, drawn from the same governmental sources as the rest of the table, suggest that the number of workers in Russia tripled between 1879 and 1900, whereas the number in Moscow increased by 75 percent. The ruble value of Russia's output grew by 172 percent, whereas Moscow's increased by 130 percent. The disparity between Moscow and the rest of Russia would be even greater if the totals had included extractive and metallurgical industries of the South. The work force in the metallurgical industry of southern Russia, for instance, increased more than tenfold between 1882 and 1900; the number of coal miners tripled between 1887 and 1900; and the work force in the petroleum industry increased sixfold.[20]

Comparing growth of factories, work force, and output in

Moscow, one finds that the number of factories showed the smallest increase; the number of workers grew more rapidly; and the output increased at a still higher rate. This pattern is consistent with a general Russian trend and is a natural consequence of mechanization and concentration of production.[21] Besides showing rapid overall growth, Russia's industries were becoming concentrated in ever-larger enterprises. Between 1879 and 1902, the number of workers at small (100-to-499 workers) factories grew by 75 percent; at medium-sized ones (those with 500 to 999 workers), by 116 percent; and at enormous ones (those with 1,000 or more workers), by 280 percent.[22]

The largest enterprises tended to be the more advanced and innovative ones, and they played a more prominent role in Russia's economy than in any of the older capitalist nations. Statistics from the turn of the century suggest that, despite Russia's relative backwardness, both the proportion and even the actual number of workers in such enterprises was greater than in Germany.[23]

Despite their prominence in Moscow, such enterprises played a somewhat different role there than in other parts of Russia. In a celebrated article first published in 1952,[24] Alexander Gerschenkron analyzed the large size of Russian factories and suggested that it arose from a series of "substitutions," through which a scarcity of certain resources was overcome by emphasizing others. Labor, in Gerschenkron's view, was a scarce resource, for although Russia had a vast supply of potential workers, most lacked the skills and habits necessary for modern industrial production. Entrepreneurship was also scarce, for Russian merchants had been stifled by centuries of restriction and social exclusion and were ill equipped to play the dynamic, innovative role their counterparts had played in the West. Given these deficiencies, Gerschenkron argued, the Russian economy achieved rapid growth through substitutions that minimized their effects. Direct state intervention in the economy became a substitute for private entrepreneurship; foreign investment provided capital and expertise on a greater scale than native-born investors could muster; and enormous capital-intensive enterprises with imported technology used scarce resources—managerial expertise and skilled labor—to maximum effect. The range of possible substitutions was greatly enhanced by the nation's backwardness, for Russia could draw upon the experience and technology of previously developed economies.

Gerschenkron's analysis provides a persuasive account of Russia's overall development but not necessarily of Moscow's. Although the city and province, and indeed most of the industrial region surrounding them, participated in national trends, their distinctive heritage was never lost. The "substitutions" that were so conspicuous in, for example, the extractive and metallurgical industries of the South were hardly visible in Moscow. Here the state intervened less; the supply of experienced laborers was greater; heavy industry was less important than textile manufacturing; and native Russian capital and management predominated.[25]

Moscow's entrepreneurs in the postemancipation era have been variously described. Western writers have emphasized their conservatism, patriotism, religiosity, and patriarchal attitudes; their mistrust of Western influences and resentment of the cosmopolitan financial-entrepreneurial elite of Saint Petersburg; their support for autocracy and reluctance to become involved in politics except when immediate self-interest was involved (e.g., in the tariff question).[26] Soviet historians, on the other hand, have written of a nascent bourgeoisie whose development was retarded by the survival of certain precapitalist habits and institutions.[27] There is general agreement, however, that the largest firms—Morozov, Prokhorov, and Konshin—were direct descendants of the preemancipation entrepreneurs, most of whom had arisen from the peasantry. These businesses continued to operate along family lines, although later generations usually dissociated themselves from their forbears' peasant origin and sectarian affiliations. Toward the end of the nineteenth century, the largest firms were reorganized as corporations or joint-stock companies, but the shares continued to be held by the original families with few if any outsiders participating.[28] At the turn of the century, some of the older Moscow industrial families (notably the Riabushinskiis) began to shift their capital from industry into banking, but there, too, familial patterns continued; the banks themselves followed the practice of industrial Moscow, remaining apart from the economic life of the rest of Russia and serving mainly the needs of the textile industry.

By the end of the century, the upper stratum of Moscow's commerical and industrial leaders consisted of a small and inbred elite, a charmed circle no longer open to prosperous artisans or traders. Although new factories continued to be built at a good pace throughout the postemancipation decades, successive periods of industrial crisis or depression regularly eliminated the weaker competitors and thereby enabled the stronger older ones to consolidate their position. Of the twenty-two largest cotton mills in 1900, none was less than thirty years old, and all but eight had been founded before 1860.[29]

Predictably, this pattern discouraged innovation and led to entrenchment in Moscow's industries. The Moscow industrialists' cautious, conservative attitude can be seen in their avoidance of new fields of investment and also in the way in which technological advances were introduced. Moscow's factories often lagged behind those of Saint Petersburg and Russian Poland in efficiency and productivity. In cotton spinning, for example, Moscow's mills had 1,060,000 spindles in 1890 and employed 42,000 workers to operate them; Saint Petersburg had 860,000 spindles but only 12,000 workers.[30] In general, Muscovite entrepreneurs were the last to introduce technological innovations and did so only when their competitors had proven their advantages.[31]

It seems that Moscow's backwardness was of a different order from Russia's. The lack of skilled hands and entrepreneurial ability Gerschenkron described were less apparent here. Moscow was relatively well supplied with experienced workers and with enterprising traders and manufacturers, but they were enmeshed in a set of traditional and only partly economic relationships. Their habits and patterns of interaction, as can be seen in Chapter Five, were often inherited from an earlier age. They could adapt, albeit reluctantly, to changing technology and market conditions but would do so only when the older system was challenged by external forces.[32]

The continuity of Moscow's industrial development can also be seen in the coexistence and interaction of large and small textile enterprises. Instead of dying out, the small-scale factories and workshops of earlier years continued to exist alongside giant mills. Despite their low levels of technology, some handcraft operations were integrated into the structure of larger enterprises, which took advantage of the so-called sweating system to farm out certain tasks to cheap cottage workers.[33] Thus, in spite of the growth of enormous factories, the number of small-to-medium enterprises in Moscow's cotton industry increased by 40 percent between 1879 and 1900. The smaller enterprises offered little threat to their larger competitors and could even play an auxiliary role in their operations. They were also a familiar institution to peasant entrepreneurs from surrounding provinces, who provided a steady influx of capital into small-scale industrial and commercial operations.

In other centers such as Saint Petersburg, the tradition of small-scale, peasant-owned factories and workshops was weaker,[34] and in the newer industrial centers of the South it was almost nonexistent. In Moscow, however, such enterprises continued to play a vital role, not just in textiles, but in most other branches of light industry. At the turn of the century, 57 percent of Moscow city and province's factory work force was in enterprises with fewer than five hundred workers; in Saint Petersburg, the comparable figure was 40 percent, and in Ekaterinoslav province, the center of the burgeoning metallurgical industry, it was 12 percent.[35] These figures may even understate the difference, for officials had great difficulty in keeping track of small-scale craft, workshop, and cottage industries. For the smallest enterprises, statistical evidence may be hopelessly inadequate; contemporary estimates of the number of such enterprises ranged as high as seven million in all of Russia in the 1890s, but more recent and detailed studies have been unable to come up with solid figures.[36] The territorial distribution of the various nonfactory crafts and trades was no easier to identify, but they flourished in the northern and north-central provinces, particularly Moscow and the seven or eight provinces closest to it. In Moscow city, the municipal census of 1902 recorded a total of 107,000 factory workers—a figure, incidentally, almost identical to the one compiled by the Ministry of Finance—and an additional 104,800 in nonfactory "extractive and manufacturing" industry.[37] In Moscow province in the 1890s, *zemstvo* statisticians estimated that there were 190,000 craft workers, compared to 180,000 workers in factories.[38] This situation must surely have reinforced the traditionalism of both employers and workers.

The traditionalism and continuity outlined here were much less characteristic of Moscow's metal industry than of textiles or light manufacturing. The relatively slow pace of growth and mechanization in textiles, and the relatively low levels of skill required for most factory tasks, enabled those industries to assimilate many workers from the older cottage and artisan traditions. The metal and machine-building industries, on the other hand, grew abruptly and relied more heavily on advanced, imported technology, which often required workers to have a higher level of skill and specialized training. It is surely no accident that this was the one branch of Moscow's industry in which foreign entrepreneurship was predominant.

One final aspect of industrial Moscow's heritage deserves mention: the dispersal of large-scale factory enterprise through rural areas of Moscow province. This pattern was strongly developed at midcentury and did not diminish in later decades. In 1900, 37 percent of Moscow's industrial work force was in Moscow city and 63 percent was in the rest of the province. A similar pattern prevailed elsewhere in the Russian empire at this time, especially in the central industrial provinces (notably Vladimir and Nizhnii Novgorod) and in the South, and it was regarded by contemporaries as one of the peculiarities of Russian development.[39] In some localities, industries grew up in the country to be close to fuel and mineral resources, but in the Moscow region the attraction was cheap labor and long-standing semi-industrial craft traditions.

The clearest example was the cotton industry, in which less than 20 percent of all enterprises were located in the city. In one form or another, cotton manufacturing was carried out in all of the province's thirteen counties, but the greatest centers were in Bogorodskii, Serpukhovskii, and Kolomenskii counties, which between them accounted for 47 percent of the industry's workers and 47 percent of its output (in ruble value). All of these had been major centers of cotton weaving and printing since the early decades of the nineteenth century. Their largest factories had been founded before emancipation: the Morozov mills in Glukhovo (Bogorodskii county, 1847) and the Konshin mills in Serpukhov (1822), each of which had close to ten thousand workers in 1900. Significantly, Moscow city's share of the cotton industry's work force (13%) was lower than its proportion of enterprises (19%); the largest mills were more prominent in the hinterland than in the city, where small and medium-sized enterprises predominated.

The hinterland, however, should not be imagined as open fields and countryside. Factories were often located in or near fair-sized towns, such as Serpukhov, with its population of twenty thousand (1897). In other cases, industrial centers, although not officially designated as cities, included upward of ten thousand workers and would seem to meet most of the criteria of urban settlements. The "noncity" areas of the province also included Moskovskii county, which surrounded the city and became a major industrial region as larger factories created their own suburbs in Izmailovo and Danilovo. (These latter enterprises were exceptional in several ways, being owned by foreigners and having considerably higher levels of productivity than the province's other spinning mills.)[40]

In one sense, all the outlying communities were urban areas whose full-time population was wholly engaged in industrial or nonagricultural activity. At the same time, however, they did not display any of the cosmopolitan, heterogeneous qualities of larger cities; in extreme cases, factory towns became self-contained total communities, a closed universe whose members obtained food and shelter from the employer and were effectively sealed off from the rest of society.[41]

Like cotton, the other textile industries tended to remain in the regions where they had flourished since the eighteenth century. The silk industry was concentrated in Bogorodskii and Moskovskii counties, although by the end of the century the older small-scale factories faced stiff competition from the enormous Zhiro and Moscow silk companies in Moscow city. Woolen mills were located primarily in Moscow city, but the older centers of broadcloth manufacture—Bogorodskii and Dmitrovskii counties —also remained important.

The newer industries, on the other hand, were often concentrated in Moscow city or around its perimeter in Moskovskii county. The largest machine works and metalworking plants were all in this region, with the single exception of the Kolomna machine works, which produced railroad locomotives and rolling stock and was situated on the Moscow-Riazan' line about 100 miles south of Moscow city. The food and beverage industries, relative newcomers with a fairly high level of mechanization, were also located almost exclusively in Moscow city, as was the chemical industry. Brick production, a relatively backward industry, was concentrated in Moskovskii county, presumably in order to serve the construction needs of the expanding metropolis.

In their overall rate of economic growth, Moscow city and the surrounding Moskovskii county kept pace with the province as a whole. They were surpassed by Bronnitskii, Klinskii, and Kolomenskii counties, each of which increased its work force by more than 150 percent between 1879 and 1900. The older textile centers of Bogorodskii, Dmitrovskii, and Serpukhovskii counties grew much more slowly, each with less than a 50 percent increase in the work force in the stated years. The remaining counties (Mozhaiskii, Podol'skii, Vereiskii, Volokolamskii, and Zvenigorodskii) had insignificant numbers of factory workers.

The Factories' Heritage

In sum, the circumstances of Moscow's industrial development created an atmosphere in which old habits and customs changed slowly and innovation was resisted. Many enterprises were located in the countryside, and even those in the city were owned and staffed by individuals with a strong peasant heritage. Large factories developed out of small ones, and new industries such as machine building were slow to displace the long-established branches of textile production. The continuity and traditionalism outlined here is symbolized by the sleeping quarters at one major cotton mill: built in the 1840s, they bore the names of individual serf owners who had supplied laborers to the factory owner on a contract basis. In the 1880s, the sons and grandsons of serfs continued to eat and sleep in the very same buildings, and the former serf owners' names could still be discerned over the doorways.[42] Under Russian law, these later inhabitants were free men, but their lives were circumscribed by the economic and social legacy of an earlier age.

Chapter Two

Migration to Industrial Moscow

Throughout the nineteenth century, Russia's urban population was increasing more rapidly than the population of the empire as a whole. In 1811, an estimated 6.6 percent of the entire population resided in urban centers, but by 1914 the figure had climbed to more than 15 percent.[1] For most of this period, urban fertility rates were lower than mortality rates, and cities therefore grew almost entirely through in-migration. Millions of peasants flocked to the cities and towns in search of wages, and countless others moved to rural factory centers such as the ones described in the latter pages of Chapter One.

The fact of such migration has long been recognized, but its social implications remain a subject of controversy: What ties did migrants retain to village life? Did they cast off a patriarchal heritage, as many Soviet authors have argued, and become assimilated to a new proletarian existence? Did they yearn for a return to the soil, as some early Russian populists suggested? Were they uprooted, disoriented, or dehumanized by the conditions they encountered in city and factory? Were the city and countryside polar opposites: could an individual draw sustenance from both, or would he or she be pulled to one extreme or the other?

Clearly more is at stake here than mere resettlement. Before one can begin to answer questions such as these or speculate about the significance of labor migration, one must understand more clearly what kind of movement was occurring. How far did migrants travel? How long did they remain in the cities and towns? What ties, if any, did they retain with their place of birth? To answer such questions one must attend closely to the distinctive traits of each individual city or region. In Moscow's case, the long-term economic trends outlined in Chapter One strongly affected migration. Urban growth over several centuries was steady and continuous, and there was a long-standing tradition of nonagri-cultural labor among peasants of the surrounding provinces.

The Juridical Framework of Migration

The fact of rural-urban migration was, in itself, unremarkable. Similar movement occurred in England and Western Europe throughout the early modern period and accounted for the greater part of urban growth before the nineteenth century.[2] Russia differed from other nations, however, in the social context in which migration occurred. In other countries, the movement from the countryside tended to be unidirectional and permanent, the classic example being England in the eighteenth and early nine-teenth centuries, where single-heir inheritance, rapid population growth, and the enclosure movement created a labor army that had no claim on the land.[3] In Russia, on the other hand, hundreds of thousands of peasants traveled annually to and from the cities and factories without ever severing their ties to the village.

The peculiarities of Russian serfdom, as outlined in the previous chapter, enabled and obliged peasants to depart from their native villages in search of wages but discouraged or prevented them from severing their ties to the serf economy. Whether they worked in factories or as itinerant craftsmen, pedlars, navvies, or barge haulers, the overwhelming majority of peasant wage earners before 1861 continued to pay *obrok* through their village com-munes, and only a tiny handful went through the expensive and cumbersome process of altering their social estate (*soslovie*). To many contemporaries, the combination of peasant communal institutions and temporary departures (*otkhodnichestvo*) seemed a shield against the social evils of England and Western Europe: the emergence of a landless, rootless, unstable and potentially explosive urban working class.[4] In the late 1850s, as the tsarist government began preparations for the abolition of serfdom, many voices were raised in defense of traditional patterns of peasant existence, and when the Emancipation reform was finally promulgated in 1861, it retained many features of the old order.[5]

Under the new law, peasants continued to be assigned at birth to their fathers' social status (*soslovie*) and village commune. Many of the responsibilities formerly entrusted to the gentry were now vested in the commune: issuance of passports, collection of taxes, and adjudication of local disputes. The most important feature of the emancipation settlement, however, was the system of land tenure it created. The peasantry was given permanent possession of specific amounts of land but was required to pay for it through a long-term mortgagelike system of redemption. In many parts of the empire, including the central provinces surrounding Moscow, this land (and the burden of redemption) was assigned not to individuals but to the commune, to be divided equitably among member households. Periodically a general meeting of the commune would be held to pool and redivide members' holdings in accordance with each household's changing circumstances.

This system supposedly guaranteed the economic security of the peasantry, but it also gave the commune considerable influence over members' nonagricultural activities. In principle, an individual had the right to renounce his land allotment, withdraw from the commune, and move permanently to some other place. This right was hedged about with so many obstacles, however, that only a minuscule proportion of peasants ever made use of it.[6] Others, unable or unwilling to sever legal ties to the village, sought outside income through the time-honored system of *otkhodnichestvo*, but their movement was restricted by the commune. By paying various sums, they could obtain passports for periods of three months, six months, one year, or five years; in order for these to be renewed, however, the departing member had to satisfy the commune and local officials that he and his household were keeping up their share of taxes and land-redemption payments.[7] The law on passports also allowed a commune to revoke a passport on other grounds such as election of a departing member to local office.[8]

It would be wrong to conclude that the state sought to discourage peasants from migrating. *Otkhodnichestvo* was an established tradition in many parts of Russia. Without it, cities could hardly have grown; factories could hardly have operated; and peasants in many regions could not have made ends meet. This was recognized by many Russian lawmakers; thus despite the cumbersome provisions of the passport system, other legislation of the emancipation period encouraged peasants to seek wages away from their villages.[9] If in sum the postemancipation system seems inconsistent or unfavorable to industrial progress, this was not the legislators' intent. They can better be described as preoccupied with noneconomic issues: the threat of disorder and violence, the stability of peasant life, and the well-being of the landowning gentry.

By the turn of the century, many of the assumptions underlying emancipation had proven unrealistic and a younger generation of statesmen was ready to discard the commune as inimical to national security and well-being.[10] The essential point here, however, is that in the last decades of the nineteenth century the vast majority of the working population in Russian cities and factories was obliged to maintain at least a nominal tie to the village. Precisely how important, or how nominal, was that tie in industrial Moscow?

Patterns of Migration, 1880 to 1902

By the end of the nineteenth century, Moscow was Russia's second-largest city (after Saint Petersburg) and was growing more rapidly than most of its neighbors. Its population in 1902 was 1.17 million, of whom 73 percent were migrants from other places and 67 percent were legally peasants.[11] The extent of in-migration can be gauged from the fact that just under 10 percent of the city's inhabitants reported that they had resided there less than one year.[12]

Employment was the city's chief attraction, and the proportion of migrants was higher among wage earners than in the urban population as a whole. In Moscow city in 1902, migrants made up 93 percent of the work force in factories, 90 percent in handcrafts, and 86 percent of the entire working population.[13] In the thirteen counties of Moscow province, the influx of outsiders was substantially less (48 percent), but the peasantry was still the chief source of labor, accounting for 93 percent of the factory work force in the early 1880s.[14]

In view of many authors' assertions that factory workers were uprooted from the countryside, it is interesting to trace the migrants' geographic origins. They came, for the most part, from a narrow radius of surrounding provinces. Moscow province alone provided 27 percent of all migrants residing in the city in 1902, while the seven closest provinces accounted for an additional 54 percent.[15] The 1902 census provides more detailed information about these provinces' migrants and indicates that the majority came from the counties closest to Moscow province's borders, a radius of barely 100 miles from Moscow city. For example, 32 percent of all migrants from Smolensk province came from a single border county.[16]

The radius of migration was widening from year to year, however. In 1872, the eight surrounding provinces had supplied 91 percent of all migrants; in 1882, 80 percent; in 1897, 77 percent; and in 1902, 80 percent.[17] This last figure illustrates the influence of economic conditions on migration. The proportion of migrants from distant places was greater in 1897, a year of full employment and rapid economic growth, than in 1902, when the Russian economy was suffering the effects of a worldwide depression. Migrants, it seems, moved to the city when jobs were plentiful and departed when they were not. This pattern would seem to bear out Reginald Zelnik's suggestion that "each new cycle of economic growth required the recruitment of new cadres of inexperienced workers from the countryside . . . tending to submerge the 'proletarian' workers in a semi-proletarian mass."[18] On the other hand, the radius of recruitment for factory workers was significantly narrower than for the total migrant population of Moscow city. In 1902, 29 percent of the city's factory workers came from Moscow province, compared to 27 percent of all migrants; 75 percent of workers were drawn from a radius of 100 miles, compared to 60 percent of the total migrant population.[19] Migrants from more distant localities often wound up working as day laborers or in other unskilled occupations. Those from closer districts, being more familiar with the city, were more likely to have acquired useful skills and may have been less intimidated by the prospect of factory work.[20] They may have been a semi-proletarian mass, but they were probably not raw recruits with no experience of urban life.

Despite the exceptionally high proportion of migrants, Moscow city's population, and even more its industrial work force, constituted an essentially homogeneous mass, not just in geographic origin, but also in language (in 1897 95 percent of the city's inhabitants were native speakers of Russian), religion (93 percent were Orthodox), and a fairly uniform peasant subculture.[21] In these respects, Moscow differed from other urban and industrial areas of the Russian empire. Saint Petersburg and the large southern cities drew their migrant populations from greater distances and often, as in the case of Odessa or Kiev, from several distinct nationalities.[22] In such centers, Russians worked side by side with Poles, Jews, Letts, Finns, or Ukrainians. But in Moscow this rarely occurred; the peasant migrant, having traveled a relatively short distance from his birthplace and surrounded by people very much like himself, may thus have found the new environment both more familiar and less threatening or alienating than some authors have supposed (see Chapters Four and Five).

In the rest of Moscow province, migrants were a smaller but still significant proportion of the industrial work force. Although the proportion of migrants was less than 50 percent in all but two of the thirteen counties (Moskovskii had 76 percent and Kolomenskii, 60 percent), it was highest in the more industrial districts.[23] The largest factories tended to draw their work force from a wider radius than the smaller ones, a pattern found on a national scale as well.[24] Districts closest to Moscow city, however, also showed a higher proportion of migrants; Podol'skii county, one of the least industrial of the thirteen, had a work force that was 48 percent migrant, compared to 42 percent in Serpukhovskii county's much larger work force. Migrants were 76 percent of the work force in Moskovskii county as a whole, but in the outlying townships the proportion dropped to 42 percent.[25]

In contrast to the city, which drew large numbers of migrants from all the surrounding provinces, other industrial centers tended to draw them only from the nearest ones. In Kolomenskii county, for example, 47 percent of the work force was recruited from nearby regions of Riazan' and Tula provinces, and only 5.8 percent of workers came from other provinces.[26] Factories in the outlying counties were sometimes located close to the provincial border, so that "migrants" were in fact as close to home as those who were recorded as locally born.

In the overall pattern of migration, Moscow city should perhaps be pictured as a magnet whose force of attraction extended in all directions. Migrants from surrounding provinces moved toward the city, sometimes stopping before they reached the center but rarely going beyond it. Those who came from the southern provinces did not often settle to the north of Moscow, and those from western ones traveled no further east than Moscow city. Similar patterns have been found in other industrializing societies, such as England in the early nineteenth century, where short-distance migration was characteristic of the newly emerging industrial centers of Lancashire and the midlands.[27] Both in England and in the hinterland of Moscow the departure of migrants to the factories created a demand for other forms of labor (e.g., hired hands in agriculture) in the districts of out-migration; this demand was met by additional waves of migrants from more remote districts.[28]

Judging from the 1902 statistics the greatest numbers of migrants came to the city from regions where industry was less developed.

Of the six adjacent provinces, Vladimir, which far surpassed its neighbors in industrial output, supplied the smallest number of migrants (27,000), whereas Riazan', Tula, Smolensk, and Kaluga, whose combined industrial output was less than half of Vladimir's, sent over three-hundred thousand migrants to Moscow.[29] Looking more closely at the particular counties that supplied the greatest number of migrants, one finds that they were usually not the most industrial ones; in Riazan' province, for example, industry and crafts were most developed in Egor'evskii, Spasskii, and Kasimov-skii counties, all of them close to the Moscow border, but migrants to Moscow came predominantly from Mikhailovskii, Zaraiskii, Riazanskii, and Pronskii counties.[30] Migrants, in other words, came to Moscow to find something not available closer to home. This is not to imply that they were unskilled or inexperienced in their crafts or trades; on the contrary, migrants tended to develop regional specialties and to follow trades their fathers and grandfathers had been practicing for many years. The point is that they did this not by working at home but by following a well-beaten path to the cities and factories.

City-born workers, on the other hand, had less difficulty finding employment at their place of birth and were much less likely to migrate. More than half of the population of *meshchane* ("towns-men") residing in Moscow city were locally born,[31] and the remaining 47 percent included a certain proportion of in-migrants who, although they had been born into other estates, had legally altered their status to become *meshchane.* In the factories of Moscow province, significant concentrations of *meshchane* were found in only two localities, Bogorodskii and Serpukhovskii counties, and in both cases the great majority were locally born.[32] Local officials concluded that they were more deeply attached to their place of birth than peasants were;[33] a likelier explanation is that coming from industrial localities they had less need to travel in search of employment.

The fact that migrants were seeking wages outside their native villages does not, of course, mean that all of them were destined for the factory. In Moscow city, factories provided the largest single category of employment but accounted for just over 15 percent of all self-supporting migrants. Handcrafts were second with 14.6 percent, followed by domestic service with 11.5 percent and transport with 5.5 percent.[34] The larger population of nonfactory migrants was subject to many of the same stresses as factory workers—long hours, low wages, and overcrowding in unhygienic conditions—and in terms of *soslovie* and place of birth, the factory and nonfactory migrant populations were virtually identical. For these reasons, census data on the entire migrant population can often be used to illuminate the details of factory workers' lives.

Year-round Employment

According to one popular stereotype, Russian workers regarded industrial employment as a supplement to their agricultural earnings and returned home each summer to work their fields.[35] This view was called into question as early as the 1890s, however, by a series of studies of factories in the Moscow region, the best known of which was the work of E. M. Dement'ev, who inspected factories in three southern counties of Moscow province in 1884–85.[36] He observed that mechanized factories could not afford to close down for the summer and that year-round labor was the rule rather than the exception at the province's more modern factories. Only the more primitive factories, where hand labor still prevailed, allowed their workers to depart in the summer. An especially clear contrast was found among dyers and printers of cotton cloth: 67.7 percent of those working on a "cottage" basis (*razdatochnye*) ceased work in the summer, as did 34.5 percent of those who worked by hand in factories; but only 6.5 percent of those in mechanized dye factories followed their example.[37]

Statistics compiled by the factory inspectorate for the Russian Department of Trade and Manufactures in 1893 follow the same pattern as Dement'ev's figures, though the proportion of departing workers in the later figures is significantly lower. Of all workers at 1,263 factories in the Moscow industrial district in the years 1882–93, only 18.36 percent departed for summer work in agriculture.[38] Although these figures do not distinguish manual from mechanized labor, the trend toward year-round operation in large-scale enterprises is clear, as the figures in Table 2.1 indicate.

The trend toward year-round employment was a nationwide phenomenon. By 1893, only 29 percent of the factory workers in Russia were employed on a seasonal basis, and by 1900 the figure had dropped to 9 percent. In the metal industry, 97 percent of the entire work force was employed year-round, and in textiles, 92 percent. Industries that had previously operated on a seasonal basis now registered dramatic changes; in the food industry, for example, the proportion of year-round workers jumped from 35 percent to 86 percent between 1893 and 1900. Even the most backward industries—brick and other mineral products, wood, and

Table 2.1. **Trend toward Year-round Operation**

Kind of enterprise	Number reporting	Average total work force per factory	Percentage departing
Weaving (hand and mechanized)	110	105	31.64
Spinning and weaving combined in a single enterprise	11	1,865	0.93
Dyeing, bleaching, and finishing	60	43	20.06
Enterprises combining all the above operations	3	4,087	0.00

Source: Report of factory inspector (Moscow district) Nikitinskii, 4 September 1893. Reprinted in *RD*, vol. 3, pt. 2, pp. 567–93.

Note: All enterprises listed in this table were located in Moscow city or province.

leather—hired from 75 percent to 85 percent of their workers on a year-round basis.[39]

The decision to work through the summer was of course not made by the workers but by the employers, who could not afford to leave expensive facilities standing idle. Through a combination of incentives and coercive measures—six- or twelve-month contracts, withholding of wages, bonuses for workers who finished their term, fines for those who departed early, and refusal to return workers' passports—employers and managers tried to bind the workers to their factories.[40] Their efforts were directed specifically at summer departures, that is, at departures for agricultural work, rather than at movement from one factory to another. The fact that many employers considered such measures necessary suggests that workers had not fully accepted the idea of year-round employment and that many engaged in it unwillingly.[41] This inference is supported by the evidence of a series of disputes and petitions in which workers demanded the right of summer departure.[42]

Willing or unwilling, the great majority of workers in Moscow and elsewhere stayed on at the factory through the summer. Dement'ev presented his statistics in conjuction with others indicating that more than one-fifth of all factory workers in his study had spent more than twenty-five years at their jobs. He concluded that there existed "a class of workers without a shelter of their own, having in fact no property . . . living from day to day" and totally alien to the countryside.[43] Many other students of this question, from Lenin down to the present, have repeated his figures and accepted his rather sweeping conclusions. A closer examination of the evidence, however, suggests that rural ties may have been more widespread and persistent than Dement'ev recognized.

The main difficulty is that the duration of employment can only provide indirect evidence of workers' ties to the village. Long-term or year-round employment per se was not necessarily an obstacle to maintaining rural ties. Dement'ev himself acknowledged that industrial veterans were often concentrated in occupations with the highest rates of seasonal departures.[44] This observation is borne out by more detailed statistics compiled in Moscow city in 1881 by P. A. Peskov, who surveyed seventy-eight textile factories with a total work force of 8,600. The factories in his study were smaller and less mechanized than those Dement'ev surveyed, and summer departures were still the rule rather than the exception. As Table 2.2 indicates, occupations with the highest proportion of long-term workers (those with fifteen years or more at the factory) all had high rates of summer departure, and the three groups with the highest rates of departure—cotton, wool, and silk weavers—were all above average in their proportion of long-term workers. In other words, the two criteria Dement'ev used to demonstrate the proletarianization of factory workers produce inconsistent results: some of the fifteen-year veterans must have continued to make the annual journey back and forth to the country.

Even those who worked year-round in factories were able to return to the countryside periodically, usually at holidays, and at other times wives and other relatives could come to the factory. Contemporary accounts of factory life suggest that both practices were routine.[45] By long-standing custom, the workers' contracts expired at Easter and the factories closed down for a week or two for repairs and renovations; as late as 1896, the enormous Prokhorov cotton mill in Moscow city was using this occasion to "cleanse" its work force of undesirables, who would not be rehired after the holiday.[46] Elsewhere workers who traveled to the countryside were expected to bring back "gifts" of produce for their foremen and were punished for failing to do so.[47]

Other sources describe workers as returning to their native villages because of age, infirmity, and unemployment. In 1885, a

Table 2.2. Length of Employment and Rates of Summer Departure in Separate Occupational Groups, Moscow City, 1881

Occupation	Percentage of all males with 15 or more years' experience in factories	Percentage of males departing in summer months
Warpers	82	62
Dye printers (hand)	70	55
Broadcloth weavers	59	58
Silk weavers	59	75
Machine-loom operators (*Samotkachi*)	58	57
Wool weavers	54	91
Cotton weavers	47	96
Carpenters	35	40
Engravers	27	59
Bleachers and dyers	24	67
Pressers	24	49
Miscellaneous	23	55
Spinners	23	63
Shearers	19	37
Scutchers	9	67
Overall average	45	71

Source: P. A. Peskov, *Sanitarnoe issledovanie fabrik po obrabotke voloknistykh veshchestv v gorode Moskve*, pt. 1, p. 134.

bad year for the textile industry, *zemstvo* statisticians in Moscow province noted that many workers who had lost their jobs were returning to the countryside, even though they were no longer accustomed to agricultural work.[48] Precise statistics on such movement are unavailable. The same is true with respect to illness and disability; factory doctors are quoted as complaining that ill workers often returned to the village instead of seeking care in the infirmary,[49] and descriptive accounts of village life make the same assertion,[50] but comprehensive figures were not gathered.[51]

The foregoing accounts indicate that labor migration was not incompatible with the maintenance of some sorts of ties with the peasant village. They shed little light, however, on the precise nature of these ties or on the migrants' motives for maintaining them. Two other considerations illuminate these issues: an assessment of the migrants' role in the agricultural economy and of the dimensions of out-migration from Moscow city.

Economic Ties to the Countryside

Although agriculture was the principal activity of the greater part of its population, the hinterland of Moscow was by and large a region of low fertility and poor agricultural yields. Of the eight provinces that surrounded Moscow city, one (Tver') had soil described as "very meagre," six were of mediocre fertility, and only two (Riazan' and Tula) were counted among the relatively fertile black-soil provinces.[52] Even in the last two provinces, however, poorer soils predominated in the areas closest to Moscow, that is, the districts that supplied the greatest numbers of migrants to Moscow's cities and factories.[53]

Despite their fertility, the eight provinces were among the most densely settled in European Russia, thus putting great pressure on available resources. Per capita land allotments were low, especially in the southern provinces of the region, and as a result pastureland was often sacrificed in order to bring the maximum possible area under cultivation.[54] Although cultivation was relatively intensive, agriculture of the Moscow region was not highly productive. The open-field system was still in use and with it the primitive three-field system of crop rotation. The communal system of land tenure, moreover, was often, though not always, one of repartition in which the arable land was periodically pooled and reapportioned to adjust to the changing capacities of each household.

As a result of all these factors, the Moscow region was a net importer of grain on a large scale, a pattern that had appeared as early as the middle of the nineteenth century and continued well beyond the years of this study. In extreme cases, a household's own produce would suffice for only two or three months of the year. More modern and rational methods of land exploitation would have improved the region's agricultural yield, but social and economic structures impeded most kinds of innovation.[55] Soviet historians have noted the persistence of "semi-feudal" land practices such as labor-rent and share-cropping in the central provinces around Moscow. Peasants rented extra land from their former lords or from a new generation of enterprising businessmen in small parcels that precluded the use of machinery or innovative techniques. The term of rental was short and the price was set by the magnitude of peasant land hunger rather than the profitability of the land itself.

In this situation, outside earnings came to play an extremely important part in the peasant economy. Without such earnings, a household might find it impossible to pay its taxes, meet its land-redemption payments, purchase additional grain for consumption, or rent or purchase additional land. In general, such outside earnings seem to have been integrated into the existing structures of village life. A recent study of the peasantry of Tula province in the years 1900–1917, the period when communal ties to the land were seriously weakened by the Stolypin reforms, concluded that "rather than destroy the peasant farm, outside employment was helping to maintain it. . . ."[56]

Factory workers differed from other *otkhodniki* in the duration of their outside employment. If they were gone for years at a time, making only short visits to the countryside, did this weaken their attachment to the land or reduce the level of their monetary contributions? Available evidence, admittedly sparse, suggests a negative answer to both questions.

The fullest data on Moscow factory workers' ties to the land were compiled at the Emil' Tsindel' cotton-printing mill in 1899. This was one of the largest and most modern cotton factories in the region, with a work force of over two thousand, 94 percent of them peasants. The factory operated year-round, and the interviewed workers had an average of 10.4 years of experience in factory labor. Of 1,335 male peasants interviewed, just over 90 percent possessed a land allotment, and almost all of the remaining 10 percent came from families that received no land at all at the time of emancipation.[57]

What, though, was these workers' stake in a land allotment? Was this a burden, carried unwillingly because of the legal restrictions described earlier? The Tsindel' study results suggest several answers to these questions. In the first place, only 64 percent of respondents were able to supply detailed information about the size of their landholdings. Absent from the countryside for several years, they had not kept track of changes in the household allotment. They were much better informed about family livestock, however: only one of the workers queried was unable to give an exact answer on this point. Livestock, as Lenin and many other investigators appreciated, was an important indicator of a family's well-being, for without it even a better-than-average land allotment could not be worked.

The workers' responses reveal that a large proportion came from the most impoverished stratum of the peasantry, those whose households did not own even a single horse. Comparing these figures with others for the entire peasantry of Moscow province, however, one finds that the proportion who were horseless was virtually identical in the two populations. The proportion with two or more horses was also identical.[58] Thus it would be wrong to suggest that only the poorest peasants were being forced off the land into the factories. The more prosperous elements of the peasantry were also represented, and one must conclude that the Tsindel' workers represented a cross-section of the entire peasant population.

Data on these workers' landholdings are, as noted above, less complete. Of 780 workers who were able to supply information about their holdings, 79.3 percent held less than 1 *desiatina* (2.7 acres) for each member of their family, and only 3.4 percent held more than 2 *desiatiny*. The overall average was 0.57 *desiatiny* per person. When these figures were compared with average allotments in the workers' native provinces, they turned out to be from 32 percent to 59 percent below the provincial averages. This would suggest a conclusion opposite to the one advanced above, but the statistics on landholding should be used with greater caution. In the first place, the chance of imprecision would be much greater for the measurement of allotment land, which was customarily divided into numerous small and scattered strips, than for the measurement of livestock. In addition, the stated figures applied only to lands allotted from the communal holdings and did not include lands rented or purchased on the side.[59] For these reasons, although it seems clear that some of the Tsindel' workers came from land-poor households, the question of just how poor they were cannot be answered conclusively.

Data on the disposition of land suggests that the great majority of workers retained an active interest in agriculture. Only 0.5 percent left their lands idle, and 14.3 percent rented them out to other peasants. The remaining 85 percent left their allotment in the care of relatives, and 7.3 percent even hired laborers to assist them.[60]

In sum, though the Tsindel' workers rarely took an active hand in the working of their lands and were often uninformed about changes in their allotments, their ties to agriculture seem more than a legal formality. Data from two other sources, though less complete, support this conclusion.

The first of these sources is a survey, carried out by the Moscow factory inspectorate in 1893, covering seven Moscow factories employing a total of 2,015 male workers. Of these workers 23.5 percent retained allotments and departed in the summer to work them. A further 51.2 percent had turned their allotments over to relatives or rented them out to others. Unfortunately the source does not indicate what proportion of workers was in each of these categories. A more detailed breakdown is given for only one of the factories, the Nosov broadcloth factory. Of 220 year-round workers who retained land allotments, 70 percent had left them to be worked by relatives; 21.4 percent had turned them back to the village; and 8.6 percent had rented them to others.[61]

Yet another study was carried out in the spring of 1907, after the promulgation of the so-called Stolypin laws, which removed most legal obstacles to permanent withdrawal from the village commune. It surveyed the landholdings of 4,982 workers in printing establishments in Moscow city. In this group, whose skill, experience, and high wages were far above the average, 45.8 percent maintained households (*veli khoziaistva*) in the countryside. An additional 16.4 percent were classified as "intermediate," keeping a land allotment but renting it out, or maintaining only a house in the village. Data on the extent of landholding of either group is not given, but information about their families and budgets gives an indication of the extent of their participation in the village economy. Of all workers in the first group, 89.6 percent sent regular payments to their relatives. The average annual contribution was 94.1 rubles, approximately one-fourth of the group's average annual wages. Workers in the intermediate group were less likely to send money; 32 percent did so, with an average contribution of 59.5 rubles—still more than two months' average wages. Data on the workers' families help to explain the differences between the "peasant" and "intermediate" groups of printers. Only 3.5 percent of those in the first group had their immediate families living with them in the city as opposed to 68.2 percent of the "intermediate" workers.[62]

These data suggest that, despite differences of degree, the Tsindel' workers were not atypical in maintaining close ties with the countryside despite prolonged absences. Although an increasing proportion of all workers was moving permanently away from the village, the majority's ties could not be characterized as merely a legal formality.

Assessing the Permanence of the Move to the Cities

If workers were unenthusiastic about remaining at the factory year-round, and if many retained serious economic ties to the countryside, one would expect to find a pattern of reverse migration, of migrants leaving the cities and factories to return to their native villages. On the other hand, if migrants were putting down permanent roots in the city, there would be no reason for such reverse migration to occur. The question, How long did they stay? is thus fraught with broader implications for the history of the Russian working class. Census data and factory studies permit at least a partial answer to this question.

A movement of older workers away from city and industry was noted by many authors, among them P. M. Shestakov, author of the aforementioned study of the Tsindel' factory. He observed that, although many workers quit or were laid off because they were physically unable to continue, others left around age forty to assume personal charge of their households in the country; at this age, Shestakov hypothesized, workers were stepping into the shoes of their fathers who had died or were no longer able to head the households themselves.[63]

If a significant proportion of factory workers retained close ties to the village and returned there in time of need, one would expect this fact to be reflected in statistics on turnover in the industrial work force. Unfortunately, as noted above, the industrial studies described here include few such statistics. The same must be said of municipal censuses, which provide at best incomplete information about broad (and ill-defined) occupational groups. The published census results, moreover, often omit the particular combinations of variables (e.g., occupation and duration of residence) that would be most useful for present purposes.

Although complete statistics on factory workers' migration patterns are not available, aggregate census data can be used to trace departures from the city of Moscow.[64] The movement of workers into and away from the city can be inferred from statistics on peasants and migrants, the two overlapping categories from which, as noted earlier, the vast majority of workers were recruited. Municipal censuses taken in 1882 and 1902 indicate how long Moscow's inhabitants resided there; these figures can in turn be manipulated to compute approximate rates of out-migration for the entire population and for specific sub-groups (e.g., separate social estates).

One way of estimating out-migration is to compare the annual influx of migrants with the overall increase in the city's population. Of all the people counted in the 1882 census, 100,530, or 13 percent, had arrived in the city during the preceding year. The comparable figure in 1902 was over 113,000, just under 10 percent of the city's population. Statisticians estimated Moscow's overall population growth in the years preceding both censuses at roughly 2.5 percent per annum, an annual increment of approximately 20,000 people. This figure included both natural increase (births exceeded deaths by 2,500 per annum in the years 1897–1902) and net increase through migration (estimated at 17,000 per annum).[65] If more than 113,000 people moved to Moscow in 1902 and the net population growth was 20,000, then some 90,000 people must have moved away from the city in that year.

Precisely who were these 90,000? The census results suggest that many were migrants who had lived in Moscow for only a few years. Table 2.3 lists the duration of residence of all migrants counted in the censuses of 1882 and 1902. If one supposes that the influx of migrants in 1901 was typical of other years,[66] in other words, that approximately the same number moved to the city in 1899, 1898, and so forth, then the first row of Table 2.3 can be compared with each successive row to determine the rate of out-migration. In other words, if 113,000 migrants moved to Moscow in 1900, more than half that group was no longer living in the city by 1902. If the influx was the same in 1897, only 37 percent of that group was still living in Moscow in 1902, and so on down the table. By the time one reaches the group living there for sixteen-to-twenty years, each year's cohort of migrants is less than one-sixth as great as the in-migration of 1901. If the initial assumption of a steady rate of in-migration is correct, then five migrants must have died or moved away for every one who remained in the city for sixteen-to-twenty years.

Because the two censuses were taken exactly twenty years apart, a further computation of out-migration is possible. The 1902 census divides the entire migrant population according to duration of residence. The number of migrants who had resided in the city for twenty years or more as of 1902 can be compared to the total migrant population of 1882. Of 555,910 migrants residing in Moscow in the earlier year, 136,091 (24 percent) remained in 1902. This works out to an annual rate of decrease of 3.8 percent over the entire twenty-year interval.[67] In contrast, the 1882 census counted 196,559 native-born Muscovites, of whom 38 percent still resided in the city in 1902.

Undoubtedly part of the decrease in both groups was due to mortality. Moscow's overall mortality rate in these years, however, was around 2.8 percent per annum, and for the age group ten to fifty, in which most migrants were concentrated, it was much lower.[68] It appears that many individuals moved away from Moscow and that those who had been born elsewhere were more likely to leave.

Table 2.3. **Migrants (Excluding Foreigners) Residing in Moscow City, 1882 and 1902, by Duration of Residence**

Number of years' residence	1882 Total	1882 As percentage of one year's in-migration	1902 Total	1902 As percentage of one year's in-migration
Less than 1 year	100,530		113,715	
1 year	43,672	43	52,768	46
2 years	40,425	40	56,088	49
3-5 years	76,168		124,589	
Yearly average	25,389	25	41,526	37
6-10 years	87,604		134,201	
Yearly average	17,520	17	26,840	24
11-15 years	61,360		83,466	
Yearly average	12,272	12	16,693	15
16-20 years	41,633		75,837	
Yearly average	8,326	8	15,167	13
More than 20 years	87,927		134,304	
Total migrant population[a]	556,910		781,067	
Total city-born	196,559		297,027	
Ages 20 and above			114,787	

Sources: PM 1882, pt. 2, pp. 41-42; *PM 1902*, pt. 1, table 5, p. 11 (my calculations).

Note: Suburban districts were not included in the 1882 census and are here excluded from 1902 results as well for the sake of consistency. These districts had a total population of 20,361 Moscow-born and 61,469 migrants in 1902.

[a]Includes "unknown duration" (27,591 in 1882; 6,119 in 1902).

One can determine more precisely who was entering and leaving Moscow by comparing census figures for different social estates (*sosloviia*). Table 2.4 shows the duration of residence of peasant and nonpeasant migrants counted in the 1902 census. The proportion of peasants with one year or less of residence was half again as great as that of other unprivileged *sosloviia* (i.e., the groups whose working and living conditions most closely resembled those of peasant migrants). This pattern was reversed in the over-twenty-years group, which included 14.5 percent of all peasant migrants but 31 percent of migrants of other unprivileged *sosloviia*.

As the last column of Table 2.4 indicates, the proportion of newly arrived migrants was lower among factory workers than in the total peasant population,[69] but the proportion of long-term

Table 2.4. Duration of Migrants' Residence in Moscow, as Percentage of Total Migrant Population

Number of years of residence	Peasants (N = 604,299)	Migrants of other unprivileged *sosloviia*[a] (N = 99,989)	Factory workers[b] (N = 99,849)
1 full year or less	22.3	15.6	18.2
2–5 years	24.2	17.3	24.8
6–10 years	17.9	14.6	19.4
11–15 years	11.1 ⎫	10.4 ⎫	
16–20 years	9.8 ⎬ 35.4	10.6 ⎬ 52.5	37.1
21 years and longer	14.5 ⎭	31.5 ⎭	

Source: PM 1902, pt. 1, table 5, p. 11; ibid., pt. 2, table 2, pp. 8–9 (my computation).

Note: Because of rounding-off of percentages, totals may not equal 100 percent in all cases.

[a] Includes *meshchane, tsekhovye,* and "other unprivileged."

[b] Overlaps with the other categories.

residents was only slightly higher. Of factory workers, 37.1 percent had been living in Moscow for eleven years or more compared to 35.4 percent of peasants and 52.5 percent of other migrants. Evidently peasants who moved to Moscow were more likely than nonpeasants to move away, whether or not they worked in factories.

The foregoing figures provide a number of clues to the patterns of out-migration from Moscow. Although they suggest that many peasants who migrated to Moscow did not remain there permanently, they do not indicate where the out-migrants went. Did they return to the villages or continue to work in other industrial centers? Once again, statistical sources do not provide a direct answer to this question. An indirect answer can be found, however, if one can determine the age breakdown of out-migrants. If they were mostly young and able bodied, one might reasonably suppose that they were going to work elsewhere. If they were older, their chances of finding work in other localities would be smaller, the likelihood that they were returning to the countryside greater.

The age distribution of Moscow's population is summarized in Table 2.5. One finds that in 1882 the proportion of peasant males aged fifty to fifty-nine was just half that of other *sosloviia,* and in the age group sixty and over it was less than one-third. In 1902, differences between peasants and nonpeasants were less pronounced, but Table 2.5 leaves some doubt as to who was re-

Table 2.5. Age Distribution of Males (Percentage in Each Age Group) in Moscow City, 1882 and 1902

Age	1882				1902			
	Peasants (N = 249,933)	Meshchane (N = 70,290)	All non-peasants (N = 182,514)	Peasants (N = 437,618)	Factory workers (N = 107,781)	Meshchane (N = 94,658)	All non-peasants (N = 168,551)
0-9	5.1	15.9	15.9	9.6	20.9	18.7	17.8
10-19	25.8	21.0	19.4	21.1	36.0	19.7	19.7
20-29	32.7	22.2	19.1	31.9	23.9	22.8	22.2
30-39	19.5	15.5	16.1	19.9	13.3	17.0	16.7
40-49	9.6	12.0	13.2	11.3	4.6	10.9	11.4
50-59	4.7	8.0	9.7	4.5	1.0	6.1	6.7
60 and above	1.9	5.4	6.0	1.9		4.9	5.3

Sources: PM 1882, pt. 2, table 2, pp. 3–11; *PM 1902,* pt. 1, table 6, pp. 12–13 and pt. 2, table 2, pp. 2–7 (my calculations).
Note: Because of rounding-off of percentages, column totals may not equal 100 percent in all cases.

sponsible for this change; between 1882 and 1902, the proportion of males over the age of fifty remained constant for peasants but declined for other *sosloviia*. In any event, the proportion of peasant males over age sixty was barely one-third that of other *sosloviia*. (Among factory workers, the proportion over age sixty was lower still, but at that age one would expect a change of occupation whether or not out-migration occurred.)

Was this disparity caused by out-migration, or could other factors have produced the same pattern? Two such factors seem possible. The first is that a constant influx of peasant migrants in the younger age brackets would reduce the proportional weight of the older group. In other words, the low proportion of peasants over age fifty might not mean that anyone was moving away but only that many more young peasants were constantly arriving. One can check this possibility by following one age cohort from the census of 1882 to 1902. Individuals who were thirty to thirty-nine years old in 1882 would have been fifty to fifty-nine in 1902; comparing peasant and nonpeasant males of these ages in the two censuses, one gets the results shown in Table 2.6. These figures indicate that the size of this cohort decreased absolutely and that the decrease was greater among peasants than among *meshchane*. In other words, the low proportion of peasants over age fifty was not caused solely by the influx of younger migrants.

Even though the number of peasants in this cohort decreased more sharply than the number of *meshchane*, this still does not prove that out-migration was occurring. One must also consider a second possibility: that mortality rates were different for the two groups. Perhaps the conditions under which peasants worked and lived were significantly worse than those of other city dwellers, making the mortality rate significantly higher. To assess the validity of this argument, one can compare the age distribution of peasants and nonpeasants in specific occupational categories. Census data are unavailable, but data from the aforementioned study of Moscow printers are well suited to this purpose.

As noted earlier, the 1907 study divided printers into three groups: city born (38 percent of all workers), peasant (46 percent), and "intermediate" (16 percent).[70] As Table 2.7 indicates, the proportion over age forty is lower among "intermediates" than among city-born workers and is lowest of all among workers who retained strong peasant ties. This pattern is found not only in the printing trades as a whole but in specific occupational groups such as typesetters and bookbinders.

The inference is clear: older printers were more likely to leave

Table 2.6. **Progression of a Single Age Cohort of Peasants and Meshchane, 1882-1902**

Soslovie	Population of males aged 30–39, 1882	Population of males aged 50–59, 1902	1902 as percentage of 1882
Peasants	48,913	19,505	40
Meshchane	10,984	5,740	52

Sources: PM 1882, pt. 2, table 2, pp. 3–11; *PM 1902*, pt. 1, table 3, p. 6 and table 1, p. 4 (my calculations).

the factory if they had retained ties to the land. If such a pattern could be found in this relatively highly paid, skilled occupation at a time when involuntary ties to the land had been relaxed, then surely it must have been more common among less educated, less assimilated workers in the pre-1906 period.

To summarize, a comparison of the age distribution of peasants and nonpeasants shows a disproportionately small number of the former in the age group forty and above. This disparity cannot fully be explained by differences in the rates of in-migration or mortality of different *sosloviia*. Moreover, when the comparison is restricted to people whose living and working conditions were

Table 2.7. **Age Distribution (by Percentage) of Workers in Printing Trades, 1907**

Occupation	Percentage of workers by age group				
	Under 20	20–40	40–45	45–50	Over 50
Typesetters[a]					
Urban	5.4	75.3	10.0	5.8	3.7
Intermediate	9.2	84.8	4.1	2.0	
Peasant	10.7	83.1	4.8	0.5	1.0
Bookbinders[a]					
Urban	11.5	71.3	9.0	4.9	3.3
Intermediate	11.1	77.7	9.7	1.4	
Peasant	10.2	78.2	5.3	3.3	2.9
All printing trades					
Urban	8.2	74.2	8.9	5.0	3.7
Intermediate	10.1	75.8	7.2	4.8	2.4
Peasant	12.8	77.4	4.5	3.6	1.9

Source: A. Svavitskii and V. Sher, *Ocherk polozheniia rabochikh pechatnogo dela v Moskve*, app., table 1 (my calculations).

[a]These occupational groups had the greatest number of workers (877 typesetters and 437 bookbinders), hence the least possibility of random distortion.

identical, peasants are still found to be less numerous in the older group. One is left with the impression that a significant proportion of peasants departed from Moscow after age forty. It cannot be proven that they returned to their birthplaces, but this inference is consistent with evidence of workers' landholding and family ties to the countryside.

Tradition Outweighs Innovation

The data presented here suggest that it would be wrong to describe village and factory as polar opposites or to picture the peasant-worker's condition as a transitory stage of development. In the Moscow region, only a small proportion of the peasant population was present in the cities and factories at any given moment; yet many more had been there but had returned to the countryside. Those who stayed in the factories still took the opportunity to return periodically to the country, and in hard times the village could still be a place of refuge. The typical worker had one foot in the village and one in the factory but showed little inclination to commit himself irrevocably to either alternative. On the contrary, as can be seen in Chapter Three, some *otkhodniki* were following in their fathers' or grandfathers' footsteps as they traveled back and forth.

Census statistics for Moscow city suggest a constant two-way movement between the countryside and urban centers. Other evidence suggests that this movement was not confined to unskilled occupations but could also include industrial veterans. In the long run, the proportion of thoroughly citified or proletarianized workers may have been increasing, as some of the data in Tables 2.3 and 2.4 suggest, but other evidence indicates that such workers were still an exceptional minority at the turn of the twentieth century.

The migration patterns of the Moscow region provide little basis for describing peasant-workers as disoriented, uprooted, unconscious, or primitive. On the contrary, elements of historical continuity seem to have outweighed disruptive or innovative influences. Like the factories themselves, the workers' movements to and from the city were strongly influenced—one might even say dictated—by customs and patterns inherited from previous generations.

Chapter Three

Migration and Family Patterns

What sort of family life did the typical Moscow worker lead? The answer to this question has far-reaching implications, not just for the study of proletarianization but for an understanding of other social and economic trends as well. *Family life* in the broadest sense encompasses patterns of marriage, childbearing, and socialization; household size and composition; residence, property ownership and inheritance. On a national scale, such factors help to determine rates of population increase, social mobility, and capital accumulation. In short, they help to determine the course of a nation's development.[1]

The family patterns of nineteenth-century Russia stood in sharp contrast to those of most of Western Europe. There private land ownership and single-share inheritance were predominant throughout the modern era. Bachelorhood and spinsterhood were relatively common; many individuals did not marry until their late twenties, and the average household included not much more than four members.[2] In Russia, where land tenure was often communal and a father's inheritance was divided among his sons, different patterns prevailed: households were larger, marriages were earlier, and bachelorhood and spinsterhood were extremely rare.

Not surprisingly, the growth of cities and the expansion of factories seemed to threaten many of these patterns. Nineteenth-century observers attached great significance to the movement of families into industrial centers. Populists saw in it the disintegration of a traditional way of life and the undermining of inherited values and authority; advocates of capitalist development believed that a hereditary class of skilled workers would be a cornerstone

of future industrial development; revolutionary Marxists expected
such workers to become the vanguard of future struggle.[3] All
agreed, however, that the worker whose family was with him in
the city or factory was in a very different position from the one
who had left wife and children behind in the village.

How were traditional peasant family patterns affected by industrialization and urbanization? Was a new, factory-based family
unit emerging? Did family life become more "European" or did
it retain its distinctive qualities? Did traditional family patterns
put their own stamp on the future course of industrial and urban
growth? Here, as in Chapter Two, the most interesting questions
are the hardest to answer. Certain aspects of family behavior are
easily described: the age at marriage, the proportion of the population that ever married, the size of the average household in city
and country. Describing the family environment of workers or
peasants, or the transmission of attitudes and habits from generation to generation, is a much more difficult task, but from the
limited evidence available one can still draw some cautious in-
ferences about the interaction between village and factory life.

Family Life in the City

The conditions of city and factory life, in Moscow as elsewhere
in Russia, tended to discourage workers from maintaining families.
Low wages and the terms of employment made it virtually impossible for workers to secure separate living quarters of their own.
In the more primitive industrial establishments, those who slept in
the workshops could keep their families beside them in extremely
unhygienic conditions. One example was the bast-matting industry,
in which workers customarily slept on the floor under their hand-
powered looms, children entered the work as early as age five, and
most workers lived with their families. Elsewhere, however,
workers were crowded into factory-owned barracks or rented a
fraction of a room in nearby flophouses (*koechno-kamorochnye
kvartiry*). Toward the end of the nineteenth century, an "enlightened" minority of employers began to build living quarters to
accommodate workers' families, but the families were often
crowded several to a room, making domestic life quite difficult.
Often, too, these facilities were available only if the husband and
wife were both working: if either quit or was fired, the family
could be evicted.[4]

Employers, moreover, made little if any provision for the exigencies of child rearing. Nurseries or kindergartens were almost nonexistent, and mothers might even be denied permission to nurse their babies during work hours.[5] The employers' motive was mainly financial: building and maintaining nurseries cost money, and so did any interruption of the work schedule, especially where expensive machinery was involved. To avoid this expense, some factory owners hired only childless women, but even where this was not an explicit policy most mothers found it impossible to keep young children with them.

As a result of these conditions, only a minority of city dwellers, and a much smaller minority of factory workers, lived with their families. As Table 3.1 indicates, only about one-third of the 650,000 people who occupied ordinary living quarters in Moscow city in 1882 were independent householders or members of their immediate families. Altogether there were 84,000 independent households, of which roughly 60 percent included children of the head of household. Of the total population 12.6 percent were clerks and workers who resided in their employers' households, and an additional 20 percent resided in nonfamily units such as factory barracks.[6] As Table 3.1 indicates, units of the latter type were especially common in the Lefortovskaia and Serpukhovskaia districts, which at that time were the greatest manufacturing districts in the city. The distinctiveness of Moscow's residential pattern can be seen quite clearly in comparison to Berlin's. There householders and their descendents comprised almost four-fifths of the entire population: servants, relatives, and boarders were less common; workers and clerks rarely lived with their employers; and group living units were nonexistent. In Berlin the conjugal or nuclear family predominated, whereas in Moscow it was almost a rarity.

It was especially rare at factories, where residence was effectively limited to those who were capable of joining in the work. This can be seen from Table 3.2, which lists the number of dependents per capita of workers in various industries. Even among the better paid metalworkers and machine builders, the census takers counted only four dependents for every ten workers, whereas textile workers were found to have less than one dependent for every ten workers.

A comparison of figures from 1882 and 1897 suggests that the number of dependents was increasing over time, but even so, such individuals remained an insignificant minority at the end of the

Table 3.1. Percentage Distribution of Population by Position in Household

	Head of household	Children and grandchildren of head of household	Relatives and their children	Servants and their children	Workers and clerks	Boarders of various kinds	Group living units
Moscow 1882	17.3	16.5	6.1	11.0	12.6	17.2	19.3
Lefortovskaia precinct	12.5	12.9	4.4	5.2	7.9	13.38	43.7
Serpukhovskaia precinct	12.8	11.8	6.1	5.9	6.1	15.8	41.5
Berlin 1875	39.3	34.7	4.3	6.8	2.1	12.9	

Sources: *PM 1882*, pt. 1, sec. 1, pp. 73–76 and sec. 2, table 4, pp. 156–57.

Table 3.2. **Dependents per Capita of Workers and Other Self-supporting People in Moscow, 1882 and 1897**

| | Dependents per capita | | |
| | Workers alone | Workers and employers together | |
Group	1882	1882	1897
Metalworkers	0.27	0.47	0.69
Machine and instrument makers	0.39	0.54	*a*
Chemical workers	0.23	0.37	0.40
Textile workers			
Total	0.08	0.14	0.17
Weaving and spinning (factory)	0.06	0.10	0.12
Food preparation workers	0.10	0.25	0.25
All workers in industry (craft and			
factory)	0.17	0.31	0.39

Sources: PM 1882, pt. 2, sec. 1, table 15, p. 223 and pt. 3, sec. 2, table 10, p. 153; Tsentral'nyi Statisticheskii Komitet, *Pervaia vseobshchaia perepis' naseleniia Rossiiskoi imperii, 1897 g.*, vol. 24, pt. 2, table 10.

*a*The two censuses divided this group in such different ways that no comparisons are possible.

century. In 1902 fully four-fifths of all migrants living in Moscow city were self-supporting; in contrast, just over one-third of city-born residents were self-supporting.[7]

Who were these workers without families? In the early decades of the nineteenth century, the population of Moscow's factories had consisted almost entirely of males.[8] With the spread of mechanization, however, many factory tasks (especially in the textile industry) no longer demanded much strength or skill and greater numbers of women and minors began to be hired. By the end of the century, women accounted for almost one-half of the total work force in textile manufacturing, and in certain divisions such as cotton spinning, males had become an insignificant minority.[9] Between 1871 and 1902 the proportion of women in Moscow city's entire population rose from 40 to 45 percent.[10] Some observers, including the eminent Soviet demographer A. G. Rashin, have taken this growth as a sign that the number of permanent city-based households was increasing—evidence, in other words, that capitalism was advancing and old patterns of life were eroding.[11] Although it would be wrong to deny that *any* such households were formed, a close examination of female labor and

migration patterns indicates that they were the exception rather
than the rule.

Moscow's female population grew through in-migration. The
women who moved there, like their male counterparts, were mostly
from the peasantry and came to Moscow to find wages. Roughly
two-thirds of them were self-supporting, with domestic service
accounting for the greatest proportion (33 percent) followed by
factory work (13 percent) and small-scale manufacturing (9
percent).[12] The conditions of their work and living arrangements
generally prevented them from having children with them (true
not just for factories but for domestic service and most other
employment), so those who were mothers commonly left their
children to be raised by relatives in the country. Even so, women
of childbearing age who moved to Moscow tended to depart
within a short time.[13] The peasant women who stayed longest in
Moscow were older, mainly widows and spinsters, who faced
fewer obstacles if they wished to renounce their land allotment
and depart permanently from the village.[14]

Thus, although the overall proportion of women in the population of Moscow city was increasing, the ratio of women to men
remained least favorable for the ages of marriage and childbearing.
It was lower for migrants than for the city-born population,
and lower in the industrial suburbs than in the central districts.
Among migrants aged fifteen to thirty-nine in the suburbs, there
were only thirty-nine women for every one hundred men.[15]

In short, only a small minority of the women who came to
Moscow were likely to stay there, marry, and raise children. An
increase in the overall proportion of women did not necessarily
mean that the proportion of marriageable women increased, nor
did an increase in the number married necessarily lead to an increase in the number of families. When migrant women did bear
children, they were more likely to raise them in the countryside.

The Bifurcated Household

In view of the migration patterns described in Chapter Two,
it is not surprising that many factory workers and city dwellers
chose to maintain households in the countryside. The extent of
this practice can be gauged from the fact that there were almost
twice as many married men as married women living in Moscow
city in 1902.[16] The population of factories and urban centers was
composed largely of husbands without wives, and parents without

children. In the countryside, thousands of households relied on the monetary contributions of absent members in order to make ends meet.

What effect did this system have upon family composition? Did departing wage earners still follow the marital patterns of the village, or were new proletarian patterns beginning to appear? Demographic statistics provide partial answers to these questions. The simplest way of approaching these questions is to look at statistics on marriage and compare the behavior of peasant migrants with that of townspeople and nonmigrant peasants. As Table 3.3 reveals, there were indeed sharp differences between the marital patterns of native Muscovites and those of the rest of Russia; migrants and factory workers, instead of falling between the two, seem to follow one extreme or the other, with males maintaining the patterns of peasant Russia and females assimilating to the patterns of the city.

The urban and rural extremes seem to represent what J. Hajnal has called "European" and "non-European" patterns of marriage.[17] City-born Muscovites seem to have married much later than the rest of the population, and a greater proportion never married at all. Their rates are comparable to those found in such countries as Sweden in the nineteenth century, whereas the national Russian figures resemble those of Asia or southeastern Europe (e.g., Serbia). Knowing that the Russian national statistics pertain to a population composed predominantly of peasants, one could easily picture the city and countryside as two opposite poles, analogous to the differences between Western Europe and the rest of the world at the end of the nineteenth century. At one extreme, Moscow city could be taken to symbolize modernity and technological progress. The factors that discouraged or prevented marriage in this setting might include increased labor mobility, more years devoted to education and specialized job training, and a work situation in which, in contrast to agrarian society, a spouse and children are more a liability than an asset. At the opposite extreme, peasants who spent their entire lives in the villages could be expected to follow age-old patterns, marrying early and producing large families.

Following this line of reasoning, migrants and factory workers who spent much of their adult lives in cities and towns should have been exposed to most of the same "modernizing" pressures as the rest of the population. They should therefore have occupied a position between the extremes of city and peasant marital patterns. The males in Table 3.3, however, do not fit this predic-

Table 3.3 **Age and Marital Status of City-born, Migrants, and Factory Workers in Moscow City, 1902, Compared to Russia as a Whole, 1897**

Age	Percentage married males	Percentage married females
15–19		
City-born	0.5	8.7
Migrant	3.6	12.5
Factory	4.1	13.3
Russia	4.4	15.4
20–29		
City-born	29.5	52.7
Migrant	54.3	55.6
Factory	63.4	59.7
Russia	58	76
30–39		
City-born	65	61
Migrant	83	61
Factory	89	60
Russia	90	88
40–49		
City-born	71	48
Migrant	86	52
Factory	90	50
Russia	92	81
50–59		
City-born	70	30
Migrant	80	35
Factory	83	33
Russia	87	66

Sources: PM 1902, pt. 1, sec. 1, table 4, pp. 9–10 and pt. 2, table 3, pp. 12–15; Tsentral'nyi Statisticheskii Komitet, *Obshchii svod po imperii rezul' tatov razrabotki dannykh pervoi vseobshchei perepisi naseleniia, proizvedennoi 28 ianvaria 1897 g.*, pt. 1, table 5, pp. 78–79.

tion. Instead of postponing or avoiding marriage, workers and migrants appear to have married at least as early as other peasants. Male factory workers, in fact, married even earlier: 63 percent in the age group twenty to twenty-nine were married, compared to 58 percent of males throughout Russia.

These figures cannot readily be explained by reference to a peasantry in transition whose members were progressing step by step from the backward village to the modern city. Employment away from the native village seems on the contrary to have reinforced or exaggerated the preexisting marital pattern of peasant men. The apparent paradox can be explained if one looks again at the idea of rural-urban interaction. Given the possibility of maintaining families in the countryside, peasant-workers may have encountered fewer obstacles to marriage than did pure peasants or city-born workers. Unlike other workers, they might not have been inhibited by the lack of housing or the high cost of living in the city; unlike other peasants, they were receiving a relatively reliable money income independent of their land allotments. From the available statistics, one cannot determine whether wage-earning peasant youths were defying their fathers by contracting early marriages, or whether the migrant's wages, by enhancing the prosperity of the parental household, encouraged the parents to seek a daughter-in-law. In either case, however, the logic of the rural-urban nexus would seem to encourage young men to marry early.[18]

Indirect support for this suggestion can be found in marriage statistics for the whole of Moscow province. In the years 1883–97, the crude rate of marriage (number of marriages per annum per thousand population) was found to vary directly with the state of the job market, especially in the more industrial sections of the province. Elsewhere in Russia, nuptiality was strongly influenced by the state of the agrarian economy. In Moscow, however, industrial employment was a better determinant of economic security and a better predictor of marriage. The rate of marriage dropped as low as 7.45 per 1,000 during the depression years around 1885 and 1891 and went as high as 8.7 in such boom years as 1888 or 1897.[19]

Moscow's municipal census of 1902 provides further evidence of the connection between nuptiality and *otkhodnichestvo* in its statistics on the marital patterns of separate occupational groups. Comparing male factory workers with two other categories—nonfactory extractive and manufacturing (*dobyvaiushchii, obrabatyvaiushchii*) workers and those in transport—one finds that artisans and craftsmen showed slightly higher rates of marriage than factory workers in the fifteen-to-nineteen-year-old bracket, though slightly lower than factory workers in the older brackets. The transport workers, on the other hand, had a rate more than twice as great as any in Table 3.4 for ages fifteen to nineteen and a significantly higher rate than other occupations for ages twenty to twenty-four and twenty-five to twenty-nine. All three categories of workers were recruited predominantly from the peasantry, and the range of wages was approximately the same for all of them. The nonfactory and transport workers, however, had more opportunity than factory workers to travel back and forth

Peasant and Proletarian

Table 3.4. **Age and Marital Status of Males in Selected Occupational Categories, Moscow, 1902**

Age and occupation	Percentage married
15–19	
Factory	4.1
Other extractive and manufacturing	5.4
Transport	9.8
20–24	
Factory	48.8
Other extractive and manufacturing	47.8
Transport	54.1
25–29	
Factory	77.9
Other extractive and manufacturing	73.7
Transport	78.5

Source: PM 1902, pt. 2, table 3, pp. 12–13.

between Moscow and the countryside; railway workers had the right of free travel, carters brought their own horses to the city, and artisans commonly traveled together to work in the city on a seasonal basis. This mobility seems to have reinforced the effects of rural-urban ties, with the result that these workers married even earlier than their brethren at the factories.

The same factors that encouraged male migrants to marry early may also have led them to produce large families.[20] Preliminary investigations suggest that migrants' households were no smaller than those of nonmigrant peasants and may even have been larger. Workers at the Tsindel' cotton mill in Moscow city, for example, reported an average family size of 7.3, whereas the average household in the regions from which they had migrated was just over 6.[21] In general, the provinces surrounding Moscow had exceptionally high birth rates in the last decades of the nineteenth century; Moscow province's rate was falling in those years, but the rates of several neighboring provinces rose spectacularly.[22] It appears that Moscow's migrants were producing children in the hinterland, thereby inflating the neighboring provinces' birth rates and deflating Moscow's.

If labor migration encouraged men to marry early and have large families, it seems to have had the opposite effect on women. Instead of maintaining the "peasant" marital pattern, female migrants and factory workers appear to have quickly assimilated themselves to the "city" one. Their rates of marriage for all ages were lower than the rates for Russia as a whole; for all ages over twenty-five, they are virtually indistinguishable from those of city-born women. The reasons for this phenomenon are not hard to find, especially in light of the previous discussion. Male migrants married earlier because they could leave their families in the countryside; to the extent that they did so, however, their wives would be excluded from the population of cities and factories. The proportion of unmarried, childless, and widowed women in cities and factories would thereby be inflated.

Women, it seems, had to choose between raising families and migrating for wages. To the extent that they did assimilate themselves to the urban-industrial order, their rates of marriage went down. The Moscow provincial *zemstvo's* survey of factories throughout the province in the early 1880s found that the proportion of married women in different populations varied inversely with the degree of urbanization or industrialization: rates were highest in the nearby nonindustrial province of Tambov; lower throughout Moscow province; and progressively lower in Moskovskii county, in the female factory population of the province, and in Moscow city. When female workers were divided by occupation, moreover, those in traditional, unmechanized branches of production were found to have higher rates of marriage than those in such technically advanced industries as cotton spinning or silk weaving.[23] Studies of a somewhat later period found a negative correlation between literacy and the rate of marriage, and this, too, suggests that assimilation to urban-industrial life inhibited women from marrying.[24]

The city and factory, it seems, were not preventing marriage and may not have reduced fertility. They were, however, attracting (and rejecting) specific segments of the peasant population. Males with families were encouraged to migrate, as were unmarried and childless women; but given the apparent integration of *otkhodnichestvo* with the village economy, traditional family patterns stood a good chance of survival in the country.

This seems likely to have intensified a pattern, still enduring today in much of the Third World, in which able-bodied young adults go off to the city and leave agriculture to the very old and the very young. (It is true that able-bodied young women also stayed behind, but the reason was usually that they were burdened with young children, and this necessarily limited their role as agricultural producers or potential innovators.) An indirect effect of *otkhodnichestvo* may thus have been to perpetuate small-scale production and inefficiency in the countryside.

Fathers and Sons at the Factory

One further way of measuring the influence of cities and factories on family life is to ask whether sons followed their fathers to the factory. If many did so, this could mean that acquired skills and attitudes were being passed on from generation to generation, helping to create a hereditary proletariat.[25] On the other hand, if each successive generation was recruited anew from the peasantry, there might be more disruption and discontinuity in migrants' lives and less opportunity to come to terms with the conditions or problems of a new environment.

The implications of this issue were recognized ' as early as the 1880s, with the result that several different studies collected information about workers' origins. The data they compiled suggest a high degree of continuity and generational succession at the factories of Moscow combined with the continuance of strong rural ties. Children followed their parents to the factory, but they still spent their formative years in the village. If their work was hereditary, this did not necessarily make them proletarian.

The first such study, carried out in Moscow city in 1881, found that 43 percent of male textile workers were the sons of workers.[26] Three years later, E. M. Dement'ev interviewed more than eighteen thousand workers in Bronnitskii, Serpukhovskii, and Kolomenskii counties and found that 55 percent of them were "hereditary" (*potomstvennye*)—sons of factory workers.[27] Shestakov's study of the Tsindel' cotton-printing factory in Moscow city in 1899 reached the identical figure: 55 percent of all male workers were second- (and in some cases even third-) generation factory workers.[28]

This pattern would seem to follow logically from the pattern of child labor mentioned earlier in this chapter. Young people entered the factory at a tender age, and those whose parents or relatives were already working there may have found their way to the factory more readily than other peasants.[29] Is it proper to conclude from this, however, that the younger generation constituted a true proletariat? Were these younger workers really cut off from village life—propertyless and, in Dement'ev's words, "living from day to day"?[30] In the main, nineteenth-century researchers answered these questions in the affirmative, and later generations of economists and historians, from Lenin and Tugan-Baranovskii down to Soviet scholars of the 1960s, have tended to agree. A close scrutiny of the available evidence, however, reveals several flaws in this argument.

In the first place, the factories described by Dement'ev, Peskov, or Shestakov did not employ substantial numbers of women or children. The majority of their workers were male, and like the males discussed earlier in this chapter, most lived in barracks without their families. Their children were raised in the country-side by their mothers (or if the mothers were also working at the factory, by grandparents or other relatives). The existence of a second generation at the factory was no proof that its members had severed ties with the "patriarchal" village.

In the second place, Dement'ev's and Peskov's statistics were compiled during the depression of the early 1880s, when many workers had been laid off and few new ones had been taken on at the factories. This may have inflated the proportion of long-term experienced workers and understated the proportion of green new recruits.[31]

In the third place, most of those who were listed as second-generation factory workers retained land allotments in their native villages. At the Tsindel' factory more than 90 percent of all peasant-workers had allotments.[32] A more extensive study of workers in Vladimir province in the years 1894–97 found that, out of a total of some 35,000 hereditary (i.e., second-generation) peas-ant workers, 40 percent (13.8 thousand) possessed allotments.[33]

An allotment, as discussed in Chapter Two, might have been an involuntary tie to the village; yet additional evidence suggests many workers had more than a nominal tie to agriculture. In Peskov's study, occupational groups with the very highest propor-tion of second-generation workers were also the ones with the highest proportion of summer departures to the countryside: handweavers in silk, cotton, or wool and hand dye-printers.[34] Dement'ev's study, meanwhile, reveals an unexpected pattern in the ages of hereditary workers: in the two largest occupational groups, spinners and weavers, which between them accounted for 40 percent of his respondents, the proportion of "hered-itary" workers was higher in the older age brackets than among younger workers.[35] (Outside the textile industries, the reverse pattern was found: each successive age group had a lower propor-tion of hereditary workers than the one before it.) Dement'ev's explanation for this phenomenon was that the textile industry was expanding so rapidly that the available pool of second-generation workers was insufficient, forcing employers to take on inexperienced first-generation laborers.[36] As indicated in Chapter One, the cotton industry did indeed expand quite rapidly in the late 1870s, but in the years of Dement'ev's study it was suffering badly from the effects of a general economic depression. In addition to cotton production, moreover, the textile industry included silk and woolen manufacturing, which grew at a much slower rate even in times of general prosperity. Dement'ev's argument can therefore provide at best an incomplete explanation of the ages of hereditary workers.

Peskov's breakdown of occupational groups, more detailed than Dement'ev's, suggests a different explanation: hereditary workers were actually concentrated in several traditional occupational groups in which mechanization had had little impact (handweaving) or had been introduced at a very early point (spinning). The data do not suggest that such individuals were likely to acquire new skills or move into trades other than those of their fathers. When factories mechanized and needed new categories of workers, they were more likely to seek them among first-generation recruits; this was so even for better paying positions that should have been especially attractive to experienced workers.[37] At the textile factories, the succession of generations does not seem to have entailed much occupational mobility.

If hereditary workers were more common in handcrafts than in mechanized labor, and if sons were most likely to remain in the same occupation as their fathers, this casts doubt on the process of proletarianization that Lenin and most Soviet historians have postulated. Far from undermining outmoded customs or opening workers' eyes to the new realities that surrounded them, the hereditary occupations that existed in Moscow seem to have locked workers into a system reminiscent of the era of serfdom, when sons involuntarily inherited their fathers' trades.[38] This impression is reinforced by other evidence from Vladimir province (1899) that suggests that the proportion of hereditary workers was highest among those who lived less than 1 *versta* (6/10 mile) from the factory and that it fell off in direct relation to the distance traveled from home to the workplace.[39] In this instance, the workers' hereditary experience would seem to have bound them to a particular enterprise, thereby limiting their horizons literally as well as figuratively.

In Moscow province, one of Dement'ev's colleagues in the *zemstvo* factory studies of the early 1880s made an even more striking observation: the hereditary proletariat was concentrated at the former votchinal factories.[40]

> Only there does one encounter the type of fundamental (*korennoi*) factory worker, alienated from the land and farmstead, having nothing to his name except the strength of his own hands—accustomed to only

one type of work, and except for that having no other source of even the scantiest existence. In the fundamental factory population, the occupation of factory work was passed on and is passed on hereditarily from grandfather to father, and from father to son . . . investigating the physical well-being of the factory worker, [the investigator] usually is dealing with two successive generations of former serf-factory workers.[41]

By the 1880s these factories, as indicated in Chapter One, had fallen far behind all others in their level of output, rates of growth, and adoption of technological advances. As shown in Chapter Seven, their levels of labor unrest were substantially lower than those of other industries even though wages and working conditions were generally worse.

The hereditary workers described in these latter studies were not skilled craftsmen and should not be equated with the relatively privileged and better paid artisans of western Europe. The Russian textile workers, unlike European artisans, had no guild tradition to look back to nor any independence or group status to lose. They were not labor aristocrats but rather semiskilled or even unskilled laborers whose forebears had been performing the same tasks for many decades at subsistence wages. Their hereditary status was associated with an unchanging environment and bound them all the more tightly to the countryside.[42]

In short, the existence of second-generation, or hereditary, workers was sometimes associated with traditionalism and backwardness rather than with progress and change; thus it need not imply the deterioration of patriarchal family structures in the countryside. It was not necessarily associated with geographic or occupational mobility (it may even have inhibited both), nor did it automatically encourage the acquisition of "modern" skills and attitudes.

Endurance of Village Family Patterns

The conditions of city and factory life were not at all conducive to the formation of new family units. As a result townspeople married later than peasants, had fewer children, or avoided marriage altogether. Male peasant migrants, however, showed no tendency to assimilate to this pattern. It appears that their non-agricultural earnings, when combined with their families' traditional agricultural pursuits, gave migrants a certain measure of economic security and enabled them to continue the rural pattern of early marriage and large households. There was more incentive for a migrant to divide his life (and his family) between factory and village than to move away from the countryside and begin a truly proletarian existence.

This discussion tends to reinforce the suggestion that tradition and continuity outweighed disruption and innovation in migrants' lives. A distinctively Russian pattern of family life was perpetuated, in turn helping to perpetuate other traditions. In the countryside, migration seems likely to have reinforced conservatism: a household whose adult members were residing elsewhere was less likely to experiment with new crops, techniques of cultivation, or patterns of landholding. At the factory, each new generation of workers was recruited from the countryside. True, many were the sons of older workers and may thus have been prepared in some ways for the transition to factory life. Nonetheless, most had spent their childhood in the countryside, making them likely to retain some psychological or cultural allegiance to the village in later life, a point examined more thoroughly in Chapters Four and Five.

Certainly there were some innovative or disruptive forces at work in the family patterns of the Moscow hinterland. The abandonment of village traditions was most apparent among female migrants. As they grew older, women without families may have found agricultural activities too difficult to continue. The city offered such individuals a meagre but possibly less strenuous existence in such fields as domestic service. The important point for this discussion, however, is that these older female migrants were destined for a solitary life in the city. They would have little direct impact on the lives of future migrants or proletarians, and the next generation of workers, like its predecessor, would have to be recruited from the countryside.

In assessing the traditionalism of Moscow's family life, one more point must be reiterated: the factories themselves were part of the region's tradition. Moscow's peasants had been traveling to urban and industrial centers for a century or more, thus village family patterns were shaped by long interaction with cities and factories. The data in this chapter, as in Chapter Two, suggest that the village and factory were not opposites but were joined together in a symbiotic relationship. Each helped to meet the needs of the other, and each in turn was shaped by the other's needs. The bifurcated household described in these pages was not an innovation of the 1880s or 1890s but had been in existence for as many decades as the Moscow region's oldest factories.

Chapter Four

Migration and
Regional Loyalties

Migrants in many historical and cultural settings have shown a tendency to settle together and provide various kinds of assistance to one another. In North America, this pattern was widespread among many immigrant groups. Jewish immigrants formed *lands-manshaftn*, mutual aid societies whose members were drawn from a single town or village in Eastern Europe. For Italians, whose regional dialects and traditions were strongly developed, ties among *paesani* from a village or district provided a basis for employment and settlement in the New World. Analogous patterns can be found among internal migrants in other parts of the world, especially in the rapidly growing cities of the Third World, whose inhabitants are drawn mostly from the countryside.[1]

The migrants who flocked to the factories and working-class districts of Moscow had traveled a much shorter distance than immigrants to North America. Their background was essentially homogeneous, without major differences of speech, religion, ethnicity, or life experience. They thus lacked some of the incentives that have kept migrants together in foreign lands, the multi-tribal cities of Africa, or the multiracial ones of Latin America. Migration, moreover, was a long-standing tradition in Russia, a nation whose entire history had been shaped by a constantly expanding frontier. Russians have always been, in Sir John Maynard's phrase, "land sailors," and this has led some historians to conclude that regional loyalties were unimportant or non-existent.[2] All the same, many of the peasants who streamed to Moscow in the 1880s and 1890s came with no previous training or craft skills, and even those such as cottage weavers who had acquired such skills might be bewildered and distressed by the complexities of city or factory life. It was natural that the newly arrived migrant should seek support and assistance from someone. Evidence suggests that "someone" was most often a *zemliak.*

The Idea of *Zemliachestvo*

Smirnitskii's dictionary defines *zemliak* as "fellow-country-man, person from the same land." In popular usage today, the term may be applied to people from an area as large as Siberia, yet it connotes a special kind of relationship. Two Siberians living in Moscow, even though their homes may be thousands of miles apart, really do have something in common that sets them apart from native Muscovites. The "land" a Russian claims as his own is often a much smaller territory—a province, a district, or even a village: to the novelist Vladimir Soloukhin, writing in the 1950s, the western region of Vladimir province was "my native land" (*zemlia rodnaia*).[3] Russian university students in the nineteenth century, like their counterparts in Germany and Scandinavia, were organized in fraternal societies by province of origin (*zemliachestva*). These organizations provided loans and mutual assistance and sometimes served as a vehicle for struggle against the university authorities.[4] The Russian government's suspicious attitude toward public organizations, together with employers' regulation of everyday life, made the establishment of such formal associations among workers or migrants impossible at least until 1905. (Even after 1905, when some of the legal obstacles to organizations had been removed, peasant-workers seem to have shied away from formal, legally constituted associations.) Peasant *zemliaki*, however, continued to seek one another out, and their informal contacts became an important bridge between village and city life. Years later, workers recalled how they had kept up ties with *zemliaki* across many decades: "They still remember their fellow villagers (*odnosel'chane*), migrants from a neighboring village or from the same county."[5]

I. I. Ianzhul, a Moscow factory inspector, noted in 1884 that children often came to work at large factories in the care of a *zemliak* while their parents remained behind or traveled elsewhere to work.[6] F. P. Pavlov, an engineer at an unnamed textile factory in central Russia, asked a woman worker how she and her husband could stand sharing a room with another family and received the reply, "What of it? They're our own people (*my svoi*), from the same village."[7] In Russian literary works of the nineteenth century, ties among *zemliaki* are often mentioned in passing, a detail of everyday life that authors and readers took for granted. In Dostoevski's *Crime and Punishment*, for example, an important secondary role is played by two house painters who are *zemliaki* from Riazan', working together in Saint Petersburg.[8] The protagonist of Gorki's novel *Mother*, whose husband and son are described as long-term factory workers, is initiated into revolutionary activity by (among others) a *zemliak*.[9]

Just how widespread was *zemliachestvo* among workers?[10] Statistical evidence suggests that the clustering together of fellow migrants was a common pattern in the factories of Moscow. At the Tsindel' cotton mill, for example, more than 50 percent of all workers in 1899 came from a single province (Riazan'), and 22.5 percent came from a single county of that province.[11] This concentration of peasant migrants seems much too great to have occurred by chance; according to the municipal census of 1902, migrants from Riazan' were just 8.6 percent of Moscow city's population.[12] A more detailed breakdown of the work force at another major cotton mill reveals that migrants from different provinces were concentrated in different divisions of the factory; there too, the degree of concentration was too great to be explained by chance.[13]

A study of workers at still another cotton mill provides more exact information on workers' places of origin and supports the suggestion that migrants from a particular village or township tended to band together:[14] five out of six workers from one village were carpenters; nine out of ten from another were dye printers; and so forth.*

Surveys of whole branches of industry reveal an analogous phenomenon: workers from a particular place were concentrated in a particular occupation, not just at one or two factories but throughout an entire industry. In brickmaking, for example, workers from a single county of nearby Kaluga province constituted an overwhelming majority of all workers.[15] A survey of male textile workers in Moscow city (1880/81) showed patterns of

---

*In all, six such clusters are listed, accounting for forty-five workers out of a total of fifteen hundred. The author, referring to these groups for a different purpose, does not indicate whether the rest of the work force followed the same pattern. This could be determined from the records of individual enterprises, whose payroll sheets and worker passbooks have sometimes been preserved in Soviet regional archives. Unfortunately, I did not have access to these archives for my study.

regional concentration on an even larger scale. For example, 43 percent of all cotton weavers came from Kaluga; yet that province provided only 3.8 percent of all dye printers and 6.6 percent of all shearers. The same study presented a further breakdown of workers from Moscow province, indicating that occupational specialization was more localized, with each county having its own particular trade or skill. Bogorodskii county, for example, provided 26 percent of all silk weavers in the survey and 11 percent of all warpers but almost no workers in other branches of production.[16]

Was this occupational concentration peculiar to a few industries, or was it part of a larger system of bonds among *zemliaki?* Data from Moscow's municipal censuses of 1871 and 1882 provide a partial answer by presenting the distribution of different provinces' migrants through the seventeen police precincts (*chasti*) of the city. In general, migrants from each province tended to cluster together in two or three precincts. Each province, however, had its own distinctive pattern of clustering. In 1871, for example, over 21 percent of male migrants from Kaluga province lived in Lefortovskaia precinct compared to 4.6 percent of males from Iaroslavl' province.[17]

A province was, of course, a large unit whose territory extended over thousands of square miles and included millions of people. The regional loyalty of *zemliaki* was undoubtedly more localized, but the census figures are not generally broken down into smaller units. The one exception is the 1882 census, which gives a detailed breakdown of migrants from different parts of Moscow province. Here once again, people from each county are concentrated in a few precincts, and each county's pattern is different from all the others.[18]

Occupational Motives

There are several ways of explaining this clustering of migrants. One factor of considerable importance was the existence of handcraft traditions through which the peasant population of a region specialized in a particular craft or trade. As peasants moved further and further from their villages and into factory production, some of the old regional distinctions were preserved. Thus, workers from Vladimir were known as carpenters; those from Tver' province, as stove makers and stonecutters.[19] An extreme example of such specialization was the production of bast matting.

Of 1,040 workers in this industry in three counties of Moscow province in 1884/85, all without exception came from a single county of Kaluga province.[20]

In other cases, peasants acquired particular skills in one industrial center, then migrated elsewhere. For example, concentrations of workers from Ardatovskii county (Nizhnii-Novgorod province) and Tambov province at the Kolomna machine-building works (Kolomenskii county) could be explained by the existence of metalworking enterprises in their home provinces.[21]

Craft skills alone, however, cannot account for the phenomenon of regional concentration because many of the clearest examples of clustering involve unskilled or semiskilled workers. Textile industries, requiring in general much less skill and experience than metalworking plants, included such operations as dyeing, pressing, shearing, and scutching, which required only the "simplest manipulations, or mere physical strength."[22] Yet according to P. A. Peskov's study of seventy-eight Moscow city factories in 1881, migrants traveled relatively great distances to work in these occupations, and migrants from one or two regions were predominant in each occupational group.[23]

The pattern of regional specialization, moreover, was not consistent from one industrial center to another. A comparison of textile workers in Moscow city with a similar group in the surrounding county shows much variation. In the city, workers from Riazan' province were concentrated in dye-printing establishments and constituted 21 percent of all bleachers and dyers; in the county, however, they were only 7.15 percent of those occupational groups, which drew far more workers from Vladimir and Tula. In the city, workers from Riazan' played no part at all in broadcloth weaving, but in the county they were 13.5 percent of all broadcloth weavers.[24] Other occupational groups show similar contrasts, but craft traditions cannot explain them. If Riazan' broadcloth weavers shunned the city and Riazan' dyers passed up job opportunities in the county, their motives must be sought apart from their occupational skills.

Nor can previous work experience in other localities explain the migration patterns of most textile workers. Although particular branches of textile production were sometimes concentrated in individual counties of Moscow province, those regions were not the ones that supplied migrants to Moscow city's factories. The greatest suppliers of broadcloth weavers, for example, were Ruzskii and Mozhaiskii counties; the first had a single broadcloth factory with sixty workers within its borders, the second had none at all. In contrast, the two counties with the greatest number of broadcloth factories and workers accounted for only 1.4 percent of the city's broadcloth weavers. In almost every branch of textile production, Moscow city's workers were recruited from regions where requisite skills and experience were least likely to be found. The only exceptions were three high-skill professions that together employed less than one-seventh of all textile workers in Peskov's survey.[25]

Another reason for migrants to work or live together was the pattern of hiring. In certain regions, recruiters were sent each year to particular districts. Elsewhere work crews (*arteli*) of peasants hired themselves out as a unit.[26] Both these practices were common in small-scale or antiquated industries such as brickmaking and bast-mat weaving. In the latter case, manufacturers sent subcontractors (*podriadchiki*) to the aforementioned regions of Kaluga province; there they sometimes dealt directly with township (*volost'*) officials, who contracted to supply a stated number of workers and sent mostly *nedoimshchiki* ("people whose taxes were in arrears"). Workers recruited in this fashion were almost exclusively male, and those who had families were obliged to leave them in the countryside.[27]

Although published references are few,[28] the pattern of hiring through such agents seems to have been most common in occupations that were seasonal either by necessity (as in the digging of clay or peat) or by tradition (as in the bast-matting industry, which was carried on only in the winter months). Workers thus spent about half of each year in the countryside, though not necessarily in agricultural pursuits.[29] Hiring agents usually traveled to the country in late winter, the hardest season for peasants, in order to strike the best possible bargain over the terms of the work contract.[30]

Regionally based work groups, formed at the hiring agents' insistence, were certainly the cornerstone of this system.[31] Workers accepted these arrangements only with the greatest reluctance. Those who took part were the most unstable element of the working class and were prone to depart for the countryside without warning, even when this involved forfeiture of pay.[32] This pattern seems inconsistent with the needs of large enterprises, which operated year-round and preferred to have workers stay on for many years. In the newly developing mining-metallurgical areas of the South, employers had to take workers where they could find them, sometimes resorting to the system of *verbovka* (recruitment) whereby peasants who had worked at an enterprise for a time returned to their native villages to enlist their neighbors.[33] This arrangement was, however, viewed as a temporary expedient, and the southern enterprises did their best to recruit and retain a permanent labor force. In the Moscow region, contemporaries make no mention of such groupings at large enterprises.

Village-based *arteli*, which in principle were formed at peasants' own initiative, were parallel to, and in some cases indistinguishable from, groups recruited by *podriadchiki*. They operated under the direction or leadership of an elected "elder" (*starosta*), who collected the groups' wages from the employer and distributed them among the members. *Arteli* of this type were sometimes formed by itinerant craftsmen but were most common among unskilled workers and day laborers.[34] At large factories, this type of *artel'* was used only for auxiliary tasks, such as construction or repair work, and even then it was a rarity. Such groupings, then, can hardly explain the settlement patterns of *zemliaki*.

The term *artel'* was also used to describe a group whose members shared room and board. These groups were sometimes formed at the employer's initiative, in which case the members might not be *zemliaki*, but they also flourished among villagers who traveled together to the factory and rented quarters nearby. Old-time workers at the Sormovo metal works outside Nizhnii-Novgorod described such units as *zemliachestva*. They were most common among newly arrived or short-term workers (*sezonniki*), who sometimes traveled back and forth to the village on Sundays for provisions.[35]

Migrants seem, then, to have stayed together in the cities and factories for reasons that had little to do with work contracts or previously acquired skills. This is not to suggest, however, that employment was not a paramount concern of migrants or a prime motive for maintaining ties among *zemliaki*. Rather, *zemliaki* assisted one another in ways not directly related to skills or village-based work groups. A common pattern that endured in Russia well past the Revolution of 1917 was for a peasant to follow his *zemliaki* to a particular part of the city and factory. Petr Moiseenko, a worker-radical of the 1880s, describes his efforts to find work in Saint Petersburg in 1873: "[Having heard that the Shaw factory was hiring] I went up to the gates and asked. They were hiring. I looked for *zemliaki*, and it turned out that one of the assistant foremen was a *zemliak*. It turned out that there were a fair number of *zemliaki*. I was hired and put into a [living] *artel'* of *zemliaki*."[36]

In such a case the migrant's choice of occupation, workplace, or residence was governed by the presence or absence of *zemliaki* among the foremen or the rank-and-file.* (Although rank-and-file workers had no direct say in hiring, they could provide the "guarantees" [*krugovaia poruka*] many employers required.) The system of hiring through *zemliak* networks and of subunits in large factories being dominated by "families" of *zemliaki* was noted in many parts of Russia.[37]

The persistence of juridical and familial ties to the countryside, and the constant movement back and forth between the village and the urban or industrial centers, enabled migrants to maintain networks of communication between their two worlds.[38] These could bring the city dweller news from his family or village and could also advise villagers of opportunities in the city. In the winter of 1885 the number of passport applications in Moscow province was high, but by June the number was greatly reduced; local officials concluded that the grapevine had warned villagers that jobs were scarce that year, owing to the continuing industrial depression.[39] Similar networks are known to have existed between central Russian peasants and agricultural migrants who settled in Siberia.[40]

Peasant Culture Survives in the City

Beyond the material assistance migrants could provide to one another, *zemliaki* had other less tangible reasons for preferring one another's company. The population of Moscow's hinterland may have been homogeneous, but it was not an undifferentiated mass. Despite the basic similarities in their backgrounds, peasants from the surrounding provinces still conserved local traditions and customs. In Moscow at the beginning of the twentieth century, the pioneer ethnologist-musicologist M. E. Piatnitskii devoted considerable attention to the distinctive folk-song traditions of three central Russian provinces. Each region, he realized, had its own style of choral singing, and these traditions were kept alive in Moscow by peasant migrants. In 1911 Piatnitskii recruited a choral group whose members were mostly factory workers, and in their first concerts they performed only as groups of *zemliaki*.[41] Local folkways, although weakened, have survived in parts of Russia

---

*Such a system is described in Anton Chekhov's short story "Peasants," whose protagonist becomes a waiter in Moscow because all his fellow villagers are waiters. One *zemliak* found a position in a hotel many years before and through him a whole generation of migrants found work (*The Oxford Chekhov*, ed. Ronald Hingley, p. 200.)

down to the present, and they were undoubtedly much stronger at the turn of the century.[42]

These cultural patterns, together with the closed nature of the factory community, kept *zemliaki* together long after they had left the village. The bonds between them were especially apparent on ceremonial occasions. Petr Moiseenko recalls being asked to serve as godfather to a *zemliak's* child on Orekhovo in 1884. Moiseenko was at that time an experienced weaver who had not lived in his native village for more than ten years. He had spent time in prison and Siberian exile for his role in the revolutionary underground and the strike movement in Saint Petersburg and considered himself a revolutionary and an atheist. These experiences had not erased the ties between *zemliaki,* nor did his atheism prevent him from participating in the child's christening.[43]

Other evidence suggests that marriage between *zemliaki* was a common pattern among migrants. Although male and female migrants usually worked at different jobs or even at different factories, their patterns of migration were virtually identical. Men and women came to Moscow in identical proportions from the surrounding eight provinces, and their patterns of settlement in the various precincts of the city were almost exactly the same.[44] Aggregate census data on residential patterns cannot, of course, prove that male and female *zemliaki* were marrying one another, but this suggestion is consistent with other accounts of factory life, for example, the description, cited earlier in this chapter, of married couples who shared quarters with "their own people." Evidence from the peasant villages seems to point in the same direction. D. N. Zhbankov, who studied out-migration from certain regions of Kostroma province in the late 1880s, described courting rituals in which eligible males were introduced to young women from neighboring villages. A wife was sometimes chosen from a village as much as 20-to-40 *versty* (12-to-24 miles) away, Zhbankov reported, but more often from a much narrower radius. Girls who had never been to the city themselves were nonetheless determined to marry an *otkhodnik* and were scornful of the country manners of young men who stayed in the village.[45]

Zemliachestvo and Social Action

What influence did regional loyalties have on the pattern of migrants' collective behavior: did they promote or retard the migrants' capacity for joint action? Partial answers to these questions can be found in the records of legal and illegal organizations among workers. Such records are at best fragmentary. The most complete ones are found in Soviet regional archives and have, with insignificant exceptions, been unavailable for this study. Central police archives do, however, contain limited information about the leaders of cooperatives and mutual aid associations, as well as lists of people arrested as ringleaders in industrial disturbances. Both these sources show a recurring pattern of "clusters." Individuals from a narrowly defined region—a county, a township, or even a single village—often constitute, if not a majority, a significant minority of people listed in such records.

The fullest list of legal organizations presently available is one compiled by the Moscow city police in 1910, well beyond the period of this study.[46] This list, supposedly complete for the entire city, provides summary information about the founders or leaders of sixty-eight cooperatives, mutual aid associations, and laboring *arteli;* but it also includes other associations not open to workers or peasants. In all, forty-nine of the sixty-eight associations included one or more peasants among their leaders; and of those forty-nine, nineteen show evidence of *zemliaki* associating with one another. That is, in nineteen cases there were two or more peasant officers from a single county of some nearby province. In one instance, five of seven officers came from a single county; in other cases, officers came from several adjacent counties. In five of the organizations, all officers were peasants from a single province.[47]

This list is probably complete for cooperatives and mutual-aid associations, which were closely regulated by the government. It includes only twenty-one *arteli,* however—a figure too low to be credible. In all probability, the groups that appeared in the list were exceptionally large and visible. *Arteli* made up of ten or twenty workers or migrants were far more numerous but operated in an inconspicuous manner as living and working units and thus went unrecorded.

Lacking information both about the full membership of the listed organizations and about the manner in which officers were chosen, one can only guess at the significance of these figures. As the eight provinces from which most of Moscow's migrant population was drawn included over 100 counties, it seems highly unlikely that the observed clusters were due to chance alone. Regional loyalties could conceivably have influenced the leadership of organizations in two ways. If the leaders listed by the police were the founders of an organization,[48] they would seem to have preferred to associate with their *zemliaki;* noting that no organizations were limited to a single county, one would conclude that regional loyalty was only one of the factors at work. If, on the other hand, the leaders were elected, one might reasonably conclude that *zemliaki* were at least an influential bloc of an organization's members. I should repeat that few of these organizations were formed on a purely regional basis; rather, regional loyalty seems to have carried over into a wider, more heterogeneous environment.

Police records of worker petitions, strikes,[49] and other industrial disorders are in some ways less complete than records of legal organizations. The quality of reports varied greatly from one district to another, and from year to year, and ranged from a single terse telegram to detailed background reports. Many records have been lost altogether. Those that survive, however, occasionally contain detailed information about persons arrested or investigated. In particular, they identify such individuals by *volost'* (township) or village of origin.[50]

Fifteen instances have been located in which lists of names were preserved in connection with worker unrest (two petitions, eleven strikes, and two other disturbances). Of these, fourteen show regional clusters of the sort encountered in legal organizations. In the most dramatic instance, thirty-seven of forty-one workers fired from the Moscow (Guzhon) metalworking factory were from a single township of Nizhnii-Novgorod province.[51] Regional groupings encountered in other strikes are comparable to those described in legal organizations except that, as the geographic units listed are much smaller, the likelihood of meaningful ties among apparent *zemliaki* is greater. One finds, for example, that, of seven ringleaders arrested during one strike in Moscow city, six came from three adjacent townships in Kostroma province.[52]

Almost all of the incidents in which regional groupings were discerned took place at large, modern enterprises.[53] The longest list comes from the Prokhorovskaia factory and includes two groups of strikers and suspected troublemakers, fifty-four of whom were arrested in May 1895 and another eighteen in January 1898. Of those on the first list, eighteen came from Serpukhovskii county of Moscow province. Nine were from a single township, five of them from a single village. One village in Kaluga province supplied six of the arrested workers; one in Tula province, four.[54]

The basic unit in any strike or protest may, of course, have been a workshop (*masterskaia*) or other subdivision of a factory. If, for any of the reasons discussed earlier, people from a single region were predominant in one section of an enterprise, they would automatically play a predominant role in any incident there.[55] Detailed police descriptions of several disturbances, however, make it clear that there were other reasons for *zemliaki* to have acted jointly.

The most important of these was communication. A stream of visitors and letters back and forth between village and factory could carry word of conditions and strikes in other localities, and in at least two instances police blamed this grapevine for worker unrest. An episode on the border of Vladimir province in 1896 is especially interesting in this respect. Agents investigating rumors of an impending strike turned their attention to a contingent of several hundred workers from a nearby county who were "in constant written communication with their relatives." Accounts of recent incidents in the home county, including brutal suppression of workers, were found in one such letter seized by police. The letter, containing charges described as seditious and untrue by the police, had been circulated and read by many workers in the Zemliak colony.[56]

In other instances, police were apprehensive that *zemliaki* might communicate unrest from one factory to another. During one strike in Serpukhovskii county (1897), workers returned to their villages for a religious holiday. Local officials agreed that the workers should be given an ultimatum to return to work but were very concerned about its timing. They feared that the workers, meeting their *zemliaki* back in the villages, would stir up trouble at the neighboring mills where fellow villagers were employed.[57]

Oral history collected from other workers many decades later indicates that the Serpukhov officials' fears were well founded. The workers had clear recollections of strikes "not just at their own enterprises but at neighboring ones, where their relatives, neighbors, and *zemliaki* were working."[58] The workers also indicated that employers, when laying off suspected malcontents, used place of origin and ties to *zemliaki* as criteria for identifying them. (This occurred not just in the Moscow region, but in Saint Petersburg as well.)[59]

Ideally, one should be able to compare industries in which *zemliachestvo* was prominent to others in which it was not. If the ties among migrants promoted labor unrest, then the former group should have a higher incidence of strikes and other protests. Unfortunately the available data are too fragmentary to permit such a calculation. Statistics on strikes, however, do show one pattern that seems relevant to this discussion. The brick industry, which by all accounts was exceptionally backward, with small-scale factories on the remote outskirts of Moscow city, had higher per capita rates of unrest than any other industry in Moscow for the years 1880-1900. Perhaps more than any other, this industry based its labor recruitment on traditional ties to particular rural districts. The brick workers showed a greater awareness of events at other factories, as evidenced by a coordinated strike at seven factories in 1899, and it seems likely that networks of *zemliaki* were the source of this knowledge.[60]

Besides communicating information, *zemliaki* may have felt a sense of loyalty or solidarity with one another. Hints of such bonds appear in the memoirs of Moiseenko, who played an active part in the famous 1885 strike at the Morozov factory in Orekhovo. During the strike he fled across the river to Zuevo and then traveled to Moscow, hoping to secure support from revolutionary intelligentsia. In both places he was sheltered by kinsmen and *zemliaki*. He evidently had no hesitation to turn to such people even though they had no connection with the strike or the revolutionary underground. They in turn did not hesitate to take him in.[61]

Beyond the Urban Melting Pot

The rural-urban ties outlined in previous chapters exercised a continuing influence on social life in the city. Like migrants in other settings, central Russian *zemliaki* often lived and worked together. Without having any formal organizational structure, networks of *zemliaki* could provide information and material assistance to the newly arrived migrant. They also helped to maintain village traditions and folkways in the new setting, thereby helping to perpetuate the migrant's identification with peasant society.

The role of these networks was partially one of mediating between agrarian traditions and urban-industrial structures. The stability and continuity they provided, however, did more than just ease the transition to city life; in certain instances it provided a focus for social action and collective protest.

Chapter Five

The Organization of
Everyday Life

For most observers and students of factory life, contemporaries and historians alike, the workers' well-being has been a prime concern. Countless studies have been devoted to such issues as hours and wages, housing, safety, hygiene and nutrition, and efficacy of factory legislation.[1] Although particular details may be disputed, historians are in general agreement about the broad outlines of these issues: in Russia, wages were normally low; hours were long; living quarters were cramped; and factory life was generally unhealthy, not just in comparison to a later age but also in comparison to contemporary conditions in other countries.

To look at these issues solely from an economic point of view (the employer's profit, the worker's privation) is, however, to miss an important point about the organization of factory life: everyday life in and around the factory can also be seen as a set of social relationships, of clearly (or not so clearly) defined roles and boundaries intended to shape workers' behavior in particular directions. The routines and discipline of factory life may have made more of an impression on workers than physical hardships did.[2] Hunger, overcrowding, and material deprivation were, after all, familiar features of everyday life outside the factory. In the long run, everyday experiences of the most mundane sort— work routines, interaction with fellow workers and supervisors, leisure-time activities—helped to shape the worker's consciousness. The structure of working-class existence thereby influenced the future course of collective action and labor unrest.

The Employers' Quest for Stability

In the 1880s and 1890s, the factory owners of Moscow were a relatively conservative lot and were often contrasted to the more "enlightened" employers of Saint Petersburg and other industrial centers.[3] The practices they followed in their dealings with workers stemmed from a few basic objectives: to maximize profit through optimum use of available resources, to avoid unproductive cash outlays and keep wages as low as possible, to secure a stable and tranquil labor force, and to prevent unrest at the factories. Often, of course, one of these goals could only be achieved at the expense of others. One way to achieve a stable labor force, for example, might be to build spacious living quarters for the workers and their families, a measure actually attempted in parts of southern Russia;[4] but this would entail large expenses. Profits, on the other hand, might be enhanced if one hired cheaper female and child labor instead of adult males, but this could lower efficiency or reduce the quality of the finished product.

Thus, like employers everywhere, the Moscow factory owners were obliged to compromise among their various objectives. In addition, their choices were limited by the physical plant and labor force they had inherited from previous generations. Because of the slow, evolutionary pattern by which many factories had developed, the Moscow industrialists tended to be less enthusiastic about new facilities and innovations than their counterparts in Saint Petersburg and the South.[5] They generally favored older, more exploitative methods of dealing with workers, though these were sometimes combined with paternalistic and heavy-handed regulation of the workers' lives.[6]

Several examples of this approach have been discussed in previous chapters. Moscow employers withheld wages to induce workers to stay on through the summer; hired workers under a system of mutual guarantees, so that, if a worker left, his guarantor would be penalized; and paid wages at long intervals, offering workers credit in company stores and thereby binding them to their jobs. In some of the more backward industries, such as brick and china manufacturing in the early 1880s, wage contracts were negotiated with peasant village-elders; peasants who were behind in their tax and redemption payments were signed over to the factory, which paid a large share of their wages directly to the village.[7]

Wage relations, in other words, involved a lot more than straightforward payment for services rendered. Employers tried to keep wage levels as low as possible and sometimes used fines and other devices to reduce them still further, but they also used the wage system as a means of guiding or controlling workers' behavior. At the Moscow metal works, the management believed that it was limiting drunkenness by paying wages on Saturdays; if paid on a weekday, workers would supposedly be incapacitated on the following day, but if they got drunk on Saturday they would have all of Sunday to recover. The management also insisted on paying the workers in small installments, even though the local factory inspector opposed this practice. He contended that when the workers received larger sums they were more likely to use the money responsibly, for example, by sending contributions to their families in the country, whereas smaller wage payments were quickly dissipated on drink.[8] Such "responsibility," however, also implied a degree of independence that employers were loath to encourage.

Certain employers, in order to keep down the cost of labor and eliminate possible troublemakers from their work force, periodically "cleansed" the rolls by dismissing a large proportion of their workers and hiring inexperienced peasants, who were thought to be more docile and pliable.[9] Others, however, attached more importance to the workers' skill and thus introduced various incentives and sanctions to induce the workers to stay on from year to year. For example, workers were given bonuses for good work but received only a partial payment, the balance being paid only after the expiration of some specified number of years.[10]

The company store, which offered workers goods on credit, was sometimes the only source of provisions; where other stores existed, workers might be penalized for patronizing them.[11] Indebtedness to the company store sometimes reached such a point that the workers' entire earnings were spent before payday without any cash changing hands. This too was a way of binding the worker to his job, for he needed cash if he wished to move elsewhere.[12]

Statistics on labor-force turnover are generally unavailable. The studies cited in Chapter Two, for example, tried to determine how many years' experience workers had "at the factory" (*na fabrike*) without asking whether the time was spent at one factory or many. The system of annual or semiannual contracts would seem likely to encourage a high degree of worker mobility; yet available accounts of factory life suggest that many workers returned to the same employer year after year. At the Tsindel' cotton mill, the fourteen hundred workers interviewed by Shestakov in 1899 had an average of 10.3 years of factory experience and had been at the Tsindel' mill for an average of 5.4 years. Second-generation workers (those whose fathers had worked in factories) had spent an average of 5.6 years at Tsindel'.[13] These figures suggest that, although some movement occurred, the labor force at Tsindel' was relatively stable. The pattern of stability was evidently no weaker among second-generation workers than in the entire population.

At the Prokhorovskaia Trekhgornaia cotton mill in the 1890s, some of the senior managerial personnel were said to be personally acquainted with most of the five thousand workers. After a scandal over cheating in the reckoning of wages, the factory owner dismissed most of the supervisory personnel but retained the manager because he knew the workers well and could help to keep track of potential troublemakers. A purge of suspected malcontents was carried out just before Easter of the following year, when eighty workers' contracts were not renewed, and most of the factory's workers waited apprehensively to learn whether their names were on the list.[14] All these details suggest that the work force was basically stable.[15] Had a large proportion been newly hired, the management could not have known about their reliability. If most workers were accustomed to moving from place to place, their apprehension about contract renewal would be hard to explain.

Admittedly these accounts provide an incomplete and possibly unrepresentative picture of worker mobility. Without more detailed information, such as other factories' payroll records,[16] one can only guess at the degree of labor turnover in other localities. Because of their central location and proximity to other factories, the Tsindel' and Prokhorovskaia factories may actually have had higher rates of turnover than other enterprises. In more isolated localities, where short-distance migration prevailed, workers may have been less willing or able to move away. The rate of labor turnover could also have been reduced if migrants were bound together by mutual guarantees (*krugovaia poruka*) or if they brought their children to work with them at the factories. In the absence of more solid data, however, one can do no more than speculate about such possibilities.

The Factory as a Closed Community

The most common pattern of living arrangements at Moscow's factories was for the employer to provide living quarters, usually at a nominal cost. This system was a predictable consequence of the dispersal of factories through the province. In the countryside, a smaller factory might be able to recruit its work force from the immediate vicinity, and a small number of migrant workers might find lodging in nearby peasant households, but as the proportion of outsiders increased the provision of housing became more difficult. Employers, moreover, discovered that there were certain advantages to providing food and lodging to workers. Like the company store, these facilities were sometimes a means of lowering wages by imposing exorbitant charges. They could also be an effective means of keeping track of the workers outside of working hours. In extreme cases, almost all of the workers' material needs could be met inside the factory gates, and workers lived in near-isolation from the outside world.

The Moscow *zemstvo* survey of factories in the early 1880s found that 57 percent of all workers lived on the premises of the factories where they were employed. The practice was more common at larger factories, especially in the textile industry, in which 66 percent of all spinners and weavers lived in factory quarters.[17] This pattern was typical of other central Russian provinces and of the newer industrial areas in the South but was less common in Saint Petersburg, where the majority of workers lived on the side in rented quarters.[18] One might have expected Moscow city to follow the Saint Petersburg pattern, but the largest factories there continued to house most of their workers well past the turn of the century.

The typical living unit was a barrackslike structure consisting of large undivided rooms that accommodated anywhere from ten to over one hundred people. At the older factories, some of these facilities had been built in the time of serfdom, and were primitive in the extreme. Even the newer quarters, however, tended to be ill lit, poorly ventilated, crowded, and unhygienic, with poor or nonexistent water supply and waste disposal. Workers slept on benches or cots, and in some instances these were shared by two shifts of occupants.

Family accommodations, briefly described in Chapter Three, were equally crowded and unappealing. Despite these unattractive features, such quarters were in high demand among workers for the simple reason that the alternatives were even worse. At existing wage levels, workers could live outside the factory only in various kinds of shared accommodation such as the flophouses (*koechno-kamorochnye kvartiry*) that sprang up on the fringes of Moscow city. These were sometimes entire houses, sometimes cellars or garrets, divided up so as to accommodate the maximum possible number of people. For 4 or 5 rubles per month (i.e., one-seventh of his wages) a worker could rent a corner of a room, a bunk bed with perhaps 1 cubic *sazhen* (8 cubic meters) of breathing space. This housing, whose squalor was vividly depicted in Gorki's *Lower Depths*, was blamed for the spread of epidemic diseases, but the Moscow city government could do little but study it.[19] Factory workers, such as those at the Prokhorovskaia Trekhgornaia factory, put their names onto waiting lists in the hope of getting a place in the company barracks.

Housing at the factory thus became a kind of reward, and the threat of eviction was not to be taken lightly. If a single woman were turned out onto the street, prostitution might be her only recourse; for a married couple with children (admittedly a rarity in Moscow), the possibility of alternative accommodation was nil.[20] Employers recognized the power inherent in this situation (one reform-minded observer described the workers as "slaves of their landlords")[21] and tried to use it to regulate minutely the lives of their charges.

The principal device for regulation was the "rules of internal order," which each employer was legally required to establish and post. These rules described the hours and terms of work, but they also extended to life in the sleeping quarters. Some employers set a curfew, not just for turning out the lights in sleeping quarters but for locking the factory gates; a worker who stayed out too late, besides spending the night on the street, could be fined for his "offense."[22] Workers were prohibited from entering any workshop (*masterskaia*) other than their own and were required to leave the premises immediately upon the end of their shift. In the barracks, drinking, loud talking, card playing, and singing might be prohibited, and workers were required to keep their beds clean and tidy. Attendance at church services was sometimes mandatory. Visits to the factory by spouses or other relatives were permitted only outside the working hours; such outsiders were not permitted to live with workers in the barracks, except by special permission of the factory director.[23] At the Prokhorovskaia Trekhgornaia, husbands and wives who had not obtained shared

sleeping quarters were allowed to visit one another once a week:
"They would give you a note (*zapiska*); the wife came, you lay
down under the bunk, hung a curtain around (*zanaveshivalis'*)
and spent the night."[24]

Violation of the rules could result in dismissal from the factory
and expulsion from the barracks, but the more usual form of
punishment was the imposition of fines. Workers could be fined a
day's wages or more for various offenses (e.g., tardiness, careless-
ness, or insubordination), and some employers used the system as
a device for reducing wages. Workers often complained that fines
were arbitrarily imposed, and factory inspectors or police sometimes agreed. Officials criticized the management of the Tsindel'
factory in 1894, for example, for fining workers who failed to
remove their caps in the presence of supervisors.[25] Precisely
because they were arbitrary, however, fines could be used to
intimidate the workers and keep them off-balance. Fines became a
major issue in a number of strikes, especially in the mid-1880s
at the enormous Morozov Nikol'skaia cotton-weaving mill in
Orekhovo, on the border of Moscow and Vladimir provinces. The
Factory Law of 1886 attempted to limit and regulate the imposition of fines and required that the monies collected be used for
the workers' benefit in sickness and disability funds.[26]

To ensure that the rules were obeyed and that order prevailed throughout the factory premises, employers maintained
their own police and guards (*khozhalye* and *sotskie*). Some factories even had their own jails or drunk tanks, where a disorderly
worker could be confined for a day or two.[27] Informal networks
of spies or informers were also used, and workers could be fired on
the basis of anonymous denunciations.[28] This was still, however,
a very paternal sort of policing in which the supervisors were
keeping track of intimate details of workers' lives. In an extreme
case, the factory owner himself might personally interrogate
suspected troublemakers. After a strike in 1896, S. I. Prokhorov
interviewed every single worker at his factory, a total of more than
four thousand: "What do you do when your shift is over? Do you
go to church on the holidays? Where do you go outside the
factory? What time do you come home?" He was reportedly
very suspicious of workers who spent their time reading but
winked at those who admitted a weakness for drink.[29]

In the late 1890s, following a period of unprecedented labor
unrest, employers and government alike began to beef up the
factory security forces. In 1899, three factories in Bogorodskii
county pooled their resources to hire a force of twenty-five Cossacks

from Astrakhan, at a cost of 19,000 rubles. In that same year, the Russian government passed a law on factory police that established a national force of 2,320 police and 160 inspectors (*nadzirateli*); their salaries were to be paid by the State, but the factory owners were to provide living quarters and detainment facilities (*arestant-skie pomeshcheniia*).[30]

The factory management also relied on foremen and other supervisory personnel to keep them informed of the workers' moods and behavior. These individuals, like the guards, were generally drawn from the same half-peasant milieu as the workers. Few had received specialized training, and those who had were often foreigners whose relations with Russian workers tended to be difficult.[31] The lower level supervisors were likely to remain at a factory for many years (at the Prokhorovskaia mill several had been employed for over forty years),[32] and this probably accentuated the paternalism already described. Like the noncommissioned officers of an army, they were able to make life easier or harder for their subordinates, for instance, by assigning them to particular stations or raw materials. Workers thus had an incentive to court the foreman's favor, and many foremen actively sought various bribes or favors, including sexual ones.[33] The foreman could be a small-scale tyrant or a dispenser of patronage and was often a target of worker attacks in times of labor unrest.

Cooperation and Association

In light of the foregoing, the existence of cooperative and mutual-aid societies at the Russian factories might seem anomalous. In other nations, such associations have been the nucleus around which trade unions coalesced (e.g., the "friendly associations" of artisans in England at the end of the eighteenth century);[34] elsewhere they enabled artisans, agriculturalists, and middle-class tradesmen to pool their resources with the aim of overcoming poverty and exploitation (e.g., the *Raffeisen* and *Schulze-Delitzsch* pattern of cooperative credit unions).[35] In Third-World countries in more recent times, similar associations have sometimes played a key role in national integration and political mobilization.[36]

The notion of grass-roots initiatives and self-help seems to contradict the paternalism and regimentation of Russian factory life, and yet one finds that factory owners were often founders and promoters of cooperative societies that had hundreds if not thousands of members and sold vast quantities of foodstuffs and supplies annually. The explanation of this pattern is not hard to find. The organizations, no matter what benefits they may have provided to members, operated under close supervision and tutelage of the employers and the government. At their worst, they were a reincarnation of the company store, the operations of which had been partially regulated by the Factory Law of 1886; at their best, they provided services and material benefits to workers but little opportunity for participation. The establishment and operation of these societies can thus provide another vantage point for examining the organization of factory life.

Two principal forms of association operated at the Russian factories: the consumer society and the mutual-assistance fund. In the former case, members purchased shares and the resulting capital was used to operate a retail store in which the members could trade; profits were commonly distributed among members in the form of dividends. Mutual-aid funds, on the other hand, accumulated their capital through regular contributions from members; the funds might be loaned out or otherwise invested, but their main purpose was to provide lump-sum benefits to members (or their survivors) in the event of disability or death.

Russian law strictly regulated the operations of all private associations. Before any society or fund could begin to function, it had to submit its charter (*ustav*) for governmental approval.[37] Disagreements and long delays were routine. A minimum of six months' wait was standard form, and some societies had to wait as long as three years before receiving permission to begin operations.[38]

Patience and perseverence, it seems, were among the prerequisites for approval of a charter. An acquiescent or submissive attitude was also helpful. In submitting their charter for transmission to Petersburg, the director and founding members of the Prokhorovskaia factory's consumer cooperative designated the governorgeneral of Moscow as their representative (*upolnomochennyi*) and authorized him to accept whatever revisions the Ministry of Internal Affairs might suggest: "The administration of the company trusts you in all that you do, and will not contradict or dispute you."[39] This charter was approved in a record two months.

Charters were closely scrutinized by officials to ensure that the associations posed no threat to public order. In some instances, charters were revised to eliminate general meetings and replace them with smaller assemblies of delegates.[40] In other cases, membership requirements were rewritten to exclude rank-and-file workers or potential subversives and to establish tight official control over societies' everyday activities.[41] Governmental agencies also kept close watch to ensure that societies did not extend their activities beyond the limits of their charters. Consumer cooperatives, for example, were required to obtain special permission before they could sell commodities other than food, and authorities were reluctant to grant such permission.[42] Outside activities, such as dances, concerts, or lotteries, had to be approved by the local police chief and were extremely infrequent.[43] In addition, the provincial governor and city administrator (*gradonachal'nik*) were empowered to terminate an association's existence if they felt it posed a threat to public order; they could also adjourn any general meeting.[44]

Restrictions and bureaucratic obstacles were so formidable that ordinary factory workers found it virtually impossible to create or operate organizations of their own.[45] The cooperatives and mutual-aid societies that did exist at factories were set up on the initiative of factory owners, managers, or supervisory staff.[46] Although the officers of a cooperative or mutual-aid society were sometimes elected, office holding tended to be monopolized by a minority of better paid workers and white-collar staff, and effective control remained in the hands of the factory management.[47]

Just how far managerial involvement could go is illustrated by the Prokhorovskaia factory cooperative. To keep them from squandering their earnings, workers were not allowed to draw a full month's credit allowance all at once. Sobriety was encouraged by the society's refusal to sell alcoholic beverages. Workers protested against such policies, and the factory owner was convinced that they would ruin the society if left to their own devices; to ensure that the policies he favored would be followed, he threatened to deny credit to dissenters.[48]

Factory cooperatives and other related associations thus appear to have been organized and run by people who were not ordinary workers. One must still ask whether rank-and-file workers had any part at all to play in them: Who joined the societies, and what benefits did they receive? Analysis of membership is complicated by the fact that membership lists and similar records of voluntary associations have not been available for this study.[49] Some general characteristics of the members can, however, be inferred from other sources.

Membership fees and contributions are especially revealing in this respect. The cost of a share in a consumer cooperative usually ranged from 5 to 10 rubles,[50] whereas contributions to mutual-aid funds might be as much as 1 ruble per month.[51] In 1900, textile workers were earning an average of 12-to-18 rubles per month, depending on the particular branch of production, whereas metal-workers earned 28 rubles per month and printers, 25.[52] Under the best of circumstances, workers had trouble in making ends meet, and an outlay of several rubles was no small matter. Not surprisingly, the better paid workers played a disproportionately great role in voluntary associations. In the aid society of Moscow printers in 1907, only 6.8 percent of all members were earning less than 35 rubles per month; yet the average wage of all Moscow printers was 34.70 rubles.[53] In other associations, members' relative affluence can be gauged by the number of shares they purchased. Members of a consumer cooperative in rural Kolomenskii county, for example, had invested an average of 56.8 rubles apiece in shares; there the high cost of a share and the requirement that it be paid in one lump sum kept most workers from joining.[54]

Despite such difficulties, some workers did join cooperative associations, and many more traded in their stores. The highest rate of participation was at the Kolomna machine-building works, where more than four-fifths of the work force was enrolled in the cooperative society. At other factories, shareholders were a minority of all workers,[55] but a large minority, one that must have gone beyond the narrow circle of supervisory personnel and highly paid specialists.

The volume of these societies' sales suggests that members spent a very high proportion of their total earnings at the cooperative stores. At the Prokhorovskaia factory, workers took up to 60 percent of their monthly earnings as credit in the cooperative store. (Inasmuch as the factory payroll office deducted these sums from their wages, the cooperative took no risk.) The fact that they spent such a large proportion of their income in cooperative stores does not necessarily mean that the workers felt any loyalty toward the cooperatives or that the stores were serving their interests. As in the older system of company stores, workers had little choice about trading in the cooperatives because credit was not readily available from other sources.[56] Critics alleged that the cooperatives sold poor-quality goods for inflated prices.[57] It is worth noting that the Factory Law of 1886 had limited the deductions an employer could make for food and lodging; available evidence indicates that cooperatives were not bound by these limits, and a cynical observer might conclude that they were a means of evading the law.[58]

Members' involvement in mutual-aid funds was probably greater.

Statistics from the printers' fund show that the turnover in membership was very low. If members felt a stronger attachment to these societies, the reason was largely monetary. Having paid hundreds or even thousands of rubles into an aid fund, they were reluctant to jeopardize their investment by withdrawing from membership. For the same reason, they favored cautious and conservative policies in regard to payments and resisted attempts to broaden the membership by lowering fees.[59]

In general, then, the activities of self-help organizations were narrowly circumscribed by employers and the government. Members played a generally passive role in them, and often only a small and unrepresentative minority participated in them. These organizations, unlike societies in England or Western Europe in the nineteenth century or in many parts of the Third World today, were not permitted to become a vehicle for political mobilization or independent initiative. (After the turn of the century, and particularly in the turbulent period between 1905 and 1907, this pattern began to change, as workers won the right to operate independent organizations. Existing organizations of the older type were challenged from within by slates of reform-minded workers who wished to alter the pattern of their operations. Most such efforts were short-lived, however, and after 1907 the government was able to reassert control over associations and generally to prevent their involvement in wider political or social issues.)

Another form of organization that flourished at Moscow's factories was the *artel'*, a work crew or association whose members pooled their resources or labor toward some common end.* Such associations had been common in Russia for centuries, especially among itinerant craftsmen and laborers. They played a more limited role in mines, factories, and plants, where a single wage was sometimes paid to an entire work crew and distributed by an elected elder (*starosta*). There were also residential *arteli* in which members paid some specified weekly or monthly sum to

---

*In the nineteenth century, the term *artel'* was used loosely to describe almost any grouping based on common interest. As a more or less voluntary association, the *artel'* was found not only among craft or industrial workers but among hunters and fishermen, carters, and even thieves. Another variant of the *artel'* was for laborers from a single village or region to migrate and work together, a pattern discussed in Chapter Four. On the history of the *artel'* and its many forms, see K. A. Pazhitnov, "Rabochie arteli," and the article *artel'* in Brokhaus and Effron, *Entsiklopedicheskii slovar'*, vol. 2, pp. 184–194.

the elder, who hired a cook and rented quarters for the members to share.

As in the case of cooperatives, the factory *arteli* operated under the supervision or control of the employer. The work-crew type of *artel'* was less common at large factories, and was mostly confined to construction and repair work. Occasionally, however, employers would organize *arteli* among ordinary factory workers, paying them on a piecework basis for the work they completed. The members of a crew were thus made responsible for one another's work in the time-honored tradition of peasant life (*krugovaia poruka*). With the connivance of the elder, moreover, the *artel'* could become a device for keeping wages down. Abuses of this system led the Russian government to prohibit such wage contracts and to insist that each worker make his own contract directly with the payroll office.[60] Nonetheless certain Moscow factories, such as the Moscow metal works, retained a modified system of *arteli* as the basic work unit.[61]

Residential *arteli* were likewise dependent on the employer. As living units they were commonly housed on factory premises. Provisions were often obtained on credit from the employer, either directly or through the factory cooperative.[62] The elder, although nominally responsible to the members, sometimes wound up performing administrative (*khoziaiskie*) tasks. In certain cases the elective principle was abandoned completely and the elder became an appointed agent of the employer—a system that evoked complaints from workers on more than one occasion.[63] When one reads of residential *arteli* with hundreds of members, strictly segregated not only by sex and occupation but by wage level,[64] it is hard to imagine them as a spontaneous organization emanating from the workers themselves. Like the cooperatives, they were more often a creation of the employer and had no independent role in factory life. Workers in some localities did sometimes express an interest in electing independent elders who would negotiate on their behalf with management and officials, but such a suggestion was anathema to most employers.[65]

The Workers' World

Everyday life at the factory was thus guided and circumscribed by a fairly complex and comprehensive set of rules and practices. These were intended not only to direct the workers' behavior but to isolate them from the outside world and from one another.

Any manifestation of independence, initiative, or coalition among workers was to be discouraged or prohibited. Moscow's factories bore a strong resemblance to Erving Goffman's characterization of the "total institution":

> The central feature of total institutions . . . [is] a breakdown of the barriers ordinarily separating [the] three spheres of life [i.e., work, recreation, and sleep] . . . all aspects of life are conducted in the same place and under the same authority . . . each phase of the member's daily activity is carried on in the immediate company of a large batch of others, all of whom are treated alike and required to do the same thing together . . . [under] a single rational plan purportedly designed to fulfill the official aims of the institution.[66]

This aspect of the factory environment was enhanced by the geographic isolation of many factories and by the cultural isolation of peasant-workers from other strata of society. Even those who worked in cities retained distinctive patterns of dress and speech, and the factory milieu could be penetrated by outsiders only with great difficulty. I. V. Babushkin, a radically minded metalworker, described his shock and depression upon visiting a textile factory: the scene reminded him of a peasant village, the material conditions were "terribly depressing for me, a skilled worker living a more respectable life and having greater needs," but most of all he was struck by the workers' remoteness. "These lads and lasses would not have welcomed our interference in their affairs . . . one must talk to [a peasant girl] in her own language, [and] it is not entirely safe for strangers to do this." Babushkin tried to console himself with the thought that "even in this building there must be someone explaining things to the workers," but clearly it could not have been someone like himself.[67]

A worker who became dissatisfied with this environment had few opportunities to broaden his own horizons. In many cases, the only recreational outlet was a neighboring tavern. Factory administrations, though they tried to limit conversation and socializing in the workshops and living quarters, rarely provided any alternative space. In their recollections of factory life, workers refer to the lavatories as "our club"—the one place on the factory grounds where people could congregate without being closely observed. In the summertime, walks in nearby wooded areas were a common pastime and, in the mid-1890s, provided cover for secret meetings. The cultural opportunities of a large city such as Moscow remained terra incognita for the factory population;

even at the centrally located Tsindel' mill, only 35 percent of the workers had ever attended a concert, a theatre, a public lecture, a museum, or a circus. The expense, the distance, and the lack of free time were almost insuperable obstacles, and these were reinforced by the workers' uneasiness in any unfamiliar setting.[68]

The use of Goffman's term conjures up visions of other total institutions such as prisons, asylums, and slave plantations. This comparison has been made by other authors, among them Reinhard Bendix, who has described Russian factory discipline as resembling "the landowner's exploitation of his serfs more closely than a Western manufacturer's exploitation of his workers."[69] Bendix goes on to contrast the Western worker's "internalized ethic of work performance" with the Russian system's emphasis on fear, coercion, and submission: "Employers failed to appeal to the conscience or self-esteem of the workers; and the reliance on fear and coercion effectively precluded the development of an internalized ethic of work performance."[70]

Nonetheless, it would be incorrect to conclude that the Russian worker was an automaton whose every step was controlled. Goffman's discussion of total institutions is instructive in this respect, for he emphasizes the "underlife" of an organization. Beneath the formally prescribed roles and rules of an asylum or a prison, he suggests, inmates persistently seek ways of asserting some measure of autonomy, of defining "what sort of self and world they are to accept for themselves."[71] His examples include apathy, disaffection, and absenteeism, but also other "secondary adjustments"—maneuvering for material privileges, preferred work assignments, or sexual liaisons, for instance—that are simply irrelevant to the institution's goals and assumptions.

Seen from this perspective, the underlife of a Moscow factory was a web of relationships and routines that were not foreseen or regulated by the employer. These might overlap with officially stated goals or procedures, as when a foreman demanded bribes or treats in return for favorable treatment, or they might take place in the interstices of factory life, as when two or three workers shared a smoke and a chat in the privacy of the lavatory. To a great extent this underlife was a peasant life. For all the reasons described in previous chapters, village traditions and ties extended into the factory setting. Their traces can be seen in the relationship between workers and foremen, in the institution of the *artel'*, and even perhaps in the paternalism of some employers, which was not unlike the feudal nobleman's relations with his serfs.

Another peasantlike feature of the worker-peasant underlife was the treatment of outsiders. Factory inspectors and police, for example, were often (though not always) regarded with suspicion, even when they came to restrict some of the employer's abuses. Parents of underage workers sometimes connived with management to misrepresent their children's ages or to conceal them until the inspector had left;[72] their own well-being was threatened if the children lost their jobs, so they became, for a while, collaborators in deception. Elsewhere some workers removed or ignored safety devices in the belief that they slowed the work, or they knowingly withheld complaints from factory inspectors.[73] This was done less through ignorance or backwardness than through the unspoken rules of the factory world. The workers knew what to expect from the foreman or the manager, but they had good reason to doubt the motives or effectiveness of an inspector.

The workers' mistrust of local officials was complemented by a faith in more remote ones—the familiar myth of the good tsar who would defend the common people if only he knew their plight.[74] This was a familiar theme in peasant disturbances of an earlier era, although, as Daniel Field has pointed out, peasants were capable of manipulating it quite consciously for specific goals.[75] At the factory, a certain proportion of the workers may have placed their trust in a paternalistic owner or manager. Others, confronted with severe abuses, attempted to petition to higher governmental authorities or even to the tsar himself.[76] This faith was eroded by the authorities' consistent rejection of such petitions and by the pattern of intervention in worker–manager disputes. Workers found that officials were unable or unwilling to respond to their grievances and that they valued law and order above what the workers considered to be justice.[77] The tradition of appeal to higher authorities endured, however, at least until 1905, when the disastrous events of Saint Petersburg's Bloody Sunday dealt it a crushing blow.

The strongest bonds workers felt in the factory setting were to a close circle of kinsmen or "neighbors," the latter group including *zemliaki*, bunkmates, and members of one's own workshop or *artel'* (categories that often, though not always, overlapped). In the 1880s and 1890s, strikes and other protests often originated in such circles and were commonly confined to one or two subunits of a factory.[78] The more "advanced" workers—those who were more widely read or otherwise assimilated to city life—also sought friendship and stability in small, close-knit groups (*kruzhki*). These sometimes played an agitational role, with or without support from radical intelligentsia, but they also seem to have played a more diffuse role for their members, providing a focus for fraternization and identification.[79]

The world of Moscow's factories can thus be seen as an ongoing community, whose rules and obligations were only partially those of the employer. Indirect support for this suggestion can be found in statistics on the abandonment of illegitimate children to foundling homes. Women who worked as domestic servants, day laborers, or seamstresses account for a disproportionately high share of foundlings, whereas the share of factory women is disproportionately low.[80] What this suggests is not that factory women were not becoming pregnant; on the contrary, the evidence of factory life suggests that sexual abuse and also voluntary liaisons were not uncommon. Unlike servants or artisans, however, factory women were part of a community that maintained many of the traditions and sanctions of village life. In such a setting, a father may have found it harder to shirk his obligations, and a pregnant girl was less likely to be left to her own devices.

Despite the continuity of peasant traditions in the factories, it would be wrong to infer that this environment and its inhabitants never changed. On the contrary, observers of village life frequently noted the contrast between the citified peasant-worker and his country cousin. *Otkhodniki* came back to the village wearing leather boots and sateen shirts. They played accordians, spoke the slang of the city, and sometimes mocked the customs of their rural kin.[81] For all their insularity, workers were absorbing some of the atmosphere of a wider universe. The clearest evidence on this point concerns the workers' literacy, a highly desirable attribute at the factory and in city life generally. Among workers at the Tsindel' factory in the age group twenty to twenty-nine, 68 percent were literate, whereas in the surrounding provinces the proportion ranged from 71 percent in Moscow province to 36 percent in Tambov province.[82] Regions where labor migration was common or where factories were located had uniformly higher rates than purely agricultural districts of the countryside.[83]

Literacy is, of course, only an indirect indicator of changes in the workers' life-style or outlook, and those changes could go in many directions. Employers and police, moreover, did their best to keep changes within acceptable bounds. A worker who adopted a conspicuously citified style of dress or speech or whose reading tastes extended beyond pulp novels or ecclesiastical tracts might find himself unwelcome at the factory or harassed by the police.[84] All the same, a certain proportion of workers—smaller in textiles, higher in the metal trades, but in Moscow never more than a small minority—did move steadily away from the peasant community and all that it implied.[85]

Effects of the Factory Environment

The stability and continuity of factory life (and underlife) in Moscow are hardly consistent with existing stereotypes of Russian labor. Writers who have emphasized the turbulent and disorganized qualities of the Russian work force have given little consideration to these patterns. If a worker spent more than five years at the same factory, if his supervisor was a peasant like himself, if his father had worked at the same factory, if the manager or owner knew his name and history, and if he worked and lived in the company of fellow villagers, can one really describe him as uprooted or alienated? Clearly there is more here than coercion or sullen acquiescence, but clearly too the underlife of Moscow's factories is less than proletarian.

Outside the central provinces and the textile industry, factory life operated on somewhat different principles. In Saint Petersburg, it was less common for workers to live at the factory, and the totality of the institution, in Goffman's sense of the term, was thereby diminished. The mines, plants, and oil fields of the South, on the other hand, although they provided housing, eating facilities, and an otherwise closed environment, were dealing with a newly recruited population; if Moscow workers could feel a continuity between their past and present lives, their brethren in the Donbas or Baku probably could not. The stability of Moscow's factory population, moreover, may have had no parallel in other regions. Fragmentary data suggest an annual turnover of 100 percent or more in other regions,[86] whereas, for Moscow, equally fragmentary sources suggest a figure closer to 10 percent.

An unanswered question is whether the Moscow region's stability, with all its repressive overtones, discouraged or prevented worker protest. Social-Democratic agitators at the turn of the century generally agreed that it did, and one of them characterized the typical central Russian factory town of Orekhovo as a stagnant pond:

> vegetation grows to the surface and sinks again to the bottom, settling there to form a slimy mass which drags into itself everything that comes its way. . . . There is no intellectual life worth speaking about, and it is difficult to continue one's education even if one did have a little to start with. . . . One seldom meets educated workers; in fact, at the slightest sign of protest against oppression out you go.[87]

In contrast, the most active leaders of worker protest often showed a highly volatile pattern of employment, moving from factory to factory and city to city at intervals of a few months.[88] One cannot be sure, however, whether this was a cause or a result of their radicalism. Despite their mobility, some veteran agitators managed to retain their connection to the factory underlife of *zemliaki* and village customs and even managed to use them in their efforts to rouse the workers. To determine how well they succeeded and how the Moscow environment influenced the growth of labor unrest one must examine the course of the labor movement itself.

Chapter Six

The Radical Intelligentsia
and the Working Class

Beginning in the late 1860s, Moscow's working class became the target of propaganda from a series of revolutionary groups and factions. Lacking any opportunity to propagate their ideas in an open fashion, these groups, whose members came mainly from the intelligentsia, turned to conspiratorial methods. Their tactics and theories developed and changed over the next thirty years, but the environment in which they operated was consistently hazardous. Would-be propagandists had to contend not only with the suspicions and insularity of factory workers but even more with the vigilance of the police. As a result, underground activity tended to follow a cyclical pattern. In the typical case, a handful of radical activists would make contact with a small number of workers and, in the course of a few weeks or months, would begin to build an organization. Inevitably the police would get wind of their activities and the members would be arrested, imprisoned, or banished to distant provinces. Once the most active, articulate leaders had been removed, there would be a lull of months or years until some new group arose to resume the struggle. Despite certain evolutionary features, Moscow's revolutionary movement remained locked in this pattern until 1905.

Populist Propaganda in the 1870s

Although the first tentative approaches to workers were made in the 1860s, systematic propaganda was not undertaken in Moscow until 1873. A group led by a Siberian-born former student, A. V. Dolgushin, had been operating in Saint Petersburg since 1872, and decided for conspiratorial reasons to shift operations to Moscow. The group's outlook was Bakuninist. Its members organized propagandist circles and distributed leaflets calling on the Russian peasants to rise up and overthrow the tsar, the landlords, and the church. They established an underground press in the countryside near Moscow, but their efforts were cut short by arrests within a few months.[1]

The Dolgushin group's activities paralleled those of the Chaikovskii circle in Saint Petersburg, which had begun propaganda among factory workers two years earlier.[2] Both groups saw in the workers a means of making contact with the countryside, and their aim of a general uprising of peasants overshadowed their concern about the specific grievances of factory life. In 1874, after the arrest of many "Chaikovtsy," several experienced propagandists from Petersburg shifted their operations to Moscow, where they established contact with an estimated twenty factories. One of the most active members of this group was Petr Alekseev, a weaver of peasant background from Smolensk province, who is said to have enjoyed immense rapport with workers. Once again the police intervened within a few months, and in April, 1875 most of the members were arrested. Their activities left few visible traces among Moscow's factory workers, but the fiery speech Alekseev delivered at his trial became an underground classic that was reprinted many times in later years.[3]

The earliest populist groups disseminated their propaganda mainly through study circles (*kruzhki*). In Moscow as elsewhere in Russia, the closed world of the factory and the homogeneous worker-peasant subculture were not easily penetrated by outsiders. Members of the intelligentsia tried to make contact with workers by striking up conversations in taverns and other public places, but such efforts were conspicuous and often unsuccessful. The circles thus came to rely heavily on the efforts of their earliest converts, radicalized workers such as Alekseev, who could bridge the gap between the intelligentsia and the masses.[4] Through their factory contacts, such individuals could identify the most responsive and reliable workers, who were then invited to secret meetings where legal and illegal literature was discussed. Alekseev was especially successful in establishing a network of *kruzhki*. As an experienced weaver, he worked at different factories for short periods of time and managed to conceal his contacts from police even after his arrest.

In some cases the *kruzhki* took on the appearance of evening courses, and included such subjects as science and mathematics along with revolutionary theories. The propagandists of these early years, however, because of their interest in the "unspoiled" population of the countryside, were uninterested in the details of factory life. They opposed the idea of unions, cooperatives, or other factory-based associations that might distract workers from the more important task of making revolution in the villages.[5]

In the "mad summer" of 1874, Alekseev and others like him were encouraged to abandon factory propaganda and take their message to the countryside. The anticipated surge of peasant unrest did not materialize, and within a year hundreds of individuals, workers as well as students, were in prison or exile for their efforts. Others abandoned revolutionary activity altogether or began to reevaluate their previous assumptions. Some began to see propaganda as a slow, painstaking process that could last for generations, but others turned their thoughts to political revolution. In place of the former goal of a spontaneous, uncoordinated uprising, this latter group now contemplated seizing and altering the mechanism of the state through terrorism and tight conspiratorial organization.

In this climate of disillusionment and reappraisal, attitudes toward factory workers also began to change. Veterans of the earlier propaganda campaigns contrasted the receptiveness of factory workers with the suspicious and sometimes hostile reaction of peasants. Without yet abandoning populist tenets, revolutionaries began to show more respect for the factory workers' potential and to recognize the distinctive features that set them apart from the peasantry. The spirit of reappraisal and change was shared by experienced worker-propagandists. As a result, in 1878 a new organization, the Northern Union of Russian Workers, was founded. Its guiding spirits were two skilled workers who had been active in earlier propaganda, Viktor Obnorskii and Stepan Khalturin, and its goals included basic liberties such as freedom of speech and association. The group was based in Saint Petersburg, where it organized an underground library and printing press. Its members had hopes of extending their activity throughout Russia, and they did succeed in establishing a base in Moscow, but their efforts were halted by arrests early in 1879. Although the Saint Petersburg members are known to have played a leading role in demonstrations and strikes, the union's activities in Moscow were of a more conspiratorial nature; as a result historians have been unable to trace any public manifestations of its work in the Moscow region.[6]

Although its leadership was drawn from the working class rather than the universities, the Northern Union was in many ways a continuation of earlier efforts. As full-time revolutionaries, Khalturin and Obnorskii were pursuing different goals from those of earlier years, yet the conditions of conspiracy and police repression were unchanged, limiting the possible tactics and structure of the union. The organization was forced to rely heavily on propagandist *kruzhki* to recruit and educate new leadership cadres from the factories; yet police vigilance removed such individuals almost as quickly as they appeared.

After the suppression of the Northern Union, the revolutionary movement was dominated for several years by the People's Will party. Many of the survivors of earlier revolutionary efforts now became adherents of terrorism. (Among them was Stepan Khalturin, who took part in one of the most spectacular attempts on the life of Tsar Alexander II and was later executed for murdering a high-ranking government official.) In Moscow, the People's Will party was represented by a "Workers' Group" under the leadership of one P. A. Tellalov. Despite its adherence to terrorism and a strictly centralized conspiratorial organization, the group followed a familiar pattern in its relations with the city's factory workers. It is said to have made contact with 100 to 120 workers through thirty *kruzhki* or similar "connections."[7] Like earlier groups, this one organized readings and study sessions at which socialist ideas were expounded and workers were urged to unite. A printing press was secured in the summer of 1880, but the organization soon subordinated propagandist efforts to the immediate needs of the terrorist campaign; within a few months, the tsar was dead and the People's Will was decimated by arrests.

New Currents in the 1880s

At this point the revolutionary underground reached its nadir. Many of its leading figures were dead or in prison. Some fled abroad; some recanted; and many lived out their lives in Siberian exile. The defeats of the 1870s had challenged many of the theories and assumptions of revolutionary populism, thus a growing number of radical intellectuals in the following years began to seek alternative theories. They were especially drawn to the writings of Marx and Engels and to a reconsideration of Russia's social and economic development. Earlier writers and activists had emphasized the uniqueness of Russia and the possibility of bypassing capitalist development through timely revolution. Now, in the early 1880s, G. V. Plekhanov proudly proclaimed his allegiance to "that trend which considers Russian capitalism a historical inevitability." Socialist revolution, he insisted, would come to Russia not through the peasant commune or the conspiracies of populist intellectuals, but through the growth of a class-conscious proletariat: "Capitalism is favored by the whole dynamics of our social life, all the forces that develop with the movement of the social machine and in turn determine the direction and speed of that movement. . . . We must utilize the social and economic upheaval which is proceeding in Russia for the benefit of the revolution and the working population."[8] Capitalism itself, far from preventing socialist revolution, would create the conditions that made real revolution possible.

The debates between Marxists and populists in the 1880s and 1890s were often highly abstract and theoretical; yet they had serious implications for the everyday course of revolutionary activity. In the eyes of Marxists, the factory worker could no longer be seen as a corrupted peasant but became instead an agent of revolutionary change. The experience of labor unrest and revolutionary struggle in Western countries could no longer be disregarded but came instead to be seen as a source of inspiration for Russians. At the same time, the Russian workers' own struggles could now be seen as part and parcel of an international proletarian revolution.

The net result of this reevaluation was to encourage factory-based propaganda and unrest. Strike funds, underground libraries, and various forms of mutual aid among workers were now actively encouraged by radicals, and efforts were made to publicize the achievements of Western workers in conducting strikes and forming unions and parties. Nonetheless it would be a mistake to picture the tactics of the 1880s as a radical departure from earlier revolutionary efforts. Underground aid funds (*kassy*) and libraries had been established among workers in the heyday of revolutionary populism, and efforts toward mass organization and coordinated labor unrest had been initiated under populist slogans by the Northern Union. The swing to Marxism in the 1880s gave such tactics a greater authority than they had hitherto enjoyed, but the tactics themselves, and the environment in which they were used, had not changed drastically from the previous decade. As a result, the Marxist-inspired revolutionary organizations of the 1880s and 1890s found themselves in many instances recapitulating the experience of their populist predecessors.

In Moscow the most notable *kruzhok* of the 1880s was the so-called Society of Translators and Publishers,[9] formed by a group of university students from Siberia in 1883. Its leading members included V. T. Raspopin, a student in the faculty of physics and mathematics, and Ludwig Ianovich [Janowicz], a Polish student at the Petrovsko-Razumovskaia agricultural academy. This group stressed self-education, and most of its energy seems to have been directed toward the intelligentsia. Its chief activity was to translate, print, and distribute socialistic writings, including works of Marx, Engels, Guesde, Blanc, Lafargue, and Liebknecht. It also reprinted Russian works that had been censored or were otherwise unavailable, including Leo Tolstoi's *A Confession.* As the list of authors suggests, the group did not have a clearly defined ideological stance, though the members were somewhat more sympathetic to Marxian socialism. They corresponded with the Emancipation of Labor group, newly formed by Russian émigrés in Geneva, and with Friedrich Engels, but also with the émigré populist theoretician P. L. Lavrov.

Although most of the Moscow circle's efforts were directed to the intelligentsia, some of the members engaged in propaganda among factory workers. They are known to have issued one proclamation entitled "Comrade Workers," which called for self-education, solidarity, and the formation of mutual-aid funds by workers and which described foreign workers' achievements in the struggle for a better life. (The example of recent underground efforts among Polish workers was especially impressive to the Moscow society, some of whose members were in close contact with the Polish revolutionary movement.)[10] Such efforts had barely begun, however, before the police moved in. Raspopin was arrested in November 1883, and in April of the following year the society's press was discovered and most of the remaining members were arrested.

For several years thereafter, no trace of organized propaganda appeared in Moscow. This does not necessarily mean that no efforts were under way: on the contrary, individuals who had been associated with the earlier *kruzhki* sometimes managed to continue independent revolutionary activity without any centralized organization. One of them was Petr Moiseenko, whose agitational efforts in Orekhovo were briefly discussed in Chapter Four. After spending several years in Siberian exile for his part in the Northern Union of Russian Workers, he returned to central Russia and took a job at the Morozov cotton mills on the border of Moscow province; less than two years later he played a leading role in the factory's massive strike of January 1885—the largest and most serious labor confrontation that Russia had yet experienced—

but he was unsuccessful in his efforts to secure outside support.[11] Another independent revolutionary was a radical weaver named Osip Vasil'ev, who had been involved with Alekseev's efforts in 1875 and continued on his own for more than fifteen years after his associates had been arrested.[12]

How many such cases may have gone unnoticed is impossible to determine precisely, but the number cannot have been large. The experiences of earlier years had made the police extremely wary, as a local constable's report from 1890 demonstrates: the officer, describing the mood of workers at the Prokhorovskaia factory, noted that a certain Vladimirov had been seen in nearby taverns wearing a respectable German overcoat and that a medical student, I. O. Mikhalev, had been seen playing pitch-and-toss with workers just outside the city.[13]

In the face of such surveillance, any sustained propaganda effort among workers by the intelligentsia was likely to be detected. *Kruzhki* composed entirely of *intelligenty* were less conspicuous if they confined their activity to self-education and discussion. Similarly, a worker *kruzhok* whose leader was himself a worker could conceal its activities more easily; any effort to move from words to deeds, however, was likely to be met by prompt repression. The more successful a *kruzhok* was in arousing revolutionary feelings, the more likely it was to be detected and eradicated.

Kruzhki of the Early 1890s

Toward the end of the 1880s, efforts began once again to establish unified networks of *kruzhki*, first in Saint Petersburg and later in Moscow. (In both cases, the example of unified Social-Democratic efforts in Poland was an important influence.) In Petersburg, a circle organized by P. V. Tochisskii operated from 1884 to 1888.[14] The group, whose leaders included several skilled workers, used conspiratorial methods and tried to isolate workers from members of the intelligentsia.[15] It organized study and discussion groups among workers as well as a library with more than seven hundred books and two *kassy*, one intended to provide assistance to workers in time of strikes, the other to aid the families of arrested and exiled workers. After Tochisskii's arrest in 1888, a new Social-Democratic network, under the leadership of V. S. Golubev, M. I. Brusnev, L. B. Krasin, and W. F. Cywinski, established ties with a newly formed Central Worker Circle, which united worker *kruzhki* throughout Petersburg.

In 1891 Brusnev, having completed his studies at the Saint
Petersburg Technological Institute, moved to Moscow to work as
an engineer in the workshops of the Moscow-Brest railroad. Together with two worker members of the Petersburg organization,
Brusnev attempted to build a Moscow network comparable to the
Petersburg one. From the outset, the new Moscow circle was
divided into factions. One group, led by the forestry student
Mikhail Egupov, was closer to the terrorist traditions of the
People's Will party, whereas Brusnev and several others considered
themselves orthodox Marxists. Nonetheless, they managed to
cooperate in efforts to establish a base in the working class, not
just in Moscow but in Tula and other cities. The number of worker
kruzhki was not large, but the leaders were enthusiastic about the
progress of their efforts. Shortly before their arrest in April 1892,
they were planning to unite several separate Moscow *kruzhki*
into a single organization with an executive committee and a
treasury (*kassa*).[16]

At the time of Brusnev's arrest, several independent student
kruzhki were also meeting regularly in Moscow, notably one led
by G. N. Mandel'shtam, who had attended the first congress of the
Second International while studying in Paris in 1889. Mandel'shtam
and several of his associates were caught in the police crackdown
that followed the discovery of Brusnev's organization, but others
who had been close to his group escaped detection, and in the
following months they managed to lay the foundations of yet
another underground center.[17] Leading members of this new
group included Mandel'shtam's brother Martin (who took the
name Liadov); a medical student, S. I. Mitskevich; an ex-military
cadet from Vil'no, E. I. Sponti; S. I. Prokof'ev, a machinist's
assistant on the Moscow-Brest railroad; and a married couple, A.
and N. Vinokurov, the husband a physician and the wife a midwife.

In the first stages of their activities, members of this group
found it difficult to establish contact with workers. Mitskevich
himself was first introduced to a worker *kruzhok* by the sister of
a fellow student, A. I. Dobronravov; the latter had been meeting
regularly with shopworkers from the Moscow-Brest railroad, but
he had recently died. The workers had previously been exposed
only to populist and Tolstoyan propaganda, but they responded
favorably to Mitskevich's Marxist ideas. One member was the
aforementioned Prokof'ev, who soon was organizing and leading
kruzhki of his own.[18]

The Mitskevich-Liadov group's first tactic was propaganda,
usually in the form of lengthy sessions in which students and

members of the intelligentsia tried to explain the principles of Marxism to workers: "First we interpreted primary accumulation and the formation of capital, and later, in lecture after lecture, expounded the first volume of *Capital*, with illustrations from Russian life."[19] They cooperated with a more theoretically minded group of students from Riazan' in the translation of works by Kautsky, Engels, Liebknecht, and other Marxist writers, and they secured literature from abroad through Sponti's contacts in Vil'no.[20] Inspired by Sponti's account of unified Social-Democratic efforts in Poland and Vil'no, Mitskevich and his associates decided in November 1893 to constitute themselves a central propaganda organization for all of Moscow.

The group of six was thus reaching out in two directions. On the one hand, they were maintaining and extending contact with diverse groups of student radicals. Some of these had a populist orientation, whereas others were inclined to Social-Democratic ideas. Many, like the student *kruzhok* of A. I. Riazanov and I. A. Davydov, were preoccupied with theoretical questions, and some, like G. M. Krukovskii, were indifferent to the workers' day-to-day struggles: "Russia [he told Liadov] is still an underdeveloped country, in a period of primitive accumulation. There is still no true proletariat, and we Marxists will have to wait a long time until the necessary conditions are created. . . . It's not the Marxists' business to practice philanthropy. . . . Their task is to accumulate knowledge which they can share with the proletariat when the right time comes. . . . For the time being the worse [the condition of the workers] the better."[21] Although Mitskevich and his colleagues strenuously opposed this view, they continued to involve themselves in activities of the intelligentsia, and Mitskevich's arrest in December 1894 was a result, not of his propaganda among workers, but of an extensive police investigation of student unrest.[22]

At the same time, the Mitskevich group was extending its ties with the plants, factories, and railroad workshops of Moscow. Despite the obstacles to propaganda, they quickly made contact with a number of enterprises, and in April 1893 a new Central Workers' Circle was formed. According to Mitskevich, its first meeting was attended by representatives from eleven different worker *kruzhki*, and seven more were soon added.[23]

The apparent ease with which these contacts were made suggests that the Mitskevich-Liadov group was building on the work of earlier propagandists. In a few cases members were able to make contact with preexistent *kruzhki*, as Mitskevich did at the Brest railroad. Even where no formal *kruzhki* existed, however, small independent groups of workers had sometimes begun to coalesce. In later years, a few of the most "conscious" workers wrote memoirs describing their experiences in the 1880s and 1890s, and these accounts help to explain the successes and failures of radical propaganda. They refer, for example, to secondhand and thirdhand rumors of revolutionary activity that aroused their curiosity and led them to seek contact with the socialist intelligentsia: "[we heard] that there were socialists, who did not believe in God, killed the tsar, and wanted to live without [government] power. This made such an impression on me that I determined at any cost to go to Tula [where a comrade reported meeting such individuals]."[24] In some cases the source of rumor was an old-timer who had participated in earlier clashes with the authorities: "Whenever someone noticed that 'uncle Grisha' had been drinking, we pressed him to tell us tales, although it wasn't possible to make anything coherent of them. He told us about the government's misdeeds (*neporiadki*), about injustices, and a hatred for the existing order began to form in us."[25] Though the workers were eager to broaden their understanding of the world around them, they were sometimes hesitant to make contact with the intelligentsia, and their uneasiness was shared by some of the more experienced worker-propagandists: "Fedor Afanas'ev said that in meeting students one must be careful, [for] there are different kinds of students."[26]

The workers who were drawn to *kruzhki* were an atypical minority, and those who later wrote about their experiences were even less typical. Almost all were literate, and most had had some measure of formal schooling. They tended to be young and unmarried, but their interest in reading and discussion (and in many cases their dislike for alcohol) set them apart from most of their fellow workers.[27] They were eager for knowledge and rebellious in spirit, but the subtleties of revolutionary doctrine were, for the time being at least, beyond their grasp. Though some would later become active Bolsheviks, their accounts of the 1880s and 1890s suggest that they read populist and Marxist books and pamphlets interchangeably,[28] and in more than one instance populist and Marxist propagandists seemed to be supporting one another's efforts.[29]

As in earlier underground efforts, the propagandists of the early 1890s relied heavily on these worker activists to widen the circle of revolutionary activity. Through them, the Central Workers' Circle came into contact with a diverse membership. On the one hand, the more "conscious" workers were ready to lead *kruzhki* of their own. On the other, there was a constant influx of new recruits, strongly interested in the propagandist's messages, but often naïve, especially in matters of conspiracy. On one occasion, Liadov was brought to a meeting by F. I. Poliakov, a weaver who had been involved with propaganda for several years. To his shock, Liadov was led into a main sleeping room full of workers and told he could talk to all of them: "They're all good lads." Realizing that this was against all the rules of conspiracy, he still had no choice but to go ahead and hold the meeting. To his relief, all went smoothly, and he continued to meet the workers for some time thereafter without coming to the attention of the police or factory administration.[30]

In this situation, it was natural that the members should seek some measure of coordination and control over the circle's disparate activities. Inevitably, however, disagreements arose over the form these should take. One faction, led by Sponti, favored an elected council of delegates from the worker *kruzhki.* This proposal was opposed by Mitskevich, A. Vinokurov, and Liadov, who argued that the workers were unprepared to direct the movement, especially where conspiracy was involved (e.g., printing and other "technical" matters, transport of literature, and relations with other cities).[31] As a compromise, a two-tiered system of direction was established, with the former group of six taking care of conspiratorial and ideological matters (*vysshoe ideinoe rukovodstvo*) and with a group of active *kruzhok* members, chosen by cooptation rather than election, providing leadership in other areas. Relations between the two tiers were not clearly defined, but over the next year the "delegates" collected information about conditions in different factories and about the workers' mood; provided guidance for the distribution of literature; reviewed proposed leaflets before they were issued; established and maintained a central *kassa;* kept a library of legal literature, and a separate collection of illegal materials; and organized agitation by directing members from one factory to another and providing them with monetary assistance to acquire suitable quarters for propaganda meetings. For more than a year, the group met biweekly in the apartment of a metalworker, K. F. Boie.[32]

In December 1894, Mitskevich, A. Vinokurov, and several other Marxist *inteligenty* were arrested or banished from Moscow in the aftermath of a student demonstration. Liadov remained at liberty, however, and the central coordinating council regrouped under his leadership. In the spring of 1895, the organization began to issue leaflets under the name Workers' Union. One of its first publications was a call for workers to observe May Day as a holiday, and on May Day itself some two-hundred workers gathered to listen to speeches in the wooded district of Sokol'niki, on the outskirts of the city. Several more mass gatherings were held in the following two months, but on 10 June 1895, new arrests were made, including Liadov and most of the other student members of the organization. A printing press that the group had concealed in a Moscow suburb was confiscated. Prokof'ev and several other active members of the central circle remained at liberty and managed to distribute leaflets at several factories in the following two months, but they in turn were arrested during a new police sweep in August of the same year.[33]

The Conversion to Agitation

At the time of these arrests, the Moscow leadership was beginning to redefine its role among workers. Through its contacts with Vil'no and Poland, word had been received of the massive Lodz strike of 1892 and of the campaign of agitation that had just begun among Jewish artisans in Vil'no. Mitskevich, who traveled to Vil'no for literature early in 1894, met with A. Kremer and other leaders of the Social-Democratic movement there and requested information about the group's agitation techniques.[34] In response, Kremer agreed to write a short account of the Vil'no experience, and the resulting pamphlet, "Ob agitatsii," soon produced shock waves throughout the Russian Social-Democratic movement.[35]

In place of the former tactic of long-term propaganda among a cultured minority of workers, the new approach emphasized day-to-day issues among the rank-and-file. Broadsheets and leaflets were prepared in a simple, easy-to-read style, described specific grievances in individual factories, and called for workers to struggle against them. The assumption underlying this tactic was that any clash between workers and employers would lead to police intervention. Through the experience of repression, workers would see the connection between their own lives and the whole social and political system of capitalism; their discontents would be redirected against the system rather than against the individual employer; and their consciousness of themselves as a unified class would be developed.

The Moscow group's first efforts in this direction came from the pen of Sponti in February or March of 1894 and were written in the form of conversations. In one, two employers compare notes on their profits and on the gullibility of their workers (e.g., "we, who live without working, have a reputation as benefactors of the people"), but they are uneasy, because workers in other countries have stopped believing in God and begun to demand an end to exploitation. In the second leaflet, a factory inspector informs an employer that he must pay a higher wage for work on Sundays but allows him to fulfill his obligation by lowering the rates for weekdays; a worker, overhearing them, realizes that it is time to take matters into his own hands.[36] A few weeks later, Liadov wrote a broadsheet addressed to workers at the Veikhelt machine works, complaining about a reduction in wages and calling for united worker action—a strike, a union, and a *kassa*.[37]

Moscow's early agitational literature was sometimes moderate, even bookish, in tone, offering vague slogans about unification "to achieve a better life." A good example was the May Day leaflet of 1895, which began with the phrase, "Many of you, certainly, have no notion of this holiday." The leaflet went on to list the achievements of foreign workers: an eight-hour day and wages "three or four times higher" than in Russia. Workers from unspecified other countries were holding international congresses to coordinate their efforts, it said, but in Russia the exhausting conditions leave the workers "no time for reading or scientific pursuits." Russian workers, it suggested, must unite to fight for their rights; they must meet together to evaluate their position, form *kassy*, and use those *kassy* to support strikes.[38] This leaflet, and several others that the Mitskevich group had prepared the preceding year, could be interpreted as supporting reformist trade-union tactics such as those used by German Social Democrats.[39] Even the name of the group was left ambiguous. For a while the group operated with no name, and then chose Workers' Union instead of Social-Democratic in order to avoid frightening workers away.[40]

On the other hand, some of the earliest leaflets took a more militant line, and spoke of overthrowing the yoke of capitalism. What this suggests is that the Workers' Union had not defined its position very clearly. Other evidence of uncertainty and vacillation can be found in the members' relations with populism (at the time of their arrest, Mitskevich and several others had populist and Tolstoyan literature in their possession)[41] and in one longer pamphlet whose romanticized picture of preindustrial crafts was hardly compatible with Marxian socialism.[42]

After the arrest of Prokof'ev in August 1895, there was a lull of several months during which time radical students and *intelligenty* regrouped, this time under the leadership of M. F. Vladimirskii, a former student from Nizhnii-Novgorod. The new group continued to use the name Moscow Workers' Union, and appears to have had a greater proportion of workers among its members.[43] It further refined the techniques of agitation, paying particular attention to the development of strikes in other localities. In the spring of 1895, before the wave of arrests, the former union had sent several workers to Iaroslavl' to gather information about a violent clash between workers and troops; in December of that same year, the new union issued a leaflet entitled "Strikes and Their Significance for Workers," which presented detailed descriptions of the Iaroslavl' strike and several others. Besides providing general guidance on how to conduct a strike, the lengthy leaflet pointed out recent gains at particular factories, among them the Danilovskaia cotton-spinning mill, whose recent wage increase was attributed to the owner's fear of a strike.[44] Copies of the pamphlet were left at several factories, including the Tsindel' cotton mill, which had recently experienced a violent and unsuccessful strike.

In its early stages, the reconstituted Workers' Union spoke of the capitalists drinking the workers' blood; its references to foreign workers who had "reached their goal, and are now in a state of bliss (*blazhenstvuiut*)"[45] showed little sophistication about the international socialist movement. Within a few months, however, the union's publications were emphasizing the international character of the workers' struggle. In February 1896 the twenty-fifth anniversary of the Paris Commune was commemorated by sending a message of greeting to the workers of France "in the name of 605 workers from 28 factories and plants."[46]

A few months later, on the occasion of the famous Saint Petersburg textile strike of May–June 1896, the Moscow union held several mass meetings and issued several leaflets to describe the Petersburg events and summon Moscow workers to join in the struggle. As in earlier literature, the leaflets noted specific conditions in Moscow, pointing out that the workers there endured even worse conditions than in Petersburg and also underscoring recent concessions at several factories—apparent proof that the owners were frightened by the specter of the Petersburg strike.[47]

The city-wide council and *kassa* that had been set up in 1894 seem to have disappeared by midsummer of 1895. In later months the new Workers' Union devoted considerable attention to reviving both and to developing local factory *kassy*. One of the earliest publications following the summer arrests was a pamphlet entitled "Why Do Workers Need *Kassy*, and How to Organize Them." In the early months of 1896, the union reestablished a central committee and an assembly of delegates from local *kruzhki* and began to discuss the formation of a central workers' fund. The issue reflected some of the latent tensions and contradictions of agitation, for the members were sharply divided over the new fund's relation to local ones. Some wanted to collect contributions through a network of local *kassy*, which would retain some measure of control over the allocation of monies; they feared that there might be disagreement over the merits of a particular strike and that the central *kassa* might not be able to meet all local needs. Others, however, argued for centralized control of the fund, and, after much discussion, their proposal was approved by majorities of workers at several secret mass meetings (*skhodki*) in June 1896.[48]

At this point the reconstituted union seemed to have recovered from the previous year's arrests. Participants later estimated that it had established ties with fifty-five factories and had between one thousand and two thousand active supporters.[49] No sooner had it begun to hold open meetings, however, than the police moved in again. Strikes had been planned at several major factories and plants in and around Moscow city, but the action of the police prevented most of them. In all, sixty workers and *intelligenty* were arrested.

In later years, the theory of agitation became a matter of controversy among Russian Social Democrats. Lenin in particular objected that a movement based on economic demands could too easily be distracted from revolutionary goals and subverted into trade unionism. In Moscow, however, this does not seem to have occurred. The literature prepared by the Moscow Workers' Union and its successors, although it focused on specific grievances, rarely failed to link them to broader slogans or concerns. Far from following in the wake of events, the Moscow radicals called for the celebration of May Day as an international workers' holiday, urged solidarity with the striking textile workers of Saint Petersburg in 1896, commemorated the Paris Commune, and attacked both autocracy and capitalism as the real source of workers' distress and as the proper target for their protests.

The agitational tactics of the mid-1890s, moreover, were successful in attracting the attention of greater numbers of workers than earlier efforts had reached. If hundreds or even thousands of workers attended a mass meeting, the effect must have been exhilarating for participants, who could feel that they were part of a larger cause with city-wide (or worldwide) support. Such meetings also served to stimulate rumors and speculation among nonparticipants.

Paradoxically, these tactics were also an invitation to police intervention. The appearance of a leaflet at a factory or of workers at a secret meeting often served as a warning to police and employers, who were able to step in before any overt mass action had been taken. Cases of this sort surely gave workers ample reason to be wary of the radical underground and to resist some of its initiatives. If in certain instances worker *kruzhki* were reluctant to participate in agitation efforts or mass meetings, or if they wished to retain some measure of local control over monetary contributions, one should not be too quick to attribute this either to anti-intelligentsia feelings or to a quest for independence by the workers.[50] To the extent that workers knew the history of underground activity, they had good reason to fear that such involvement would bring the police down on them. A *kruzhok*, left to its own devices, could sometimes survive for years, even if its members were stirring up other workers and provoking strikes.[51] A *kruzhok* connected to the revolutionary underground, however, had a much shorter life expectancy. Paradoxically, it was the conspiratorial revolutionary centers, much more than the spontaneous efforts of inexperienced workers, that drew the attention of the authorities.

From 1896 onward, the details of Social-Democratic activity follow a familiar cyclical pattern, succinctly described by the future Bolshevik, I. I. Skvortsov-Stepanov: "Hardly did the members of the intelligentsia establish acquaintance with workers than they were subjected to arrest and banishment. The same fate befell practically every *kruzhok* from its very beginning."[52] After the arrest of the second Workers' Union in July 1896, a third union was formed under the leadership of a medical student, A. N. Orlov, but it too was discovered and decimated by arrests three months later. During its brief period of activity, this group seems to have adhered more strictly to the methods outlined in "Ob agitatsii" by gathering information from individual factories and encouraging workers to strike over specific local grievances; the group's leaflets called on workers to use nonviolent methods of struggle such as strikes and *kassy*, but rarely put forth political demands or proposals.[53] After a series of arrests in November and December, intelligentsia participation in the union virtually ended, but a nucleus of workers, most of them from the metal trades, continued to issue leaflets in the name of the union; this group, too, concentrated on local economic issues, especially the demand for a shorter work day. Its efforts were halted by arrests in the summer and late autumn of 1897.

In January 1898, a new group appeared, calling itself the Moscow Union of Struggle for the Emancipation of the Working Class, a name that had first been used two years earlier in Saint Petersburg. Its leadership, judging from a list compiled by the police, was entirely from the intelligentsia,[54] mostly students from the Moscow imperial technical school and Moscow university. The new group issued three leaflets before being broken up by the police in March. In April, yet another group proclaimed its existence under the same name. The new Union of Struggle issued a call for the establishment of a city-wide *kassa* and an organization roughly the same as earlier city-wide committees,[55] but its activities left few traces in the following months. In autumn the group took the name of the Russian Social Democratic Labor Party. Its activities seem to have consisted mostly of distributing illegal literature; émigré sources report that members of the organization were arrested in April, May, June, October, and December 1899 and in January 1900.[56] In terms of propaganda and revolutionary activity, Moscow had fallen behind "even the most god-forsaken corners of Russia,"[57] and this "backwardness" was to continue until 1905.

Radical Influence in the Worker-Peasant Milieu

In comparing Moscow's revolutionary groups to their counterparts in other parts of Russia, one must note the exceptionally difficult conditions the Muscovite radicals encountered. For one thing, the insularity of worker-peasants was greater here than in many other industrial centers, and it was reinforced by the geographic isolation of many factories and the homogeneity of the workers' backgrounds. More than half of Moscow province's work force was located in the hinterland, in small factory towns or villages where any outsider would be conspicuous. Even in the city, paternalistic employers managed to maintain significant barriers between their workers and external "subversive" influences. Opportunities for open, legal contact between workers and the intelligentsia were almost nonexistent; Sunday schools, for example, had a clientele of, at most, a few thousand workers and operated under close police supervision.[58] Beyond the formal barriers were less tangible ones of speech, dress, and social background, which set peasant-workers apart from the rest of the population and made them suspicious of outsiders—be they students, officials, townsmen, or even skilled craftsmen.

The most active members of the Moscow Workers' Union, and of the revolutionary underground generally, often came from a social background alien to most Moscow workers. Not only were many from upper- or middle-class families but they also came from distant regions or non-Russian ethnic backgrounds. Mitskevich grew up in Kazan and was the son of a Polish officer in the Russian army. The Mandel'shtam brothers were evidently Jewish and from a well-to-do family; Gregorii had studied in Paris, while Martin attended gymnasium in Mitava. Sponti attended military school in Saint Petersburg and was introduced to Marxism while serving as an officer in the Russian army in Vil'no. Many other examples could be provided, not just from the student intelligentsia but also from the ranks of the most active workers. The two earliest worker-members of the Moscow Workers' Union were Prokof'ev and Boie, both of them townsmen (*meshchane*) and graduates of technical schools; contemporaries noted the abundance of books in their homes and commented on Boie's outward resemblance to a middle-class radical (*raznochinets-intelligent*).[59] In their skills, training, style of life, and social background, such individuals had little in common with the half-peasant masses described in previous chapters. Such differences were probably more important in Moscow than in the factory centers of the South or in Saint Petersburg, where the work force was drawn from more heterogeneous sources.

This is not to suggest that the barriers between workers and revolutionaries were insuperable but merely that they were more formidable in Moscow than in other centers. In the 1890s, the Moscow radicals' difficulties were compounded by the intensification of police activities under the direction of Sergei Zubatov. Zubatov, who began serving in the Security (*Okhranka*) Section of the Department of Police in the mid-1880s, played an important role in developing new techniques of counterrevolutionary surveillance and intervention. (Zubatov's attempts at "police socialism" belong to a slightly later period and posed a different challenge to revolutionaries in the years 1900–1903; in the 1890s, however, his efforts were directed more toward ferreting out radical activity among Moscow's workers.) By the time that he assumed the post of director of the Moscow *Okhranka* in 1896, he had established an extensive network of agents who could keep track of the revolutionary movement and penetrate its organizations. Zubatov was especially adept at interrogation and persuasion, and he managed to convince many radicals, both workers and intellectuals, to become police agents.[60]

In these conditions, the revolutionaries' frequent defeats and setbacks seem less surprising than their tenacity and endurance. Despite the workers' insularity and the *Okhranka's* surveillance, the underground groups did manage to make contact with certain groups of workers and to win a sympathetic audience for their doctrines. There emerged a small but significant nucleus of worker-radicals, not well schooled in the subtleties of revolutionary theory but adept at disseminating simple ideas among broader masses of workers. From the time of Petr Alekseev, such individuals showed considerable skill and dedication in their efforts to build a wider workers' movement. No sooner had this stratum of knowledgeable, radicalized workers come into existence, however, than it became subject to the same perils as the nonworker intelligentsia. Police vigilance regularly removed from the scene the most visible, outspoken leaders and propagandists—workers and students alike. As a result, their less experienced comrades found themselves picking up the pieces and repeating the errors and experiments of their predecessors in a seemingly endless cycle. (The absent leaders, it should be noted, were routinely banished to out-of-the-way provincial towns, where they often managed to continue their activities. The role of such individuals as carriers of revolutionary ideas to the hinterland has been documented in a number of instances. It helps to explain both the surge of labor unrest that occurred in many hitherto-tranquil centers in 1903 and the absence of such a wave of unrest in Moscow at that time.)[61]

Although Moscow's conditions did not prevent radical activity, they did tend to define and limit the radicals' field of action. Clearly some groups of workers were more accessible than others. The Moscow Workers' Union, the Union of Struggle, and the other groups whose activities have been outlined above were concentrated almost exclusively in Moscow city. They also had far less contact with textile workers than with metalworkers or railroad workers, even though the former group far outnumbered the latter two. The reason was that city workers could be reached more easily than those in the countryside; the metalworkers, besides being concentrated in Moscow city, tended to live independently outside the factory walls and were therefore more approachable than textile workers who lived in barracks.

The organizational characteristics of particular industries also tended to promote or retard radical activity. The metal industry and the railroads operated with more advanced technology than other industries and therefore employed more highly skilled workers as well as engineers and university-trained specialists. Members of the former group, as represented by Prokof'ev and Boie, were eager to further their education and were responsive to radical propaganda. Their accessibility to radical influence was enhanced when their work put them into contact with members of the "working intelligentsia"—specialists such as Brusnev. Once recruited to the revolutionary cause, the skilled workers could play a mediating role between the intelligentsia and the worker masses. Outside the metal trades, however, this intermediate stratum of workers was less prominent, if not altogether absent, and the radicals often had to address themselves directly to the ordinary worker.

The course of radical activity was also in some measure dictated by the composition of its intended audience. The slogans and tactics appropriate to one group of workers were not necessarily suitable for others. *Kruzhki* of textile workers, for example, were described by some radicals as less sophisticated and requiring more elementary propaganda than metalworkers. At the same time, the textile workers were said to be more militant, less susceptible to "narrowly professional" slogans and tactics (e.g., the organization of *kassy*). Metalworkers, however strong their commitment to the revolutionary cause, tended to show more independence in their relations with the radical underground. They may have been better at concealing their activities (Prokov'ev's *kruzhok*, for example, resisted the call to hold mass meetings in May 1895 and was almost alone in avoiding the wave of arrests that followed), but they did not succeed in mobilizing the mass of their fellow workers.

Radical activity in the Moscow region, then, was narrowly circumscribed by the environment in which it took place: by the characteristics of the workers, the factories, and the police. Within these limitations, how successful were the radicals in formenting labor unrest or advancing the cause of revolution?

The direct and visible effects of their work were far from spectacular. They were unable to exercise a continuous, consistent leadership role in worker unrest, and throughout the 1880s and

1890s only a handful of strikes could be traced directly to agitational activity. When workers did go on strike, their demands, as can be seen in Chapter Seven, were local and economic; they did not respond to the broader political issues the underground groups had tried to raise, nor did they echo the radicals' slogans against autocracy or capitalism.

In less tangible ways, however, the Moscow underground organizations may have encouraged workers to think of themselves as part of a larger movement, thereby giving them confidence to take actions of their own. Their leaflets and slogans were constantly connecting Moscow's factories to a wider world beyond most workers' experience: May Day, the Paris Commune, or even a strike in some distant Russian city. The leaflets themselves, smuggled into the factories past the guards and police, referred to specific conditions at individual enterprises. The mystique of a vast and powerful underground organization was thereby strengthened and may have provided a further inducement for workers to engage in acts of protest.

The workers themselves, in their dealings with employers, factory inspectors, and police, often compared their own circumstances to those of other workers, threatened to follow the example of strikes at other enterprises, or demanded that wages or working conditions be improved to match those at other factories. Precisely where the workers obtained such information can rarely be determined, but as noted above, the radical underground often included such details in its publications.

In sum, after almost thirty years of *kruzhki*, pamphlets, leaflets, and underground agitational activity, the radical movement's main influence on workers remained indirect. The intelligentsia's goals were revolutionary, but they had not succeeded in building a mass revolutionary movement. Individual workers responded enthusiastically to the radicals' efforts, but the breadth and depth of their exposure was quite limited. The typical *kruzhok* was unable to develop more than a superficial knowledge of revolutionary theories before the police intervened, and any shift toward mass agitation only hastened the moment of intervention. In this situation, the radicals had little hope of leading the workers, but in indirect ways they could still encourage or inspire unrest at the factories. It is almost impossible for a historian to trace such influence—the memory of a pamphlet or conversation, the rumor of a secret organization, thirdhand stories of events and conditions in distant places—but it would be a mistake to conclude that it did not exist.

Chapter 7

The Contours of
Labor Unrest

To trace the history of labor unrest in prerevolutionary Russia is no simple matter. Before 1906, strikes and similar manifestations were illegal, as were labor unions. Even the strictest surveillance and the most severe repressions did not prevent workers from voicing their discontents, joining underground organizations, or participating in various collective acts of protest. The tsarist police machinery was much more successful, however, in suppressing news and public discussion of these events. The press was discouraged or prevented from reporting such incidents. Arrested workers, instead of being put on trial in public, were more often subjected to administrative penalties such as detention or exile.

For most contemporaries, these measures had the effect of obscuring the true contours of the labor movement. For historians, they have sharply limited the range of available evidence. The fullest records of labor unrest are to be found neither in the press nor in contemporary publications but in the archives of the tsarist government, especially the files of the police and factory inspectorate. These, besides being colored by the prejudices and preoccupations of the officials who compiled them, have been difficult to use for other reasons. Records are often incomplete or divided among numerous departments and divisions, yet the range of potentially relevant files is so great that no one individual could hope to master more than a small fraction of it. In addition, important collections such as the files of the Saint Petersburg *Okhranka* for the late 1890s either have not been preserved or have survived in truncated form.

A Data File on Labor Unrest

Soviet and non-Soviet historians alike have been forced to rely heavily on the efforts of teams of archivists to bring to light the most important documents. The most important work of this kind has been the eight-part *Rabochee dvizhenie v Rossii v XIX veke*,[1] a collection of documents and reference material that totals well over six thousand pages. Intended for an audience of both specialists and generalists,[2] these volumes were produced in the early 1950s. Of the eight volumes, the fullest listing of strikes and related incidents ever assembled, five deal with the period between 1875 and 1900. Because this publication has been the principal source for the following discussion, a few words about its strengths and weaknesses are in order.

The documents are of three basic kinds: petitions and correspondence emanating directly from workers; pamphlets, leaflets, and other illegal publications produced by the revolutionary underground; and reports of various governmental agencies, especially the police and factory inspectorate. From the mass of available material the editors have attempted to provide a representative sample of documents that would illuminate the main trends of worker protest and revolutionary unrest. In most cases, the documents have been published without abridgement, and some preference has been given to sources that were hitherto unknown or unpublished. In addition to the full documents, the editors have provided a year-by-year chronicle of strikes and related events derived from a survey of a broader range of documents and published accounts.

The authenticity of the documents seems unquestionable. In a few cases, I was able to compare the published version with the archival original, and no major discrepancies were found.[3] The reliability of the evidence, however, is another matter. Although most of the accounts emanate from eyewitnesses or participants in the events described, their authors' objectivity is disputable at best. Police officials, for example, were often preoccupied with the revolutionary threat any strike or related incident might pose; hence they dealt with strikers heavy-handedly, both on the streets and in their reports. If such officials imputed strikes to subversive conspiracies and outside agitators, the historian must treat those claims with caution.[4] Revolutionary leaflets, on the other hand, attempted to arouse the workers by depicting factory life in the blackest tones, denouncing the brutality of the police and the blood-sucking bosses. The authors of such documents naturally emphasized the strength and unity of the working class, and they were quite capable of making exaggerated claims on the workers' behalf.

The problem of credibility is compounded by the question of the editors' selectivity. Given the vast range of potentially relevant sources, how can a reader be satisfied that the chosen documents provide a fair sampling of the whole, much less a true reflection of events? A Western reader's misgivings are not assuaged by the editors' introduction, which states that preference was given to documents emanating from Social-Democratic underground groups and that the *Rabochee dvizhenie*'s format was designed to show the role of such groups in leading the strike movement.[5] These hints of bias or a priori assumptions about the nature of unrest should put the reader even more on guard.

Unlike the documentary section of the *Rabochee dvizhenie*, however, the volumes' chronicle is less likely to be distorted by the sympathies of authors or compilers. It attempts to provide an exhaustive listing of strikes, petitions, and other forms of worker protest, as well as the activities of (Social-Democratic) revolutionary organizations. The entries are extremely brief, often including nothing more than the name of factory, date, kind of incident, and source of information. Fuller entries indicate the number of participants, the duration, the issues that were mentioned, and (in a rather small number of cases) the outcome. In compiling this chronicle, the editors used not only archival documents but also the legal press, memoirs, and other studies published in later years. Roughly 75 percent of the entries for Moscow city and province were taken from the archives of the police, 15 percent from the factory inspectorate, and 10 percent from the publications of the radical underground. Precisely because of the abbreviated format of the entries, opinions and preconceptions are virtually excluded; yet statistical trends and patterns can be computed and analyzed.

One can still not be certain that the chronicle provides a complete, accurate, or representative listing of incidents. Volumes in the companion series, *Krest'ianskoe dvizhenie*, have been criticized on these grounds by Soviet scholars, who have been able to make extensive comparisons with the original documents and have reported a number of serious omissions.[6] The main problem in those volumes, it seems, is that relevant provincial archives were not consulted, but this was not the case with the *Rabochee dvizhenie.* Here provincial archives were used extensively, especially in the case of the largest industrial centers such as Moscow, Saint Petersburg, and Vladimir.[7] Thus it seems unlikely that any large number of records went unnoticed in the archives.

Close scrutiny of the chronicle does reveal a small number of mechanical errors, such as misidentification of a factory's location, and a few cases of apparent double counting in which two almost-identical entries seem to be referring to only one event. A few of the incidents are listed on the basis of secondhand sources that seem ill informed about the course of events. Nonetheless, only a very small minority of cases exhibit problems of these kinds— errors too few and random to impart any systematic bias to the chronicle. The editors do seem to have consistently chosen the higher of two figures whenever their sources disagreed about the number of participants in an incident. This poses a more serious problem, for it could systematically inflate the total number of strikers; nevertheless, because the procedure seems to have been followed throughout, it should not distort comparisons between different years, localities, or branches of industry. Needless to say, such totals are used with caution in the following pages.

This still leaves the possibility that the archives themselves are incomplete because some incidents were never recorded. Only about 3 percent of the incidents reported in Moscow, for example, involved twenty-five workers or less. Were small-scale incidents so rare, or small-scale enterprises so tranquil, or did the police simply pay less attention to them? Similarly, there are known incidents in which employers tried to keep police and other officials from interfering in a labor dispute, fearing that this would only complicate matters.[8] Were there perhaps cases in which employers succeeded in keeping incidents secret? Inasmuch as questions such as these cannot presently be answered, the only possible response is to treat the chronicle with caution, especially when discussing factories small enough or remote enough to escape the notice of government officials. Most of the factors that made for distortion, however, would probably have remained constant over time. If the data show changing trends and patterns, these are probably reflections of real events, not of differing patterns of reporting them.[9]

The *Rabochee dvizhenie*'s chronicle has been the principal source of this chapter. It lists a total of 452 incidents of unrest at the factories of Moscow city and province in the years 1880–1900.[10] Whenever possible, the chronicle entries have been double-checked against other sources.[11] To facilitate statistical computations, this information (referred to hereafter as the data file) has been converted into machine-readable form and processed by computer. This quantitative approach is supplemented whenever possible by reference to more traditional qualitative sources such as memoirs, press reports, and the documentary sections of the *Rabochee dvizhenie*.

Year-by-year Distribution of Unrest

Labor unrest was no novelty in Moscow by 1880. Protests were not unknown even in the time of serfdom,[12] and the immediate postemancipation period witnessed strikes at several major enterprises, including the Morozov and Konshin cotton mills. The Saint Petersburg area was more turbulent than Moscow in this period, with major confrontations at the Alexandrovsk machine works (Saint Petersburg, 1860) and the Krengholm cotton mill (Narva, 1872), compared to which Moscow's strikes were mere skirmishes. Nonetheless, Moscow's strikes far outnumbered those of other regions.

In the 1870s, the tempo of unrest increased sharply over that of the previous decade. In all of Russia in the decade from 1870 to 1879, there were 350 instances of unrest compared to 118 in the preceding nine years. Saint Petersburg, with one-fourth of all strikes and disturbances, continued to have the greatest number of incidents, but Moscow was not far behind with one-fifth of the national total. Labor unrest was spreading, albeit in a sporadic, uncoordinated fashion, and in the 1870s Moscow was averaging between 6 and 7 incidents per year. Unrest was confined almost entirely to the textile industry and was greatest during the period of economic boom from 1878 to 1880.[13] The total dropped abruptly in the period between 1881 and 1884 but soared to unprecedented heights from 1885 to 1888. In 1887 alone, Moscow city and province experienced 32 strikes; and in the four-year period between 1885 and 1888, the city and province had just under half of all the strikes in Russia.

There followed another period of decline, which lasted from 1889 to 1894, after which the number of incidents again began to climb, both in Moscow and throughout Russia. Moscow's events were increasingly eclipsed by unrest in other localities, however, and in the latter 1890s the city and province provided barely one-tenth of the national total of strikes. At the end of the century, there was another nationwide lull in the incidence of unrest, but in 1903 Russia was swept by the greatest wave of strikes yet recorded. Although Moscow participated in this trend, the intensity of unrest was much lower there than in the southern industrial areas; when the incidence of unrest is compared to the total work force in each province, Moscow's per capita rate for 1895 to 1904 is among the lowest in all of Russia.[14]

In order to analyze more closely the pattern of Moscow's labor movement between 1880 and 1900, I have collected information, in the above-mentioned data file, on a total of 452 cases identified by the *Rabochee dvizhenie* chronicle. More than half of the incidents were strikes,[15] of which I counted 271. The second-most numerous category can best be described as "disturbances"—cases of unrest in which no work stoppage occurred. These are usually listed as *volneniia* (agitation, nervousness, perturbation), but the total also includes illegal mass meetings (*skhodki*), secret organizations among the workers (*kruzhki*), and abortive strikes that were prevented by dismissals or arrests; of such incidents, I counted 97, including three that were officially described as riots (*bunty*).

Third on the list were collective complaints and petitions addressed to employers, police, or factory inspectors. The *Rabochee dvizhenie* lists 72 cases of this sort, evidently excluding the routine complaints factory inspectors received concerning infractions of the factory code. The events the chronicle lists were collective actions by groups of workers and sometimes included processions to the local police station, threats to quit work, demands for permission to depart from the factory, or public confrontations with managers or officials.

The final category of incident was mass departure from a factory. Twelve such cases were listed.

Table 7.1 shows the distribution of incidents over the twenty-one years of the data file. Several general trends are immediately apparent. The number of incidents was greater in the second decade of the study than in the first, but in both decades unrest was concentrated in relatively short periods: from 1885 to 1887 and from 1895 to 1898. Between them, these two periods accounted for two-thirds of all incidents, whereas the remaining one-third was spread over fourteen years. These trends are generally in line with the national patterns mentioned above.

A breakdown of incidents according to location shows the same pattern. In Moscow city, 65 percent of all incidents occurred in the stated years; and in eight of the province's thirteen counties the comparable figure was greater than 60 percent. Figure 7.1 shows, in the form of a graph, the distribution of all incidents over the

Table 7.1. **Year-to-year Distribution of Strikes and Other Labor Protests**

	Kind of incident				
Year	Strike	Disturbance	Complaint	Mass departure	Total
1880	10	2	3	1	16
1881	3				3
1882	1	1			2
1883	4		3		7
1884	6	2			8
1885	11	12	17	6	46
1886	7	5	13	3	28
1887	32	7	12		51
1888	11	3	3		17
1889	6	3	4		13
1890	7	1	1		9
1891	5	2			7
1892	5	2	3		10
1893	7	1	2	1	11
1894	7	3	4		14
1895	19	5		1	25
1896	33	27			60
1897	32	13			45
1898	31	5	6		42
1899	20	2	1		23
1900	14	1			15
Totals	271	97	72	12	452

Source: Data File on Labor Unrest (see pp. 121-24).

entire period of twenty-one years. It is evident that the curve of labor unrest is approximately the same for all areas even though a slight time lag is visible in a few instances.

The same year-to-year pattern is visible in Figure 7.2, which shows the distribution of protest incidents in the principal branches of industry. In the textile industry as a whole, 65 percent of all incidents, and in metal trades, 85 percent of all incidents, occurred in the years 1885-87 and 1895-98. Only two branches of industry showed a slightly different pattern: brick production and woolens, each with less than 45 percent of all incidents falling within the stated years. Even so, the trend of unrest in these industries still rose and fell along with that of other industries.

Despite this general uniformity, each separate district or industry showed some local variation; for example, the wave of unrest in the 1890s reached its peak in Moscow city in 1896, in Bogorodskii county in 1897, and in Serpukhovskii county in 1898. This would suggest that whatever common causal factors were at work did not operate uniformly or simultaneously throughout the region. Long-range economic or political forces might produce such a pattern, but single decisive events such as a famine, a violent conflict, or the promulgation of a new labor law would not.

What sorts of long-term trends or forces might account for the up-and-down pattern of unrest? In the political sphere, the tsarist government followed a relatively consistent conservative course from the accession of Alexander III in 1881 to the end of the century. Significant legislation such as the ending of the poll tax in 1886–87 or the enactment of the *zemstvo* counterreforms between 1889 and 1893 did not coincide at all with changes in the trend of labor disturbances, nor did the passage of factory laws in 1882, 1885, 1886, and 1897; the first of these dates was followed by an eighteen-month period of labor tranquility, whereas the others came in times of widespread unrest. Far from causing this unrest, the laws of 1886 and 1897 have usually been seen as the government's response to the massive strikes of the preceding years (the Morozov strike in Vladimir province in January 1885 and the city-wide textile strike in Saint Petersburg in 1896).

In the economic realm, the two peak periods of unrest were times of expansion, as can be seen in Table 7.2, which presents several year-by-year indexes of economic activity. The boom years of the 1890s coincided closely with one period of maximum unrest, and the labor turbulence of the mid-1880s also took place against a background of economic growth. In contrast, the more uncertain economic conditions of 1888–94 and 1899–1900 were associated with relative tranquility on the labor front, and the years of deepest depression, 1881–84, had fewer incidents of unrest than any other years.

Does this mean that prosperity caused labor unrest? If prosperity is taken to mean a rising standard of living, the answer would probably be no, inasmuch as workers' incomes tended to lag behind the expansion of the economy as a whole. Without materially improving the workers' income, however, economic boom could have a direct effect on their lives through its influence on hiring patterns. As the third and fourth columns of Table 7.2 indicate, the peak years of economic growth were also ones of peak employment.

Three aspects of this situation should be mentioned. First,

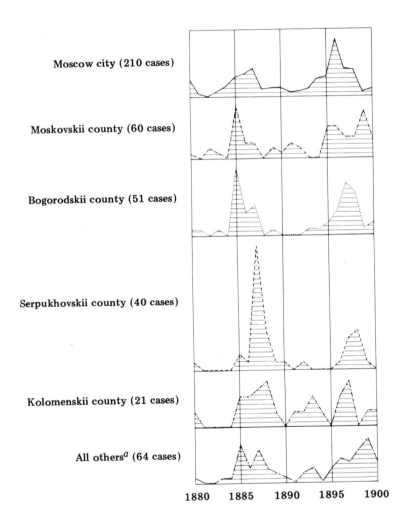

Moscow city (210 cases)

Moskovskii county (60 cases)

Bogorodskii county (51 cases)

Serpukhovskii county (40 cases)

Kolomenskii county (21 cases)

All others[a] (64 cases)

1880   1885   1890   1895   1900

Figure 7.1. **Percentage distribution of labor unrest, by locality and year (each locality equals 100 percent).**
[a]Klinskii county (18 cases), Dmitrovskii county (17 cases), Podolskii county (10 cases), Vereiskii county (6 cases), Zvenigorodskii county (6 cases), Bronnitskii county (5 cases), Ruzskii county (1 case), and Volokolamskii county (1 case).

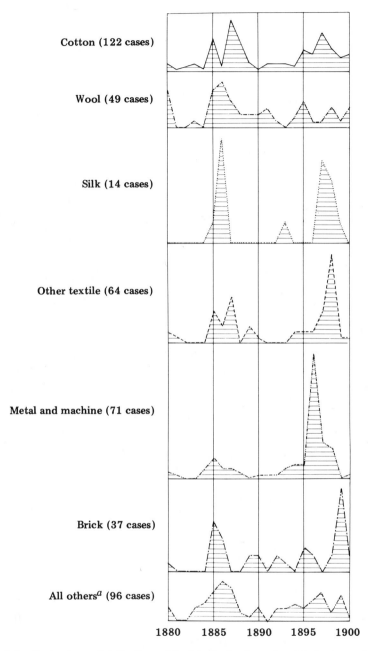

Figure 7.2. **Percentage distribution of incidents, by branch of industry and year (each branch of industry equals 100 percent).**
[a]Wooden products, paper, chemical, mineral, products of animal origin, food and drink, rubber. These are not listed individually because of the small number of cases in each.

Table 7.2. **Year-to-year Distribution of Labor Unrest, Together with Indexes of Trends in the Russian Economy**

Year	Labor unrest in Moscow (number of incidents)[a]	Estimated ruble value of output of Russia's 10 main industries (million rubles)[b]	Total Russian factory labor force (1,000s)[c]	Work force at Tsindel' cotton mill (Moscow)[d]	Combined index of economic growth, using 1913 as base year (= 100)[e]
1880	16	461.0		1,183	
1881	3	487.6		1,296	
1882	2	503.4		1,222	
1883	7	469.8		1,296	
1884	8	450.7		1,282	
1885	46	428.9		1,427	20.57
1886	28	426.9		1,316	21.28
1887	51	465.0	995	1,299	24.24
1888	17	527.9	1,034	1,384	22.65
1889	13	507.8	1,058	1,403	26.74
1890	9	497.0	1,069	1,507	27.29
1891	7	495.3	1,067	1,479	29.30
1892	10	521.6	1,105	1,830	31.14
1893	11	619.4	1,196	2,033	35.29
1894	14		1,178	2,061	36.26
1895	25		1,177	2,343	39.38
1896	60		1,308	2,379	41.94
1897	45	908.7	1,490	2,555	45.85
1898	42			2,757	50.24
1899	23			2,598	55.80
1900	15			2,500	61.05

Sources:
[a] Data File on Labor Unrest (see pp. 121–24).
[b] S. G. Strumilin, *Ocherki ekonomicheskoi istorii Rossii i SSSR*, pp. 501–5.
[c] Ibid., p. 504.
[d] M. I. Gil'bert, "Dvizhenie zarabotkov rabochikh v kontse XIX veka" [The movement of workers' wages at the end of the 19th century], in *Iz istorii rabochego klassa i revoliutsionnogo dvizheniia*, ed. M. V. Nechkina, p. 329.
[e] Alexander Gerschenkron, "The Rate of Industrial Growth in Russia Since 1885," p. 146.

in years of economic expansion the total factory population was increasing, bringing many new hands to the factory; this may have led to crowding and pressure on housing and other facilities.[16] Second, a certain proportion of the new recruits came directly from the countryside and had no previous experience. This group was often described as highly volatile and prone to violent protest.[17] Third, the years of expansion were years of relative security for the workers. Factories were less likely to lay anyone off, and a worker who left his job at one enterprise stood a good chance of finding work elsewhere; this in turn may have given workers a sense of security and self-confidence in their dealings with employers and made them more critical of the terms of employment. In times of economic recession, layoffs and cutbacks in production may have made workers more anxious to preserve their jobs, however unsatisfactory the terms might be.

Of these three factors, the third appears to have been most important in Moscow's unrest. The years 1885–86 in particular were a period of recovery more than expansion and followed a five-year depression during which many businesses had failed and many more had experienced sharp cutbacks in their operations. In this situation, many, perhaps most, of the "new recruits" who were hired must have been workers with previous experience who were returning to the factories after a period of involuntary absence. Overcrowding of sleeping quarters, dining halls, and other facilities would not have been an immediate problem; these facilities would in all likelihood have been underutilized during the years of depression, and the slack would not immediately be taken up. At the same time, any change in the number of workers employed would quickly become apparent to all workers, because contracts were customarily renewed at six- or twelve-month intervals. If an awareness of such changes affected workers' willingness to protest, one would expect a wave of protest to follow soon after any dramatic improvement in hiring conditions.

Such an analysis can provide at least a partial explanation for the surge of labor protest in 1885. In that year the pace of economic growth was slow; indeed, by some measures no growth occurred at all. After four years of depression, however, even a leveling off of production could have been a very positive factor from the workers' point of view. In place of the widespread layoffs of previous years, 1885 saw a moderate increase in the number of workers hired—not enough to crowd the barracks or exhaust the pool of experienced unemployed workers but perhaps enough to overcome the uncertainty and precariousness that workers felt in preceding years.[18]

According to available figures,[19] the total number of factory workers in Russia continued to grow from 1885 to 1887, just as the number of strikes did. After this a downward economic trend set in. For the following six or seven years, the patterns of economic growth and hiring were uneven, with rapid increases one year and none at all the next. Only in 1894-95, as the Witte system got into full swing, did the Russian economy enter a period of sustained rapid growth. The trend of labor protests, which reached a peak in 1887, fell off rapidly in the following year and remained at a uniformly low level until 1895 (the level, however, was never as low as in the years 1881-84).

If the workers' sense of security was in fact a major determinant of labor unrest, the up-and-down course of industrial production in the years 1888-94 would appear to have inspired little confidence. (It should also be noted that 1892 was a year of famine, in which the nearby provinces of Tula and Riazan' were especially hard hit. This may have increased the number of job seekers in Moscow, thereby offsetting whatever increases might have occurred in the number of jobs available.)[20] The years 1895-98, on the other hand, like the period between 1885 and 1887 (and in a negative way the years 1881-84) showed a continuous, decisive trend in levels of employment and production. This trend began to subside in 1899, and the number of protest incidents dropped sharply. When a new depression set in in 1900, even fewer protests were recorded.

Among the factors that may help to account for year-to-year changes in the pattern of protest, at least two others should be mentioned. One is the influence of outside agitation; the years of greatest labor unrest in the 1890s were the period in which the radical intelligentsia was most active among the workers. Such activity was not in evidence, however, during the earlier surge of protest in the years 1885-87. In those years another factor seems to have played an important role: the example of labor protests in other nearby localities. The massive Morozov strike of January 1885 took place in the town of Orekhovo, in Vladimir province, just across the river from Moscow province. This incident, which involved approximately eight thousand workers, made a great impression on the government and on public opinion. As indicated earlier, the number of protest incidents in Moscow city and province soared in 1885 despite relatively unfavorable conditions in the labor market and the economy as a whole; possibly the protestors (who, as may be seen below, seem to have been well informed about events in other localities) were following the lead of the Morozov workers.[21]

If high levels of employment and industrial expansion were correlates of labor unrest, this still reveals relatively little about the incidents that occurred. Even in the years of maximum unrest, only about 5 percent of Moscow's factories experienced strikes or other incidents, and the number of strikers in any single year was never more than 10 percent of the total work force. To understand why unrest occurred at the particular times and places that it did, and why some enterprises were turbulent while others were tranquil, one must look more closely at the specific local causes of incidents and at the goals, slogans, and tactics of the workers.

Complaints and Grievances

In all but thirty-nine of the incidents in my data file, the sources indicate some of the underlying issues. The grievances and complaints that are listed should be seen as a crude and possibly incomplete reflection of the workers' concerns. In almost two-thirds of the cases the chronicle of the *Rabochee dvizhenie* lists only a single issue. Can one therefore assume that only one issue or grievance was at stake in an incident? Evidently not, for the more detailed descriptions of individual incidents almost invariably mention more than one. On the other hand, when lists of many grievances are included, one cannot assume that the workers cared equally about all of them. Typically an incident would be provoked by a single issue, but in subsequent meetings with factory inspectors, local police officials, or members of the radical intelligentsia, the workers would complain about other aspects of their lives or put forth other slogans. Many of these were undoubtedly added as afterthoughts and would not by themselves have led to an organized protest.[22]

This pattern of reformulating demands and raising new issues as a strike progressed was common in other parts of Russia as well. In May 1896, the Saint Petersburg textile workers went on strike to demand pay for the national holidays surrounding the coronation of Nicholas II, but in the course of the next two weeks the strike came to focus on the issue of a shorter workday. In December 1904, the workers at the Putilov works in Saint Petersburg began a strike to protest the firing of a few suspected troublemakers; the eventual result was a petition to the tsar, demanding a constitution and basic civil rights for all Russians.

It is thus difficult to decide which issues were most important at any given moment in an instance of unrest. I have attempted to circumvent this problem by listing all the issues that were mentioned in an incident without trying to rank them. This approach identifies the most important themes through their recurrence on a broader plane; it also reveals how the pattern of grievances and demands changed over time.

In the total file, there were 262 cases in which only one issue was mentioned, 91 with two issues, 40 with three, 15 with four, and 7 with five or more, for an overall total of almost seven hundred separate demands or grievances. These are summarized in Table 7.3. Looking at the table, it is apparent that economic issues, that is, issues related to the workers' immediate surroundings rather than some larger polity, were predominant. Pay rates alone accounted for about 30 percent of all issues, whereas, at the bottom of the table, solidarity with other factories was mentioned only once in the entire data file.

The issues shown in the table fall into four general categories. First and most numerous are those directly related to the level of wages (58 percent of all demands and grievances). This group includes, in addition to disputes over wage rates, demands and grievances involving fines, deductions from wages, and alleged abuses in reckoning and payment. In addition, closer examination of the evidence reveals that wage levels were the real issue in disputes over idle time and raw material. Almost all workers in the study were paid on a piecework basis. If a factory shut down for a few days for repairs, or if the supply of raw material was interrupted, wages would be lost. Similarly, if the quality of raw material fell, the workers' productivity might decrease (e.g., warp strings might break, causing costly delays), or the finished product might be paid for at a lower rate; in either case, wages would decline.

The second main group of issues referred to working conditions and accounted for 23 percent of all issues: hours, terms of contract, work schedule, schedule of holidays, behavior of supervisors, election of crew leaders, issuance of passbooks, and schedule of wage payments.

The third group includes all aspects of living conditions: food, housing, and the company store. This group accounts for 10 percent of all issues in the data file.

The remaining issues on the list, which account for 9 percent of the total, are harder to categorize. They include protests against arrests and firings of individual workers, and against mass layoffs;

Table 7.3. **Issues and Grievances**

Issue	Number of times mentioned
1. Wages, general	211
2. Delays in paying wages	53
3. Terms of contract, including right to depart	50
4. Hours	48
5. Fines imposed by employer	35
6. Working conditions, general	27
7. Company store (prices, quality of goods)	24
8. Deductions from wages (for heating, stringing loom, provision of water for tea, etc.)	22
9. Wages improperly reckoned	21
10. Idle time caused by employer	21
11. Supervisory personnel	20
12. Holidays, including coronation of Nicholas II	18
13. Raw material (complaints about quality)	17
14. Housing	16
15. Dismissal or arrest of individual workers	15
16. Oppression, arbitrariness, harshness, indignities	14
17. Living conditions, general	13
18. Issuance of passbooks; passbooks improperly kept	12
19. Food	11
20. Mass firings or shutdown	6
21. Politeness, respect	5
22. Enforcement of law	4
23. Schedule of wage payments	3
24. Free election of crew leader (*starosta*)	3
25. Corporal punishment	1
26. Wage rates not posted	1
27. Compensation for fire damage	1
28. Pay for strike time	1
29. Solidarity with other factories	1

Source: Data File on Labor Unrest (see pp. 121-24).

demands that the factory code be observed by employers; expressions of solidarity with other workers; demands that foremen and managers treat the workers with politeness and respect; and complaints against harshness, arbitrariness, or oppression. The one characteristic that all of these issues share is their extension beyond the details of everyday life.

In the case of layoffs and shutdowns, the workers' very existence at the factory seemed threatened. References to the factory code, whether positive or negative, indicate that workers were becoming more aware of wider political and administrative influences.

Further evidence that some workers were moving beyond immediate self-interest in their demands are their expressions of solidarity with arrested comrades or with strikers in other localities. And the demand for polite treatment suggests that their sense of dignity and self-respect was increasing. Complaints against oppression and arbitrariness seem more diffuse; they are reminiscent of the slogans put forward in agrarian disturbances, when peasants demanded a freedom or justice that defied precise legal definition. For want of a better term, in the discussion that follows all the issues in this fourth group will be referred to as noneconomic.

The relative importance of the four general categories of issues can be measured in two ways: the number of incidents in which they appeared, and the number of times they were mentioned. As Table 7.4 shows, wages appear at the head of both lists, followed by working conditions, living conditions, and noneconomic issues. Significantly, wage issues often appeared as the sole issue or grievance in an incident, whereas working and living conditions were usually mentioned in conjunction with other issues. Among the noneconomic issues, protests against layoffs, arrests, and shutdowns followed the same pattern as wage issues, but references to the factory code, harsh treatment, and politeness appeared only when other issues were mentioned. Wages and layoffs, in other words, can be seen as more basic concerns; by themselves, working and living conditions and most noneconomic grievances were not enough to arouse collective protest from the workers.

A closer examination of the distribution of issues over time discloses that wages were mentioned less frequently in the years identified earlier as peak periods of economic expansion and unrest. In boom years workers were more disposed to raise issues of working and living conditions, but in years of depression and insecurity only wage-related issues could arouse protests. This, too, makes wages seem a more basic concern.

Most issues and grievances were distributed fairly evenly through the twenty-one years of the data file, but a few were concentrated in particular years. Fines, deductions, company stores, terms of contract, dining halls, mass layoffs, and delays in wage payment were all mentioned more often in the first decade of the file. In later years hours became an important issue. Complaints against supervisors and idle time, and references to the factory code, were also more common in the 1890s than they had been in the previous decade. Most of the issues concentrated in the file's earlier years were dealt with by the Factory Law of 3 June 1886; the fact that they were mentioned less frequently in later years

Table 7.4. **Main Categories of Issues (Frequency of Occurrence)**

	Number of cases in which only this category of issue was mentioned	Number of cases in which this category was mentioned along with others	Total number of demands and grievances mentioned
Wages	221	98	383
Working conditions	66	114	148
Living conditions	10	45	65
Noneconomic	14	40	60

Source: Data File on Labor Unrest (see pp. 121–24).

may mean that these abuses were at least partially curtailed in Moscow's factories. The length of the working day, on the contrary, was an issue raised in the Saint Petersburg textile strike of May 1896 and it subsequently became important in Moscow. In this case, the Moscow Workers' Union was partly responsible, for it took up the issue in its pamphlets and broadsheets. In both the eighties and nineties, Moscow workers presented demands and grievances that were tied in some tenuous way to national trends, whether administrative or agitational.

Another indication of the workers' changing moods and outlook is the predominance of offensive or defensive demands and grievances. For this reason, I have coded issues to distinguish between those cases in which workers were challenging the status quo or demanding that it be changed in their favor (e.g., by shortening the workday) and those in which they were defending the status quo against some challenge (e.g., reduction of wages). Defensive issues outnumber offensive ones in the years in which the fewest strikes and incidents occurred—1881-84 and 1888-94— those also characterized as years of depression or economic uncertainty. In addition, the years 1885 and 1886 show a predominance of negative or defensive issues. As indicated earlier, the total number of protests was high in these years, but unlike other periods of high unrest these two years did not show a decisive economic expansion. The years of most favorable economic conditions—1887 and 1895-99—all recorded more offensive than defensive demands and grievances, and so did 1880 and 1900.

In short, favorable economic conditions were associated not just with a higher incidence of unrest, but with a more optimistic or aggressive spirit among the workers. The very tone of the disturbances changed, as workers demanded higher wages, shorter hours, and better conditions, and turned their attention to issues which had gone unmentioned in less prosperous times.

Number of Participants and
Duration of Incidents

Estimates of the number of participants are available for roughly three-fifths of the incidents in my data file. As one might expect from the diversity of incidents, the estimates are not uniformly reliable. In some cases, leafleting for example, the conspiratorial nature of an action made it almost impossible to guess the number of active participants, much less the number of outwardly passive bystanders who might have been in sympathy. At the opposite extreme there are a number of cases in which participants were clearly identified because of arrest or dismissal from their place of work; unfortunately for the historian, the persons thus identified were usually a small minority of participants.

The duration of some kinds of incidents is also difficult to calculate. A mood of discontent might develop among workers over a period of weeks or even months, with sporadic outbreaks of one sort or another. After a strike or disturbance had apparently run its course, unresolved grievances might remain to trigger a new confrontation.

These difficulties were less common in the case of strikes than in other kinds of labor unrest. In most instances, the beginning of a work stoppage could be clearly delimited,[23] and the employer was in a position to estimate the number of participants. Such estimates are available for over 75 percent of the strikes in the file, whereas for other kinds of incidents the proportion of unknowns is much higher. For these reasons, the following discussion of duration and participation concentrates almost exclusively on strikes.

Table 7.5 shows the number of participants in strikes, year by year. The third column shows the number of participants as reported in the sources; because these figures include only 75 percent of all strikes in my file, I calculated a revised total based on the assumption that the median number of strikers was the same in the remaining 25 percent (sixth column).

In general, the figures in the third and sixth columns seem to parallel the trends observed earlier in Tables 7.1 and 7.2 and

Table 7.5. Participation in Strikes, by Year

Year	Total number of strikes	Cases in which number of participants is reported	Total number of participants reported	Average number of participants reported	Median number of participants reported	Projected total number of participants[a]
1880	10	8	6,000	750	200	6,402
1881–83[b]	12	5	1,140	682	75	3,640
1884	8	5	3,080	616	500	3,580
1885	46	10	3,750	375	138	3,895
1886	28	5	425	85	50	527
1887	51	31	17,546	566	250	17,807
1888	17	8	4,000	500	500	5,498
1889	13	4	1,112	278	288	1,688
1890	9	5	1,230	246	200	1,634
1891	7	5	1,360	272	250	1,362
1892	10	4	852	213	188	1,041
1893	11	5	1,580	316	88	1,758
1894	14	7	833	119	150	831
1895	25	15	2,100	140	100	6,306
1896	60	23	6,486	282	125	7,746
1897	45	26	11,128	428	262	12,716
1898	42	22	8,646	393	188	10,330
1899	23	18	3,546	197	188	3,919
1900	15	9	4,815	535	550	7,565
Total	271	215	81,899	380		98,245

Source: Data File on Labor Unrest (see pp. 121–24).
[a]For cases in which the number of participants is not reported, the yearly median has been substituted.
[b]Combined because of the small number of cases in each.

Figures 7.1 and 7.2. The years with the greatest numbers of incidents were also the ones with the greatest numbers of participants in strikes, with the exception of 1888 and 1900, each of which had few incidents but many strikers. Turning to the average and median numbers of participants (the fourth and fifth columns), however, two other trends are immediately apparent: the number of participants per strike was greater in the earlier years of the study than in the later ones, and it was greatest in years when the overall number of incidents was low, the years described earlier as times of depression or uncertain economic conditions.

The first of these trends can be seen in the fact that, in the decade from 1880 to 1890, the average number of strikers was over five hundred in five out of ten years, whereas in the following decade it reached that number only once. The median number of strikers was over two hundred in six of the first ten years, but three of the second ten. A closer examination of the data reveals that the number of extremely large strikes (over a thousand participants) declined, not only in relative terms, but absolutely. In the total data file, there were fourteen strikes with more than one thousand participants, and nine of these (64 percent) occurred before 1890.

At first glance this apparent trend toward smaller strikes would seem inconsistent with my earlier observations about the waxing and waning of labor unrest. If, as suggested earlier in this chapter, the workers' mood was more cautious and conservative whenever the Russian economy took a downward turn, would this not have reduced the average number of participants as well as the number of incidents?

The pattern of workers' complaints and grievances suggests an explanation for this apparent paradox. When negative or defensive issues were at stake, the average number of participants was consistently higher than when offensive ones were involved.[24] The issues that invariably attracted above-average numbers of strikers were life-and-death ones such as mass layoffs or individual firings. Even in the worst of times, such issues could provoke a strike, but the "critical mass" of discontent necessary to produce a strike was greater than in years of general prosperity. If workers were on the defensive, it seems reasonable to suppose that a grievance would have to be especially keenly and widely felt before collective action could occur; by the time that it did occur, the number of workers affected would be likely to be greater.

Table 7.6. **Duration of Strikes, 1880–1900**

Year	Less than 1 day	1 day	2 days	3 days	4-10 days	More than 10 days	Total
1880	9				1		10
1881–84	9	1	2		1	1	14
1885	6	2	2		1		11
1886	6				1		7
1887	19	6	4	1	2		32
1888	5		3		3		11
1889–94	28	5	1		3		37
1895	8	6	2	1	2		17
1896	25	3	2	2	1		33
1897	18	1	4	3	6		32
1898	14	7	1	4	4	1	31
1899	13	1	3	1	2		20
1900	7	1		1	3	2	14
Total	167	33	24	13	30	4	271

Source: Data File on Labor Unrest (see pp. 121–24).

Conversely, a lower degree of consensus or preparation may have been sufficient to launch a strike in more prosperous years.

This suggestion is supported by statistics on the duration of strikes (Table 7.6). The years with the highest proportion of longer strikes were 1888 and 1900, both of which have been described as times of worsening economic conditions. The average duration of strikes, unlike the average number of participants, seems to have been greater in the later years of the study.[25] Nonetheless, the longest strikes in the data file were also the largest ones, and defensive issues were more prominent in longer strikes than in shorter ones.[26] Statistics compiled by the Ministry of Trade and Industry for the period between 1895 and 1904 show a similar trend: the average duration of strikes was longest in years when the total number of incidents was low, shortest in years of widespread unrest.[27]

The great waves of strikes, it seems, consisted mainly of shorter incidents, encouraged by favorable economic circumstances or by a generalized mood of protest among workers. In less favorable times, without the example of other strikes to arouse them, workers were less disposed to step forward with their demands and grievances. Only the most serious issues could provoke them to strike at such times, but for this very reason the strikes that did

occur were larger and longer, reflecting the greater determination
(or desperation) of the participants.

Industrial and Territorial Patterns
of Unrest

Earlier I indicated that the year-to-year distribution of labor
unrest was essentially the same in each major branch of industry
and in each county of Moscow province. Nonetheless, the per
capita rates of unrest varied considerably from place to place, as
can be seen in Tables 7.7 and 7.8. From the previous discussion,
one would expect industries that were expanding rapidly to show
generally higher rates of unrest, whereas those that were declining
or stagnating would experience fewer incidents. The second part
of this prediction is borne out by the woolen and silk industries,
whose rates of unrest were considerably lower than those of other
industries. Among the faster growing industries, however, one
finds a greater diversity in the patterns of unrest. Some, such as
metalworking, had especially high numbers of incidents, but their
duration was short and the number of participants was small.
Others, including several branches of cotton production, had few
incidents, but those that did occur were longer and larger. Perhaps
these differences can illuminate the earlier discussion.

Did proletarianization foster labor unrest? As pointed out in
Chapter Two, few Russian workers were proletarian in the original
Marxist sense of being totally dependent on the sale of their own
labor. Only a very small minority of the labor force in Moscow
was totally divorced from the means of production. Industries did
vary, however, in the degree to which they uprooted peasants
from the traditions of the rural environment. Some were based on
large, highly mechanized factories that brought together thousands
of workers under a single roof, imposing a division of labor in which
each individual performed progressively narrower tasks and was
alienated from the product of his labor. Modern enterprises
operated year-round and tended to demand a high degree of skill
and long-term commitment (e.g., apprenticeship and formal education) from their workers. Some were located in large, cosmopolitan centers, which exposed workers to new cultural influences
and may have encouraged the spread of radical ideas. A few paid
high enough wages that some workers could keep their dependents
with them. If influences such as these helped to promote class
consciousness and create a true proletariat, then this should have

Table 7.7. Geographic Distribution of Labor Unrest

Location	Number of incidents			Number of participants in strikes[a]		Man-days lost to strikes[a]		Total work force 1900-1903
	Total	Per 1,000 work force	Per factory	Total	Per 1,000	Total	Per 1,000	
Moscow city	210	2.24	0.34	23,434	241	46,492	443	105,276
Bogorodskii county	51	1.07	0.31	6,245	130	14,167	295	48,198
Moskovskii county	60	1.54	0.36	10,037	250	22,079	539	40,922
Kolomenskii county	21	0.95	0.60	9,144	415	24,017	1,091	22,003
Serpukhovskii county	40	2.07	0.95	20,468	1,077	75,301	3,778	19,281
Bronnitskii county	5	0.47	0.14	2,300	182	19,540	1,550	12,621
Dmitrovskii county	17	1.75	0.63	9,766	1,006	105,536	10,891	9,699
Klinskii county	18	2.39	0.81	10,010	1,328	27,168	3,605	7,536
Podol'skii county	10	2.01	0.42	233	47	233	40	4,987
Vereiskii county	6	1.24	0.66	1,733	357	5,213	1,070	4,853
Zvenigorodskii county	6	4.39	0.46	186	136	246	180	1,365
All others	2	1.04	0.19					1,913

Source: Data File on Labor Unrest (see pp. 121–24); work force data, Ministerstvo Finansov, *Spisok fabrik i zavodov Evropeiskoi Rossii za 1900–1903.*

[a]For strikes in which the number of participants is unknown, the yearly median number of strikers has been substituted and used to compute mandays.

Table 7.8. Distribution of Labor Unrest by Branch of Industry

Industry	Number of incidents		Number of participants in strikes[c]		Mandays lost to strikes[c]		Total work force (1890)
	Total	Per 1000 in work force	Total	Per 1000 in work force	Total	Per 1000 in work force	
Cotton (total)	132	1.9	50,665	798	260,288	4,104	63,423
Spinning	31	0.7	12,993	310	124,448	2,973	41,851
Weaving	52	2.6	15,699	775	66,404	3,277	20,260
Other (including multiphase)	49		21,973		69,436		
Woolen	31	1.3	6,685	276	14,498	600	24,161
Woolen broadcloth	18	1.1	1,812	113	2,952	184	15,957
Silk	14	0.9	1,999	125	4,495	283	15,868
Dye-bleach-print (all fabrics)	20	1.0	1,823	89	2,573	125	20,464
All textiles[b]	249	1.8	74,712	526	312,084	2,197	142,005
Metal and machine	71	4.1	6,315	368	11,715	682	17,166
Railroad workshops[a]	22	4.4	4,600	920	6,285	1,257	5,000
Food processing (including beverage)	6	0.9	360	56	782	121	6,428
Rubber	6	19.7	386	1,270	386	1,270	304

Table 7.8 *(Continued)*

Industry	Number of incidents		Number of participants in strikes[c]		Mandays lost to strikes[c]		Total work force (1890)
	Total	Per 1000 in work force	Total	Per 1000 in work force	Total	Per 1000 in work force	
All consumer goods except food and rubber	22	2.7	3,203	395	4,148	512	8,109
Brick and cement	37	7.2	5,773	1,138	8,187	1,615	5,069
Peat bogs[a]	12		709		709		
All other	28	2.0	2,187	158	2,425	175	13,833
Total[a]	453	2.3	98,245	509	346,721	1,797	192,909

Sources: Data File on Labor Unrest (see pp. 121–24); work force data, P. A. Orlov and S. G. Buganov, *Ukazatel'fabrik i zavodov Evropeiskoi Rossii (Po svedeniiam za 1890 god)*; for railroad workshops, *PM 1902*, pt. 2, table 6, pp. 64–69.

[a]Available work force statistics exclude railroad workshops and peat bogs; for the former, statistics from the 1902 municipal census have been substituted, but for the latter no figures at all were available and per 1000 rates could not be computed.

[b]Includes all the above categories as well as miscellaneous and combined fibres (linen, jute).

[c]For strikes in which the number of participants is unknown, the yearly median number of strikers has been substituted and used to compute mandays.

been reflected in the patterns of unrest found among different industries. In brief, workers in the more proletarianized enterprises and industries should have shown greater cohesion and a higher propensity to strike.

The rates and patterns shown in Table 7.7 and 7.8, however, do not vary in the predicted directions. Industries closer to the countryside, either through geographic location or through the life patterns of their workers, did not experience less unrest; nor did their workers, on the whole, show any less militance, determination, or solidarity than those of more "advanced" industries.

A good example is the cotton textile industry. As noted earlier, Moscow's largest factories were in this industry, the most mechanized branch of which was spinning. According to Table 7.8, cotton mills were below average in the number of incidents per capita, and the spinning industry had the lowest rate of all industries surveyed (0.7 incidents per 1,000 workers, compared to an overall average of 2.3 per 1,000).

The cotton mills—although they were often enormous, operated year-round, and included many long-term industrial veterans in their work force—did not generally require a high degree of specialized training or skill in their workers, and in this sense their workers may have been less proletarian (i.e., less thoroughly integrated into industrial and urban life) than their brethren in the metal industries. The metalworkers too, however, were not conspicuously militant in the period of this study. They had an exceptionally high number of incidents of unrest per capita but were conspicuously low in the number of participants per capita and the number of man-days lost to strikes.

The railroad shopworkers showed above-average rates of unrest on all three indexes in Table 7.8, but in each case these rates were surpassed by the brick industry, probably the single most backward factory industry in Moscow. (Statistics on unrest in the brick industry are all the more impressive in view of these factories' small size and relatively remote location, which increased the chance that they would be overlooked by government officials.)

The figures in Table 7.7 make it clear that labor unrest was widespread even in the rural districts of Moscow province. One might have expected that workers in a large cosmopolitan center would have a different perspective on the world than those in the more remote counties and that this would produce a higher rate of unrest. One finds on the contrary that although the number of incidents per capita was relatively high in the city, the number of strikers and the number of man-days lost to strikes was low in relation to the total factory work force. In the countryside, the number of strikers per capita was generally higher; six counties surpassed Moscow city on this index, and the same pattern is found in the number of man-days lost per capita.

Undoubtedly one reason for this pattern is the dispersal of large factories throughout the hinterland. A case-by-case tabulation of unrest makes it clear that larger enterprises tended to have higher rates of unrest. In a rural county such as Klinskii, the entire work force may have been concentrated at a few such enterprises, whereas in Moscow city the larger factories existed side by side with many smaller ones; this might tend to inflate the rural counties' per capita rates of unrest and to deflate Moscow city's. To test this possibility, one can compare rates of unrest at specific enterprises within a single industry. A breakdown of unrest at the largest cotton mills (i.e., those with one thousand or more workers) reveals that the greatest number of incidents (fifteen) occurred at the Konshin mills in Serpukhov; the Voznesenskaia manufactory in Dmitrovskii county and the Riabovskaia manufactory in Serpukhov were in second place with six incidents apiece, whereas Moscow city's Prokhorovskaia Trekhgornaia mills trailed behind with just five incidents. Thus, after controlling for size of enterprise and branch of production, one still finds the outlying counties outstripping Moscow city in the incidence of unrest.

There does not seem to be any simple explanation for the distribution of unrest that appears in Tables 7.7 and 7.8. Only two factors seem to have had a consistent influence. One was the proportion of women and adolescents in the labor force: industries such as cotton spinning, silk weaving, and food processing, where females predominated, had generally lower rates of unrest. A second consistent influence was the size of enterprises, a factor which helps to explain some of the variation in unrest within individual branches of industry. Larger cotton mills generally experienced more unrest than smaller ones, and larger brickyards had more incidents than smaller brickyards. The size of factories does not, however, explain much of the variation among industries, for example the fact that unrest was more widespread in the brickmaking industry than in cotton textiles.

Other structural aspects of Moscow's industries do not seem to be evenly correlated with variations in the pattern of unrest. Some of the most turbulent areas of the province were experiencing rapid industrial growth, but the rate of unrest was equally high in others (e.g., Dmitrovskii county) that were growing slowly if at all. Some centers of unrest (such as the city of Serpukhov) had their factories clustered together, whereas others (Dmitrovskii and Klinskii counties) had them scattered through the countryside at great distance from one another. The relatively low rates of unrest in older centers such as Bogorodskii and Moskovskii counties might suggest that age and tradition were inhibiting unrest; yet Serpukhovskii county, with an equally long industrial tradition, had exceptionally high rates of unrest.

Industries also varied in their accessibility to outside agitation. The *Rabochee dvizhenie* chronicle lists fifty-one instances of underground activity that put workers from specific, identifiable factories into contact with members of radical organizations. These incidents included leafleting, secret meetings (*skhodki*), study circles (*kruzhki*), and other similar activities. All but five of these cases occurred in Moscow city and the surrounding Moskovskii county; two-thirds of them involved metalworkers or railroad workshops.[28] These enterprises had the attraction of being centrally located, with a relatively highly skilled work force. They were particularly accessible to certain members of the intelligentsia such as M. I. Brusnev, whose technical training enabled him to work as an engineer in the workshops of the Moscow-Brest railroad. Some of the earliest recruits to the underground work were skilled metalworkers such as the machinist S. I. Prokof'ev or the lathe operator K. F. Boie; such individuals were quite successful in making contact with other metalworkers but had more difficulty in penetrating the semipeasant milieu of the textile workers.

It seems possible that the underground groups' ties with metalworkers may have led police and employers to pay especially close attention to the metal plants and railroad workshops. This in turn may help to explain some of the anomalies in Table 7.8. If strikes at metal plants were shorter and had fewer participants, perhaps the reason was closer surveillance. The higher rates of participation and the longer duration of incidents at brickyards and outlying enterprises could then be seen as the opposite extreme: factories that were ignored by police until serious disturbances had occurred. On the other hand, the metal plants and railroad workshops experienced virtually no strikes in the 1880s, when both the underground and the police were concentrating their attention elsewhere. The experience of the railroads and some of the largest textile mills, moreover, indicates that intensive surveillance was no guarantee against strikes or other highly coordinated forms of labor unrest.

Even if surveillance does explain the apparent quiescence of metalworkers, the sources of other workers' unrest remain unclear. The timing and locale of most of the incidents in Tables 7.7 and 7.8 was such that even indirect influence by radicals seems unlikely. Nonetheless, workers in isolated localities or primitive enterprises produced a protest movement that equalled or surpassed the efforts of Moscow city's more proletarian workers. Regional and industrial differences appear to offer little explanation of the varying patterns of unrest. The discrepancies and anomalies discussed here, however, cast doubt on traditional explanations of unrest and suggest that other factors must have been at work.

Timing and Tactics

Perhaps the incidents themselves, if examined individually from a different perspective, can help to illuminate their causes. One of the most important questions to be answered is whether (and how) workers in any one factory were aware of events elsewhere: were demands, tactics, and slogans communicated from factory to factory, or should separate incidents be regarded as distinct and isolated events? In Moscow in the years of this study there were no clear-cut cases of coordination among workers at different enterprises.[29] One does find, however, numerous examples of chains of strikes and protests in which workers seem to be following the example of others. As early as 1880, a series of seven incidents occurred in an eight-week period at wool-weaving factories in Moscow city; five of the seven mentioned the same issues (prices in the factory stores and cheating in the reckoning of wages). In a period of six weeks in 1887, thirteen separate incidents occurred at nine separate cotton mills in Serpukhovskii county, and in all but four cases higher wages were the main demand. In May–June 1899, eleven brickyards in Moskovskii county were struck, including six on a single day, with higher wages the main demand in every case. These examples are the most suggestive in the study, but the data file includes at least twelve other chains of incidents that were close enough in time, space, and style to make it seem that some sort of communication existed among workers.

This suggestion is borne out by a few instances in which identical petitions or demands were presented by workers. One such case occurred in the city of Serpukhov in 1879, when workers at several adjacent cotton mills went on strike and were supported by other neighboring mills. When one owner capitulated to the workers' demands, the other workers demanded identical treatment.[30] Several years later, workers from two separate brickyards in Moskovskii county submitted petitions to the governor-general of Moscow, complaining of ill-treatment; the two petitions repeated each other almost word for word, and the petitioners in both instances were *zemliaki* from Riazan' province.[31] Elsewhere, workers referred to conditions in other localities or threatened employers with the same treatment other employers had received.[32]

Most of these incidents occurred at times and places that hardly fit the classic description of proletarianization. Some of the affected enterprises were in the countryside, while others were closely tied to peasant traditions, either through antiquated methods of production or paternalistic managerial practices. Almost all, moreover, were both spatially and temporally remote from the influence of the radical intelligentsia. What these incidents suggest is that there existed some measure of communication among workers that extended through the countryside as well as the largest urban centers. Evidence of such communication can be found in reports of several strikes in which employers and officials tried to isolate strikers from workers in nearby factories.[33] In at least one instance, visitors from other enterprises were arrested or detained by police during a major strike and were accused of inciting the incident.[34]

In addition to these cases, the history of Moscow's labor unrest includes many hints of communication across greater distances or time periods. One such instance was the massive strike at the Morozov cotton mill in Orekhovo in January 1885, which was echoed by a series of incidents in nearby counties of Moscow province. Unlike other waves of unrest, the incidents in Moscow in 1885 did not coincide with a general economic upturn. Contemporary observers, especially the police, were quick to attribute the later strikes and incidents to the Morozov workers' example, and even three years later, strikes in other localities were being blamed on Morozov workers who had moved on to different factories.[35]

As noted earlier in this chapter, the timing of strikes often seems to reflect a close awareness of national economic trends—a sense of how much was being risked at any given moment. Often, too, the workers seem to have been aware both of legislative changes and of the fine points of the law. They demanded that employers observe the requirements of the factory code, insisted on their rights, and complained to factory inspectors about specific issues that fell within the inspectors' jurisdiction.[36] In still other instances, they seem to have devised their tactics on the basis of careful calculation of the employer's weak points. The tea packers of the K. Popov company, for example, postponed their 1893 strike until a moment when their employer was at a disadvantage vis-à-vis his competitors and had no choice but to accept their demands.[37] All of these examples reinforce the suggestion that workers were not isolated within their own factories, rather they were receiving fairly precise information about a wider world and acting on that information.

The workers also showed a considerable measure of discipline and coordination in their protests. In a small proportion of incidents, there occurred violence of one sort or another: window breaking, looting of the payroll office or the factory food shop, or assaults on unpopular foremen or other managerial personnel. Some contemporaries regarded such incidents as typical of the workers' movement as a whole, and some historians of a later day have accepted this stereotype uncritically.[38] In point of fact, only a handful of the incidents in the data file included any reference to violence. Of those that did, several cases involved the police or military forces, whose heavy-handedness may itself have provoked violent clashes with workers. In a far greater number of cases, police and factory inspectors reported that the workers had been calm, well behaved, and determined to maintain order in their ranks. In Serpukhov in 1887, for example, almost all the cotton mills in the county experienced strikes, but only one instance of violence occurred, and was blamed (by the local police inspector) on the provocative behavior of a supervisor in the factory barracks.[39] In another strike in the same county in the following summer, a police official commented that the workers' behavior reached the point of almost acting on command (*oni kak budto postupali po komande*).[40] Numerous other examples could be provided from factories througout the province.[41]

Discipline and loyalty were not easily achieved. Any worker who showed leadership tendencies was likely to be taken away by the police;[42] in at least one instance, workers refused to elect spokesmen or representatives to negotiate on their behalf because they feared that these would immediately lose their jobs.[43] Whatever coordination was achieved in a strike was precarious, for the authorities were quite willing to play the workers off against one another. If one group appeared to be wavering, efforts would be made to isolate it from more determined groups of workers.[44] Workers sometimes retaliated by using threats and physical coercion against waverers and strikebreakers, though any open violence was likely to bring active police intervention.[45] One solution to this dilemma was the anonymous note scrawled on a wall during a strike in 1897: "Whoever of us goes to work will be anathematized by the Workers' Union—cursed."

Workers also tended to be more attached to a workshop or a division of a factory than to the entire mass of fellow workers; and many strikes, especially in the earlier years of the data file, involved subunits rather than an entire factory. Despite all the impediments to unification, however, one Soviet author has calculated that thirty out of sixty-one strikes in Moscow in the early 1890s were carried out with unanimous support.[46]

Sources of Collective Action

One is left with an apparent paradox: despite their geographic, political, and spiritual isolation, workers came together in strikes and other collective protests that showed at least a rudimentary awareness of a wider world; despite formidable obstacles, they managed repeatedly to unite their efforts in a common cause. Their greatest successes, moreover, often occurred at the least propitious times and places. How can the workers' bonds of solidarity, networks of communication, and sense of organization be explained?

The revolutionary underground was one obvious source of information and cohesion, though its direct influence was limited to a few years, a few branches of production, and a few localities. Another channel of information was the "unstable element" of the working class—workers who changed jobs frequently and could inform their fellows about conditions and protests they themselves had experienced in other localities. Police often blamed such individuals for spreading rumors and sowing discontent.[47] For this very reason, however, these independent souls were often unwelcome at Moscow's factories, whose owners went to great lengths to ferret out potential troublemakers. One can also surmise from the comments quoted in Chapter Five that the more footloose and adventuresome members of the factory population would have been more attracted to the larger cities rather than to the isolated rural factories.

Another channel of communication was informal fraternization among workers from different enterprises. Obviously this was more likely to occur in large urban and industrial centers where workers from separate enterprises could easily encounter each other outside working hours. Police reports often mention workers gathering in taverns, on street corners, or in wooded sections on the outskirts of Moscow. On such occasions they could discuss common problems, air their grievances, or even plan collective actions. Outside the cities, workers from different factories socialized on major holidays and feast days, when peasant-workers returned to their native villages and could compare notes on their experiences. As noted in Chapter Four, much of the social life of such workers centered around *zemliaki*, and a grapevine with roots in the countryside could sometimes spread rumors through factories.

Most of these incidents took place within the confines of a single factory, however, and it is there that we must confront the paradoxical combination of isolation and solidarity. However much the workers may have learned from outside contacts, they still had to operate within the institutional constraints outlined in Chapter Five—the locked gates and minute regulations, the cultural isolation that was symbolized by the workers' distinctive dress and speech—and the incidence of unrest was often highest where those obstacles were strongest. Did the very forces that kept workers apart from the rest of society also bring them together in collective protest? If one looks at factory life from the point of view of the employer or the radical agitator, such a suggestion must seem farfetched. If one thinks of the peasant-worker subculture as it has been outlined in previous chapters, however, the suggestion may seem more plausible. The factories themselves were the product of long interaction between the city and countryside, and patterns of recruitment and operation encouraged workers to maintain significant rural ties. These ties, however, gave the workers a base on which to unite, a reference group whose members shared the same background and grievances. In times of stress, workers could find comfort and support from fellow peasants or even fellow villagers. The factory community was a closed one, but its members were capable of united action against a common adversary.

This is not to say that random, uncoordinated violence (*buntarstvo*) did not occur or that workers never crossed strike lines or betrayed their comrades. Instances of such behavior were not uncommon. What the course of labor unrest in Moscow does suggest, however, is that in the midst of the industrial turmoil of the 1880s and 1890s workers showed themselves capable of independent action and organization. Some of their actions were influenced by external forces, but others seem to have occurred spontaneously and can be attributed to the historical and evolutionary factors discussed throughout this study. If the Moscow workers were indeed half-proletarian and half-peasant, then both halves contributed to their unity and organization.

Conclusion

In each of the foregoing chapters, I have examined the interaction between innovative or disruptive forces and the traditions and continuity of Moscow's life. In general, it seems that men's habits and attitudes changed more slowly than technology or the gross national product. Despite the tremendous increase in factory industry in the last decades of the nineteenth century, the patterns of workers' lives remained much as they had been in previous years. This is hardly surprising: the capacity of the human species to resist change is proverbial.

Less predictable, however, was the peculiar meshing of traditional customs or institutions and industrial change. The length of a worker's sojourn at the factory, the pattern of one's domestic life, the expenditure of one's wages, the system of hiring, and perhaps even the course of collective protest, were all strongly influenced by the demands and habits of the peasant village. Employers recognized this influence and adjusted their own demands and routines accordingly, but so did the more successful radical agitators and propagandists. The village's influence over factory life was subtle and complex and does not easily match the stereotypes that historians, East and West, have often accepted.

I began this study by contrasting two widely accepted models of Russian development: proletarianization as described by Soviet historians and peasant alienation as many non-Soviet historians have described it. Throughout the study, I have been measuring various kinds of evidence against these two models. Rarely if ever have I found a perfect fit.

The difficulty, as I see it, is that both models begin with the assumption that workers were either peasant *or* proletarian, that is, firmly attached to either the village or the factory. The weight of the evidence presented in the preceding pages suggests that most workers were firmly attached to both. The relation between village and factory, as I have suggested at several points in the preceding chapters, can be seen as one of symbiosis. Workers

155

traveled back and forth between city and countryside as their
fortunes, or those of the national economy, rose or fell. So did
their relatives, especially wives and children who could not live
permanently at the factory. So did their neighbors, their *zemliaki*,
aided by those who were already established at the factories.
Workers whose contracts ran year-round still managed to return to
the village at Easter or Christmas, and they sent a substantial part
of their wages back to their families. Living in two worlds, the
Moscow worker was nourished by both, and from this experience
developed many of the characteristic traits that set him apart
from the workers of other countries.

Wittingly or unwittingly, employers and officials encouraged
this process by blocking many of the paths that workers in Western countries had followed. This was true of specific forms of
organization such as labor unions and political parties but also of
more general sociocultural adjustment. As I have shown in Chapters Five and Six, the factory world was often walled off from the
rest of society just as the peasant one was. Any student or other
outsider who tried to fraternize with workers risked arrest or exile
from Moscow. Any formal organization that was allowed to exist
at a factory was certain to be dominated by the management, and
regular police surveillance made sure that its activities were free
of any subversive taint. Employers literally locked the gates of
many factories to seal their workers off from all contaminating
outside influences, and a workday of thirteen hours or more left
the workers little time to themselves.

Factory production was itself a jolting, contaminating influence.
The worker who experienced mechanized production or the
regimentation of factory discipline was entering a new and different world whose horizons were incomparably broader than
those of a purely agrarian society. No combination of rules or
barriers could prevent this influence, but the Moscow industrial
system did manage to mitigate its effects. Instead of abandoning
their traditions altogether, peasants were encouraged to synthesize
the old and the new.

The scope and durability of this synthesis has few parallels in
England or Western Europe at a comparable stage of industrialization. There a number of factors, including traditional patterns of
land tenure and inheritance, discouraged factory workers from
retaining ties to peasant life; the urban population soon lost track
of its agricultural heritage.[1] A much closer equivalent to the
Russian pattern can, however, be found today in many Third-
World nations. In Southern Africa, able-bodied adults may leave

their families in rural areas for months or years at a time in order to work in mines, factories, and cities; yet they remain legally connected to their place of birth, and their families remain dependent on their continuing contributions. In parts of the West Indies, peasants will spend part of each year in agriculture and the rest in fishing or other employment away from their native villages;[2] these activities are not mutually exclusive but are integrated into a continuing life pattern. Other parallels to the Russian case can be found on the outskirts of large cities throughout Latin America, Africa, and Asia, where newly arrived peasant migrants seek out networks of kin and fellow villagers in order to find work or living space.[3]

In recent decades, this rural-urban nexus has attracted attention from radical activists as well as scholars because of its implications for revolutionary (or counterrevolutionary) development. Almost all of the great revolutionary struggles of the twentieth century, after all, have occurred outside Western Europe or North America. Possibly the experience of Third-World revolutions may illuminate the Russian case. Revolutionary spokesmen such as Frantz Fanon[4] and Amilcar Cabral[5] have paid particularly close attention to rural-urban ties in developing their theories of guerrilla struggle. Fanon has gone so far as to suggest that in Third-World countries the industrial proletariat is an unreliable revolutionary force and that activists should concentrate more on the peasantry and the lumpen proletariat of the towns. Cabral has gone even further in singling out newly arrived rural migrants to African cities as channels of revolutionary communication with the countryside.

The anthropologist Eric Wolf has taken up this idea in his comparative study of peasant wars of the twentieth century and has used the term *tactical mobility* to describe the complex of economic and social forces that brings peasants into open rebellion.[6] According to Wolf, the poorest peasants are "completely within the power domain" of landlord or employer and therefore unlikely to rise up by themselves. Unrest is more likely to appear among those who have some base of security from which to challenge those who hold power. Such a base can be provided by geographic remoteness (e.g., the mountainous Oriente Province of Cuba, where Castro's guerrillas established their stronghold), material well-being (e.g., ownership of sufficient land to resist the influence of landlords or moneylenders), or involvement in "subsidiary activities not under the direct constraint of an external power domain" (e.g., casual labor). The latter group includes peasant households that divide their activities between city and countryside. In Wolf's view, these become transmitters of urban ideas and unrest in the countryside: "It is probably not so much the growth of an industrial proletariat as such which produces revolutionary activity, as the development of an industrial work force still closely geared to life in the villages."[7]

Perhaps Wolf's argument can be carried into the city as well. The transitional peasant who worked in the city but maintained ties to the countryside may have enjoyed a tactical mobility or a latitude of action that the city-bred worker did not possess. His kinship ties and landholding in the countryside gave him an extra cushion of security that the employer could not take away. The threat of dismissal from the factory may thus have been less potent as a deterrent to acts of defiance or unrest.

If the peasant-worker transmitted certain city ideas to the countryside, so too might he transmit ideas, traditions, and organizational forms in the opposite direction. In the century and a half before 1905, the discontents of rural Russia were far more manifest than those of the city. The tradition of collective action was stronger in the country, reinforced by the village assembly and, perhaps, by repartitional land tenure. Following Wolf's line of reasoning, one might reasonably expect that the peasant-worker would be more volatile than the pure proletarian, not because he was bewildered or frustrated by city life, nor because he was alienated from the means of production, but because the fusion of urban and rural discontents and propensities produced an especially explosive mix.

This line of reasoning may explain some of the anomalies of the Moscow workers' movement. Despite their isolation and backwardness, the workers of Moscow became for a time the most turbulent element of Russia's working class. Their turbulence, however, was generally of a focused and disciplined variety. Some enterprises experienced multiple strikes, as dissatisfied workers renewed their struggles and refined their tactics. In other instances, chains of strikes can be identified in which grievances and tactics were communicated from one factory to another. Despite the localized, economic content of their demands, the workers' protests seem to show a sensitivity to broader trends in the national economy and even to subtle changes in administrative policy—the role of the factory inspector, the provisions of the factory code.

The very existence of such protests presupposes the existence of some kind of bonds among workers, some communication and feeling of commonality, some sense of organization. If these did not come from outside agitators, what were their sources? As I have shown in Chapter Seven, the industries and regions that in Marxist terms should have been most advanced—those with large, mechanized factories whose workers were spiritually further from the countryside—had average or below-average rates of labor unrest, whereas some that could be considered backward—those that were, smaller, less mechanized, and had workers more closely tied to the village—had much higher rates.

Even without additional evidence, the observed variations in the rates of labor unrest would suggest that other influences were at work. In Chapters Four and Seven, I discussed several bodies of evidence that point to regional loyalties—ties among people from the same village or region of the countryside—as a major factor in promoting strikes and other protests. In some localities, a grapevine of *zemliaki* disseminated news of working conditions and protests. In others, clusters of *zemliaki* formed a nucleus out of which grew larger strikes. Industries and localities that drew their workers from a single region appear to have had significantly higher rates of unrest than those in which the work force was more fragmented.

In descriptions of unrest in the countryside, workers returning from the cities and factories often appear to have been disseminators of radical ideas.[8] In other cases, however, workers from the countryside appear to have brought radical ideas to the factory. I noted in Chapter Seven the case of identical petitions submitted to the police by workers from two Moscow brickyards, both groups being *zemliaki* from the same district of Riazan'.

The tie to the village sometimes provided more than a source of information or solidarity. In certain instances, workers who possessed a land allotment were found to be more willing to strike, for the simple reason that they had less to lose.[9] If, as I suggested in Chapter Seven, some degree of economic security was a basic precondition for labor unrest, a worker who could return to his village and his plot of land had less reason to fear dismissal from the factory.

If the peasant village did exercise a positive influence on the course of labor protest, one must ask what has become of the patriarchalism that so many Soviet historians have imputed to the peasantry, and what of the "primitive, elemental *buntarstvo*" so many Western historians have emphasized. The village, in this view, seems to have contributed to the workers' sense of organization and self-discipline in ways that confound the established stereotypes. *Zemliak* ties appear to have brought workers together to share their grievances and focus their protests. In the incidents that followed, some of the peasants' traditional beliefs and suspicions were likely to be expressed. The distrust of local officials, the generalized sense of oppression, the appeal to a sense of justice that was distinct from legal norms—all these themes had been heard in the countryside for decades and were now echoed in the workers' protests. In this way too the countryside may have given impetus to the workers' movement.

At this point an objection arises. If the workers' rural background was the cause of their unrest, why did the strike movement begin so late in Moscow? Surely the workers of the 1860s and 1870s were just as closely tied to the countryside as those of the 1880s and 1890s; yet their rates of protest were generally much lower. Why? In the first place, as noted in Chapter One, the number of workers and factories was greater in the last two decades of the nineteenth century than at any previous time; the factory population almost doubled during the years of the study, so some fairly dramatic increase in the number of strikes and protests should not be surprising. In the second place, as I established in Chapter Seven, the number of protest incidents was greatest in years of rapid economic expansion and lowest in time of depression. Taken as a whole, the period of my study was a time of substantial industrial development—especially in the period between 1895 and 1900, which had the most rapid industrial growth and the greatest number of incidents—whereas the preceding two decades were characterized by slower growth and a higher degree of uncertainty in the national economy.

In the third place, the rate of social unrest in the countryside, as expressed in acts of open disobedience and clashes with governmental authorities, fell sharply after 1861 and did not begin to rise again until the 1890s. The peasants, however much they may have resented the terms of emancipation, were either unable or unwilling to continue the widespread disorders that characterized the years 1855-61. It is possible that for this reason the peasant migrants of the 1860s and 1870s came to the factories in a more acquiescent mood and that the militancy of later decades developed slowly as the impoverishment of the village increased. Although the issue of unrest in the villages is clearly outside the bounds of this study, one can note that peasant militancy did increase around the turn of the century and continued to grow until the revolutionary outbursts of 1905-1907. The provinces with the highest rates of unrest in those years included several that had only recently begun to send large numbers of migrants to the factories (Tambov is a conspicuous example). If, as I have argued, migration was really a two-way street, then perhaps it contributed to the spread of revolutionary discontent and activism in the countryside.

I am not suggesting, then, that the countryside was the source of labor unrest at the factories but rather that the combination of factory experience with the still-vital customs and habits of peasant society produced a particular kind of unrest with quite distinctive organizational features. It seems quite reasonable to suppose that the results of this combination would be found in the countryside as well as in the industrial centers.

The patterns described in this study—migration and family composition, *zemliachestvo*, and factory paternalism as well as patterns of labor unrest—were not unique to Moscow but appeared to a greater or lesser degree throughout Russia. It seems significant that many of the landmarks of the labor movement—the Morozov strike in Vladimir province in 1885, the Saint Petersburg textile strikes of 1896 and 1897, the formation of the first soviet of workers' deputies in Ivanovo in 1905—occurred in industries and regions that most resembled Moscow in their closeness to the countryside. This is not to suggest that peasant ties were the only source of labor unrest but rather that, in combination with other, better-known influences, such ties could promote cohesiveness and enhance the workers' willingness to protest.

Having noted some of the ways in which factory–village ties seem to have promoted organization and protest, one must also recognize the limits they imposed. The same bonds that held worker-peasants together may also have acted as one more barrier between those workers and the rest of society. To the extent that peasants formed a close-knit community at the factories, they also constituted a world apart, a world that outsiders had great difficulty in penetrating. The mass of workers was often suspicious toward outsiders, even toward the better educated worker aristocracy who had severed ties with the village. Workers might accept leaflets or other logistic support from members of the intelligentsia during strikes, but they also insisted on defining their own grievances, slogans, and goals. A deep-rooted suspicion toward all intellectuals was a recurring theme throughout the years of the study and beyond.[10] This insularity, this isolation of the peasant-worker, was almost surely an outgrowth of traditional peasant attitudes carried over into a factory setting by the ties I have described.

The insularity of the worker-peasant's world may also have

discouraged workers (and peasants) from forming broader, more cohesive protest movements. Although ideas and tactics seem to have spread from place to place, the Moscow labor movement shows no clear-cut examples of coordination, of workers in different localities presenting a united front against employers or government authorities. Rather, the factories were struck one by one, just as, a few years later, the peasant villages rose up one by one to defy the landlords and the State. It would appear that the workers' collective consciousness was not a class consciousness, that they felt an allegiance not to *all* other workers but to specific groups of them, groups defined at least in part by *zemliak* ties.

Looking ahead to 1905, 1917, and beyond, one finds the workers confronting a new and substantially different set of conditions. In particular, many of the obstacles to Western-style political and economic development were removed or diminished. Peasants acquired the right to withdraw from the village commune; workers were permitted to form associations and unions, though their activities were still quite restricted; and the powers of the autocracy were modified by the creation of an elected legislative body. Nonetheless, the workers' movement continued to show many of the traits encountered in this study. The workers and peasants, now more militant and impatient, showed in later years the same ability to organize in protest. Once again, however, one finds that their strength was greatest when applied to local issues, and to negative ones. The spontaneous actions of the masses proved capable of toppling the old regime, but the task of social reconstruction and transformation proved quite a different matter. The workers and peasants, as a result of their shared experiences over the preceding half-century or more, did show a distinct set of demands, concerns, and goals, but these were mostly in the direction of decentralization and fragmentation (e.g., workers' control at the factories or confiscation and redistribution of gentry land to villagers). They did not constitute a distinct, organized force on the national level, and power soon began to coalesce about other centers. The gap between would-be leaders and the worker masses was as wide as ever, and would remain to challenge more than one generation of Soviet leaders.

Abbreviations

Abbreviations have been used for archives and a few frequently cited Russian publications:

PM 1882 *Perepis' Moskvy 1882 goda*
PM 1902 *Perepis' Moskvy 1902 goda*
     RD *Rabochee dvizhenie v Rossii v XIX veke: Sbornik dokumentov i materialov*
 SSSMG *Sbornik statisticheskikh svedenii po Moskovskoi gubernii, Otdel sanitarnoi statistiki*
  TsGAM Tsentral'nyi Gosudarstvennyi Arkhiv goroda Moskvy
TsGAOR Tsentral'nyi Gosudarstvennyi Arkhiv Oktiabr'skoi Revoliutsii
  TsGIA Tsentral'nyi Gosudarstvennyi Istoricheskii Arkhiv

Archival citations are given in the following form: abbreviation of archive, *fond* number, *deloproizvodstvo* number or *opis'* number, *delo* number, date, page number. For example:

TsGAM, f. 16, op. 76, d. 132 (1886), p. 1.
TsGAOR, f. 102, 4 del-vo, d. 121:2 (1908), p. 235

Archival collections are fully identified in the bibliography, which also includes translated titles and full details of publication of books and articles. Articles from collections of essays are cited by author in the notes, but such volumes are normally listed under the editor's name in the bibliography.

Notes

Introduction

1. V. I. Lenin, *The Development of Capitalism in Russia*, especially pp. 542-46, 595-600.
2. P. I. Lyashchenko [Liashchenko], *History of the National Economy of Russia*, pp. 542-49.
3. See in particular Theodore Von Laue, "Russian Peasants in the Factory," pp. 74-80. Writing about a slightly later period, Leopold Haimson has referred to the "alienation" of newly recruited workers from both liberal society and the veteran trade-union leaders ("The Problem of Social Stability in Urban Russia, 1905-1914," pp. 630-36). A third Western historian, Richard Pipes, argues that skilled workers constituted an "aristocracy" more concerned with self-improvement than with the struggles of the lower-paid masses (*Social Democracy and the St. Petersburg Labor Movement 1885-1897*, pp. 118-19).
4. Thus Von Laue speaks of large categories of workers who remained "on the peasant side of the divide," and suggests that "there were more peasants than workers in the common trek to the factories" ("Russian Peasants," p. 71).
5. "The spasmodic character of economic development, the rapid transformation of the methods of production and the enormous concentration of production, the disappearance of all forms of personal dependence and patriarchalism in relationships, the mobility of the population, the influence of the big industrial centers—all this cannot but lead to a profound change in the very character of the producers" (Lenin, *Capitalism*, pp. 598-99).
6. Gerhart von Schulze-Gaevernitz, *Ocherki obshchestvennogo khoziaistva i ekonomicheskoi politiki Rossii*, pp. 130-32.
7. Haimson, "Social Stability," pp. 634-36.
8. A. S. Trofimov, *Rabochee dvizhenie v Rossii, 1861-1894 gg.*, pp. 67-68.
9. Pipes, *Social Democracy*, pp. 118-19.

Chapter One

1. On the beginnings of Moscow's textile industry, see I. V. Meshalin, *Tekstil'naia promyshlennost' krest'ian Moskovskoi gubernii v XVIII i pervoi polovine XIX veka*, especially pp. 53-54; cf. K. A. Pazhitnov, *Ocherki istorii tekstil'noi promyshlennosti dorevoliutsionnoi Rossii:*

164

Khlopchatobumazhnaia, l'no-pen'kovaia i shelkovaia promyshlennost', pp. 162-64.

2. E. I. Zaozerskaia, *Manufaktura pri Petre I*, pp. 111-13, 130-36; M. I. Tugan-Baranovskii, *The Russian Factory in the 19th Century*, p. 20; M. F. Zlotnikov, "K voprosu ob izuchenii istorii rabochego klassa i promyshlennosti," pp. 63-65.

3. Tugan-Baranovskii, *Russian Factory*, pp. 25, 58-59.

4. *Obrok* was the predominant form of feudal obligation in the provinces closest to Moscow; Iaroslavl' had 78 percent of its serfs on *obrok*, and Vladimir had 50 percent (V. I. Semevskii, *Krest'iane v tsarstvovanie imperatritsy Ekateriny II*, p. 548). In Iaroslavl', 73,000 males out of a total male population of 385,000 traveled on passports in 1798; this represented one-fifth of all males but one-third or more of the able-bodied adult male population (Tugan-Baranovskii, *Russian Factory*, p. 60; cf. Meshalin, *Tekstil'naia*, p. 60).

5. M. N. Artemenkov, "Naemnye rabochie Moskovskikh manufaktur v 40-70kh godakh XVIII veka"; Zaozerskaia, *Manufaktura*, p. 113. In Moscow city, a survey of wage laborers in the 1770s discovered that only 154 out of 5,205 workers were legally city dwellers, while all the rest were manorial serfs or state peasants (M. N. Artemenkov, "Sotsial'-nyi sostav naemnykh rabochikh," as cited by John T. Alexander, "Catherine II, Bubonic Plague, and Industry in Moscow," p. 647).

6. Meshalin, *Tekstil'naia*, p. 162 ff.; cf. Tugan-Baranovskii, *Russian Factory*, pp. 171-214.

7. On serf entrepreneurs, see Henry Rosovsky, "The Serf Entrepreneur in Russia."

8. R. S. Livshits, *Razmeshchenie promyshlennosti v dorevoliutsionnoi Rossii*, pp. 94-98; cf. I. F. Gindin, "Russkaia burzhuaziia v period kapitalizma," pt. 1, pp. 70-71.

9. Livshits, *Razmeshchenie promyshlennosti*, p. 95; William Blackwell, *The Beginnings of Russian Industrialization: 1800-1861*, pp. 46-47.

10. In 1870 the managers of the enormous Morozov mills in Moscow and Vladimir provinces reported that they employed about 20,000 cottage weavers in a total work force of 35,000 (Meshalin, *Tekstil'naia*, pp. 236-38).

11. On the growth of Moscow in the first half of the nineteenth century and the role of peasant in-migrants, see Akademiia nauk SSSR, *Istoriia Moskvy*, vol. 3, p. 162.

12. On economic cycles in Russia in the decades following emancipation, see S. G. Strumilin, "Promyshlennye krizisy v Rossii (1846-1907)," in his *Ocherki ekonomicheskoi istorii Rossii i SSSR*, pp. 414-59; P. A. Khromov, *Ekonomicheskoe razvitie Rossii v XIX-XX vekakh*; Alexander Gerschenkron, "The Rate of Industrial Growth in Russia Since 1885."

13. The total length of Russian rail lines was 1,626 kilometers in 1861, 22,865 in 1880, and 53,234 in 1900 (Khromov, *Ekonomicheskoe razvitie*, p. 462). On Moscow's importance in the national railroad network, see Akademiia nauk SSSR, *Istoriia Moskvy*, vol. 4, p. 156 ff.

14. Livshits, *Razmeshchenie promyshlennosti*, pp. 157-59.

15. V. I. Lenin, *The Development of Capitalism in Russia*, p. 473. By another estimate, the number of power looms in Moscow province grew from 3,700 in 1859 to 10,200 in 1871; in the former year they

accounted for 27 percent of the province's output of cotton cloth and in the latter year 63 percent (Pazhitnov, *Ocherki . . . Khlopchatobumazhnaia*, p. 83).

16. Pazhitnov, *Ocherki . . . Khlopchatobumazhnaia*, pp. 21, 84, 92.
17. Tugan-Baranovskii, *Russian Factory*, p. 301. These statistics exclude enterprises with fewer than a hundred workers.
18. My calculation from Ministerstvo Finansov, *Spisok fabrik i zavodov Evropeiskoi Rossii za 1900-1903;* on the textile industry's shift to Moscow, see Livshits, *Razmeshchenie promyshlennosti*, p. 151; Pazhitnov, *Ocherki . . . Khlopchatobumazhnaia*, p. 89.
19. K. A. Pazhitnov, *Ocherki istorii tekstil'noi promyshlennosti dorevoliutsionnoi Rossii: Sherstianaia promyshlennost'*, pp. 139-47; idem, *Ocherki . . . Khlopchatobumazhnaia*, p. 361.
20. A. G. Rashin, *Formirovanie rabochego klassa Rossii*, pp. 28, 30, 32.
21. Khromov, *Ekonomicheskoe razvitie*, p. 217. By Khromov's computation, in the decade from 1890 to 1900 the number of factories in Russia grew by 18 percent, the number of workers by 66 percent, and the value of output by 100 percent. These figures are based on the same government publications as Table 1.1 but include a very large proportion of tiny enterprises (those with fewer than fifteen workers). Lenin, who excluded such enterprises from his calculations, reached a total of nine thousand enterprises in 1900, an increase of 50 percent from 1890, instead of Khromov's figure of thirty thousand (Lenin, *Capitalism*, p. 468).
22. A. V. Pogozhev, *Uchet chislennosti i sostava rabochikh v Rossii*, p. 42 (my calculation).
23. Ibid., p. 46. In 1895, Germany counted 5.3 million workers in small-scale establishments (those with fewer than 51 workers), 2.6 million in medium-sized ones (those with 51 to 1,000 workers), and 560,000 at enormous ones. In Russia, the Ministry of Finance counted 261,000 in small enterprises, 918,000 in medium-sized ones, and 710,000 in enormous enterprises.
24. Alexander Gerschenkron, "Economic Backwardness in Historical Perspective," in his *Economic Backwardness in Historical Perspective*, pp. 5-30. The argument is further developed in the same author's "Russia: Patterns and Problems of Economic Development, 1861-1958," ibid., pp. 119-42.
25. In 1900, metalworkers were 50 percent of Saint Petersburg's labor force, whereas in Moscow city and province they were just over 12 percent (Rashin, *Formirovanie*, pp. 195-97). In the South, foreign-owned firms accounted for more than three-fourths of Russia's steel production and 60 percent of its coal, but in Moscow only a few large enterprises were foreign owned.
26. Roger Portal, "Industriels moscovites: le secteur cotonnier (1861-1914)," pp. 10-11. Cf. Thomas C. Owen, "The Moscow Merchants and the Public Press, 1858-1868," pp. 26-38.
27. I. F. Gindin, "Russkaia burzhuaziia," pt. 1, pp. 60-67; M. L. Gavlin, "Rol' tsentra i okrain Rossiiskoi imperii v formirovanii krupnoi moskovskoi burzhuazii v poreformennyi period," p. 354.
28. Gindin, "Russkaia burzhuaziia, pt. 1, p. 63; Portal, "Industriels moscovites," pp. 34, 40.

29. My calculation, from Ministerstvo Finansov, *Spisok fabrik . . . za 1900-1903*. Gavlin, "Rol' tsentra," pp. 340–43, uses archives of the Moscow merchant guild (*Moskovskaia kupecheskaia uprava*) to determine the origins of Moscow capital in 1865 and 1898. In the wealthier First Guild, 81 percent of the registered merchants in 1865 were Moscow born and 91 percent in 1898. In the Second Guild, the figures were 84 percent and 52 percent respectively. Of the smaller-scale "outside" capital that showed such gains by 1898, over two-thirds had come from the central industrial provinces (Moscow, Vladimir, Iaroslavl', Tver', Kaluga, Kostroma, Nizhegorod, and Smolensk). Of all merchants registered in the Second Guild, 29 percent were peasants; of those who were "outsiders" to Moscow, 62 percent were peasants.
30. Pazhitnov, *Ocherki . . . Khlopchatobumazhnaia*, p. 89.
31. Soviet historians have tried to explain this pattern by citing the abundant labor supply in the central provinces and the profitability of established work routines. The Moscow industrialists, they argue, did not lack imagination or initiative but had little incentive to change a system that continued to bring them ample profit. See Gindin, "Russkaia burzhuaziia," pt. 1, pp. 64, 66–67; V. Ia. Laverychev, *Krupnaia burzhuaziia v poreformennoi Rossii, 1861-1900*, p. 9.
32. Walter Phillips, noting a similar pattern in certain regions of India, Brazil, and South Africa, suggests that an industrial system that begins with a high labor-to-capital ratio tends to become locked into primitive technology and to resist innovative pressures. In his examples, as in Moscow's factories, the relations between management and labor were colored by noneconomic considerations (e.g., paternalism, patronage), and previously established industrial forms tended to be self-perpetuating. Walter Phillips, "Technological Levels and Labor Resistance to Change in the Course of Industrialization."
33. Even the giant Morozov Bogorodsko-Glukhovskaia cotton mill, with a work force of 9,400 in the year 1900, continued to operate as a "distribution center" for some 765 cottage weavers (Ministerstvo Finansov, *Spisok fabrik . . . za 1900-1903*, p. 14); on the interaction of cottage and factory in the cotton industry, see M. K. Rozhkova, "Fabrichnaia promyshlennost' i promysly krest'ian v 60-70kh godakh XIX veka."
34. Gindin, "Russkaia burzhuaziia," pt. 1, p. 70.
35. Pogozhev, *Uchet chislennosti*, pp. 94–95 (my calculation).
36. "We must content ourselves with the fact that the subject of peasant crafts does not lend itself to statistical reckoning. In this situation, to resort to any sort of an approximate quantitative characterization would hardly be advisable and would merely create an illusion of exactness" (P. G. Ryndziunskii, *Krest'ianskaia promyshlennost' v poreformennoi Rossii*, p. 82).
37. *PM 1902*, pt. 1, table 2, p. 7.
38. Roger Portal, "The Industrialization of Russia," p. 841; cf. Ryndziunskii's assertion that the number of crafts dropped sharply after 1880 (*Krest'ianskaia promyshlennost'*, pp. 255-56).
39. Pogozhev, *Uchet chislennosti*, pp. xvi, xvii, and app. 1. In Vladimir province, 64 percent of factory workers were outside cities; in Ekaterinoslav, 75 percent; in Russian Poland and the Caucasus, more were in cities, and in Saint Petersburg only 10 percent were in the countryside.

40. V. A. Kondrat'ev and V. I. Nevzorov, eds., *Iz istorii fabrik i zavodov Moskvy i Moskovskoi gubernii*, p. 79.

41. For a discussion of the rural or urban nature of Russian industrialization, in the South or generally, see Roger Thiede, "Industry and Urbanization in New Russia from 1860 to 1910," in *The City in Russian History*, ed. Michael Hamm, pp. 125-38; and Richard H. Rowland, "Urban Inmigration in Late 19th Century Russia," ibid., pp. 115-24.

42. *SSSMG*, vol. 3:7, p. 91.

Chapter Two

1. A. G. Rashin, *Naselenie Rossii za 100 let*, 1811-1913, p. 98. Rashin's figures refer to settlements that were defined as urban by the Russian government, and they include a large proportion of essentially agricultural centers that served local administrative needs. By other estimates, only 2.4 percent of the Russian population lived in centers with twenty thousand inhabitants in 1820; by 1897 the comparable figure had reached 9.4 percent (Robert A. Lewis and Richard H. Rowland, "Urbanization in Russia and the USSR, 1897-1960," in *The City in Russian History*, ed. Michael Hamm, p. 206).

2. Adna Weber, *The Growth of Cities in the Nineteenth Century*, pp. 230-46.

3. H. J. Habbakuk, "Family Structure and Economic Change in Nineteenth-Century Europe," pp. 6-9.

4. August von Haxthausen, *The Russian Empire*, vol. 1, pp. 56, 123, 235; M. L. de Tegoborski, *Commentaries on the Productive Forces of Russia*, vol. 1, pp. 446-49.

5. The most comprehensive study of the emancipation reform is P. A. Zaionchkovskii, *Otmena krepostnogo prava v Rossii*. B. G. Litvak, *Russkaia derevnia v reforme 1861 goda*, offers a detailed analysis of the realization of the reform in five central black-soil provinces. A concise and straightforward account in English is G. T. Robinson, *Rural Russia under the Old Regime*, pp. 64-93.

6. The requirements for permanent departure (*uvolnenie*) are spelled out in *Polnoe sobranie zakonov Rossiiskoi imperii*, 2d ser., vol. 36, no. 36657 (19 February 1861), art. 130 ff. They are summarized in Robert Eugene Johnson, "The Nature of the Russian Working Class: Social Characteristics of the Moscow Industrial Region, 1880-1900, pp. 52-58. Available records provide only indirect evidence of the number of peasants who altered their *soslovie*. For example, two counties of high out-migration in Kostroma province recorded a total of 130 families transferring to other *sosloviia* between 1861 and 1891; this represented less than one household in ten thousand (D. N. Zhbankov, *Bab'ia storona*, pp. 56-62).

7. The five-year passport booklet (*pasportnaia knizhka*) could be issued only to those who paid their taxes in full, and it was validated year by year by the payment of all tax obligations entered in its pages. The short-term passport, which made no such requirement, was preferred by the vast majority of peasants.

8. *Polnoe sobranie zakonov*, 2d ser., vol. 36, no. 36657 (19 February

1861), arts. 58 (par. 10), 84 (par. 8), and 119; ibid., 2d ser., vol. 36, no. 37431 (21 September 1861); ibid., 3rd ser., vol. 14, no. 10709 (3 June 1894), arts. 44, prim. 49, 55; *Polnyi svod zakonov o krest'ianakh*, vol. 2, pp. 183-89. Cf. Johnson, "Nature of the Russian Working Class," pp. 58-59.

9. In 1861 village assemblies were given the power to compel tax defaulters to work elsewhere for wages, which would then be paid directly to the village treasury (*Polnoe sobranie zakonov*, 2d ser., vol. 36, no. 36657 (19 February 1861), art. 188 (par. 3); ibid., 2d ser., vol. 36, no. 36659 (19 February 1861), art. 133 (par. 3); also ibid., 2d ser., vol. 49, no. 53678 (27 June 1874), art. 11 (par. 13). Under later legislation, employers could apply on behalf of their workers for renewal of passports (ibid., 3rd ser., vol. 6, no. 3769 [3 June 1886], arts. 3-4) and arrange to pay part of their wages directly to village authorities (ibid., 3rd ser., vol. 15, no. 11702 [22 May 1895]).

10. Far-reaching changes in the peasantry's legal position were instituted only in 1906, when the Stolypin land program relaxed restrictions on movement and permitted individuals to choose their place of residence (ibid., 3rd ser., vol. 26, no. 28392 [5 October 1906]). On the effects of these changes in Moscow province, see S. I. Antonova, *Vliianie Stolypinskoi agrarnoi reformy na izmeneniia v sostave rabochego klassa.*

11. *PM 1902*, pt. 1, sec. 1, table 5, p. 11.

12. Ibid., pt. 1, sec. 1, table 3, pp. 6-8.

13. Ibid., pt. 2, table 2, pp. 10-11. Over the following ten years, the city's population grew by half a million, but these proportions remained virtually unchanged; the proportion of migrants in the city decreased from 72.6 to 70.9 percent, while the proportion in the work force decreased less than half as much, from 86.0 to 85.3 percent (Rashin, *Naselenie*, p. 141).

14. *SSSMG*, 4:1, table 19 and p. 297.

15. These were Tula (99.6 thousand), Riazan' (94.8), Kaluga (67.4), Smolensk (48.6), Tver' (41.7), Vladimir (39.8), and Iaroslavl' (23.1)—my calculations, from *PM 1902*, pt. 2, table 4, pp. 16-27; figures exclude suburbs.

16. My calculation, from ibid., table 5, pp. 40-45.

17. My calculation from Moscow, Stolichnyi i gubernskii statisticheskii komitet, *Statisticheskie svedeniia o zhiteliakh goroda Moskvy*, pp. 76-77; *PM 1882*, pt. 2, sec. 2, pp. 32-33; Tsentral'nyi Statisticheskii Komitet, *Pervaia vseobshchaia perepis' naseleniia Rossiiskoi imperii, 1897 g.*, vol. 24, bk. 2, pp. 24-25; *PM 1902*, pt. 2, table 5, pp. 40-45. The 1897 table contains several apparent errors, and my computation has been adjusted in accordance with the suggestions of Barbara Ann Anderson, "Internal Migration in a Modernizing Society," p. 346.

18. Reginald Zelnik, "Russian Workers and the Revolutionary Movement," pp. 217-19.

19. *PM 1902*, pt. 2, table 5, pp. 40-45 (my calculation).

20. Anderson, "Internal Migration," p. 256. Anderson concludes that peasants who were exposed to industry at their place of origin were more willing to migrate to industrial destinations whether or not they had any direct experience in factory employment.

21. Tsentral'nyi Statisticheskii Komitet, *Pervaia vseobshchaia perepis'*, vol. 24, bk. 2, pp. xxx, xxxi.

22. Even Saint Petersburg, which most resembled Moscow in the pattern of in-migration, drew 22 percent of its migrants in 1869 from Iaroslavl' province, some four hundred miles away (Rashin, *Naselenie*, p. 142).

23. *SSSMG*, 4:1, tables 19, 21, pp. 240–41. Data for the different counties were gathered in different years and are not wholly comparable.

24. Pogozhev, *Uchet chislennosti*, pp. 94–95.

25. *SSSMG*, 3:4, p. 103 (my calculation: districts were considered to be "outlying" if they were located 20 *versty* [12 miles] or more from the border of Moscow city).

26. Ibid., 3:13, p. 38.

27. Arthur Redford, *Labour Migration in England, 1800–1850*, pp. 184–87.

28. Zhbankov, *Bab'ia storona*, pp. 39–41.

29. *PM 1902*, pt. 2, sec. 1, table 5, pp. 40–45 (my calculation). At the turn of the century the value of industrial output of the central Russian provinces was estimated to be: Moscow, 287 million rubles; Vladimir, 132 million; Iaroslavl', 36.6 million; Tver', 25.4 million; Riazan', 23.4 million; Tula, 15.3 million; Smolensk, 8.8 million; Kaluga, 7.3 million (V. P. Semenov Tian'-Shanskii, *Rossiia: Polnoe geograficheskoe opisanie nashego otechestva*, vol. 1, p. 166; vol. 2, p. 253; vol. 9, p. 289).

30. *PM 1902*, pt. 2, table 5, pp. 44–45; on industry in Riazan' see Brokhaus-Effron, *Entsiklopedicheskii slovar'* (Saint Petersburg, 1899), vol. 27, p. 524.

31. *PM 1902*, pt. 1, table 5, p. 11.

32. *SSSMG*, 4:1, pp. 300–303; in Bogorodskii county *meshchane* were 11.6 percent of the factory work force and in Serpukhovskii, 10.8 percent. Some of these individuals were probably descendants of the earliest factory workers in these regions or of household serfs who received no land during emancipation.

33. Ibid., p. 304.

34. *PM 1902*, pt. 2, table 2, p. 11.

35. See, for example, Gerhart von Schulze-Gaevernitz, *Ocherki obshchestvennogo khoziaistva i ekonomicheskoi politiki Rossii*, pp. 114–19.

36. E. M. Dement'ev, *Fabrika, chto ona daet naseleniiu i chto ona u nego beret*, pp. 1–57. Dement'ev's research was part of the Moscow *zemstvo's* comprehensive survey of factory conditions throughout Moscow province, and his findings were first published in *SSSMG* 4:2.

37. *SSSMG*, 4:2, p. 266.

38. Report of factory inspector for Moscow district, 4 September 1893. Reprinted in *RD*, vol. 3, pt. 2, supp. doc. 13, pp. 567–93. See Chapter 7, note 1.

39. Pogozhev, *Uchet chislennosti*, p. 107.

40. Specific examples of these are presented in I. I. Ianzhul, *Fabrichnyi byt Moskovskoi gubernii*, pp. 76–79; Dement'ev, *Fabrika*, p. 33.

41. One exception noted by Dement'ev was the metalworking industry, in which the higher wages seem to have been incentive enough to keep workers from departing (*SSSMG*, 4:2, pp. 313–14).

42. A survey of relevant archives has disclosed a total of ten such incidents in the Moscow region. Although this total is small, eight of the ten were found in *fondy* of TsGAM (f. 16, op. 76, d. 132 [1886]; f. 46, op. 2, d. 146 [1884–85]), which between them cover a period of less than three years. My access to this archive was strictly limited; it seems

probable that a fuller survey of local records would disclose a much larger number of cases.

43. Dement'ev, *Fabrika*, p. 46.
44. Ibid., p. 49.
45. Ibid., p. 35.
46. A. Markov, *Na Presne 30 let tomu nazad*, pp. 19-20.
47. K. A. Pazhitnov, *Polozhenie rabochego klassa v Rossii*, vol. 2, pp. 179-80 (referring specifically to Moscow province).
48. *Statisticheskii ezhegodnik Moskovskoi gubernii za 1885 g.* (Moscow, 1886), pp. 78-79, 128.
49. F. P. Pavlov, *Za desiat' let praktiki*, p. 70.
50. Zhbankov, *Bab'ia storona*, p. 36.
51. On the other hand, V. I. Romashova, using the archive of the Kol'chugin brass and copper works in Moscow, has concluded that the families of most disabled workers resided not in the country but at the factory; she does not give concrete figures. "Obrazovanie postoiannykh kadrov rabochikh v poreformennoi promyshlennosti Moskvy," in *Rabochii klass i rabochee dvizhenie (1861-1917)*, ed. L. M. Ivanov, pp. 161-62.
52. Tegoborskii, *Commentaries*, vol. 1, p. 30.
53. Semenov Tian'-Shanskii, *Rossiia*, vol. 2, pp. 32-33.
54. As early as the 1850s, this pattern was clearly established in the Moscow region. The provinces of Tula, Smolensk, Kaluga, Vladimir, and Riazan' were among the seven lowest provinces in Russia in the ratio of meadow-land to arable land, each with a ratio of less than 16:100 (as compared to a national average of 67:100). Only the province of Tver' had a relatively favorable ratio, but this was due to the extremely poor quality of its soil (Tegoborskii, *Commentaries*, p. 49).
55. A. M. Anfimov, *Zemel'naia arenda v Rossii v nachale XX veka*, pp. 191-92; cf. Anita B. Baker, "Deterioration or Development," pp. 21-23.
56. R. Munting, "Outside Earnings in the Russian Peasant Farm," pp. 428-46. For evidence that the practice of temporary departures (*otkhodnichestvo*) persisted in some parts of Russia as late as the 1950s, see Stephen Dunn and Ethyl Dunn, *The Peasants of Central Russia*, pp. 81-85.
57. P. M. Shestakov, *Rabochie na manufakture tovarishchestva Emil' Tsindel' v Moskve*, pp. 25, 26.
58. Ibid., pp. 28-33; Antonova, *Vliianie*, pp. 72, 75, for overall figures on livestock of peasants in Moscow province (1907-13).
59. Shestakov, *Rabochie*, pp. 26-27.
60. Ibid., p. 38.
61. *RD*, vol. 3, pt. 2, supp. doc. 13, pp. 592-93.
62. My calculation from A. Svavitskii and V. Sher, *Ocherk polozheniia rabochikh pechatnogo dela v Moskve*, app., tables 1, 3, and 5.
63. Shestakov, *Rabochie*, p. 22.
64. The discussion that follows is based on the Moscow municipal censuses of 1882 and 1902 (*PM 1882* and *PM 1902*). The national census of 1897 (Tsentral'nyi Statisticheskii Komitet, *Pervaia vseobshchaia perepis'*, vol. 24) and the municipal one of 1871 (Moscow, Statisticheskii Komitet, *Statisticheskie svedeniia o zhiteliakh*) both lack the particular categories of information most relevant to the present discussion.

65. Moscow, Gorodskaia uprava, Statisticheskii komitet, *Glavneishie pred-varitel'nye dannye perepisi goroda Moskvy, 31 ianvaria 1902 g.* no. 1, pp. 9-10, 24.
66. In fact, because of worsening economic conditions, in-migration in both years may have been less and out-migration greater than at other times. The statistician who directed the 1902 census concluded that the population increase had been greatest from 1897 to 1900 and had fallen off somewhat in 1901 and 1902 (ibid., p. 10).
67. Ibid., no. 4, p. 25.
68. V. N. Grigor'ev, ed., *Smertnost' naseleniia goroda Moskvy, 1872-1889 g.*, pp. 20-22. The mortality rate for the total population in the years 1882-85 (including foundling infants) was 28.2 per 1,000 per annum. Age-specific rates were as follows: ages ten to fifteen, 5.6 per 1,000; fifteen to twenty, 7 per 1,000; twenty to thirty, 11 per 1,000; thirty to forty, 15 per 1,000; forty to fifty, 22 per 1,000; fifty to sixty, 34 per 1,000. Of all migrants in the 1882 census, 68 percent were in the age group ten to forty, compared to only 47 percent of the Moscow-born population (*PM 1882*, pt. 2, sec. 1, p. 50).
69. This was probably due to the poor economic conditions of 1901-2.
70. Svavitskii and Sher, *Ocherk polozheniia*, pp. 8-9.

Chapter Three

1. On this interrelation, see in particular Habbakuk, "Family Structure."
2. J. Hajnal, "European Marriage Patterns in Perspective"; Peter Laslett, "Mean Household Size in England since the 16th Century," in *Household and Family in Past Time*, ed. Peter Laslett, p. 126 ff.
3. See for example Schulze-Gaevernitz, *Ocherki*, p. 120 ff.; cf. V. I. Lenin, *The Development of Capitalism in Russia*, p. 552.
4. The Prokhorovskaia Trekhgornaia cotton mill was considered a model employer for supplying family accomodations; its barracks included 51 rooms housing four married couples each and 132 family rooms with four to seven persons in each (*Prokhorovskaia Trekhgornaia manufaktura*, pp. 50-51; S. Lapitskaia, *Byt rabochikh Trekhgornoi manufaktury*, p. 40 ff.).
5. The Moscow factory inspector I. I. Ianzhul noted in 1883 that only 4 out of 174 factories he visited made any provision for the care of children (I. I. Ianzhul, "Zhenshchiny-materi na fabrikakh," *Ocherki i isseledovaniia*, p. 391.
6. These facilities had an average of fourteen to fifteen persons per room; the total included certain industries in which workers slept in the same rooms they worked in (*PM 1882*, pt. 1, sec. 1, p. 37).
7. *PM 1902*, pt. 2, table 2, pp. 8-9 (my calculation).
8. B. N. Kazantsev, *Rabochie Moskvy i Moskovskoi gubernii v seredine XIX veka*, pp. 77-79.
9. A detailed account of female and child labor in Moscow is found in Johnson, "The Nature of the Russian Working Class," pp. 93-95.
10. Moscow, Statisticheskii Komitet, *Statisticheskie svedeniia o zhiteliakh*, p. iii; *PM 1902*, pt. 1, sec. 1, table 1, p. 4.

11. A. G. Rashin, "Dinamika chislennosti i protsessy formirovaniia gorodskogo naseleniia Rossii v XIX-nachala XX vv.," pp. 83-84.

12. *PM 1902*, pt. 2, table 2, p. 11.

13. Ibid., pt. 1, sec. 1, table 5, p. 11. Of all newly arrived migrant women in 1902, 42 percent were in the age bracket fifteen to twenty-four, but these ages accounted for just 31 percent of those who had lived in the city for five years. Out-migration was heavy for female migrants of all ages but especially so for younger ones. The same pattern was found at factories, leading one factory inspector to conclude that women were a more casual (*sluchainyi*) element of the factory population (P. A. Peskov, *Sanitarnoe issledovanie fabrik po obrabotke voloknistykh veshchestv v g. Moskve*, pt. 1, p. 122).

14. Peasant customary law varied from region to region in the rights accorded to widows or spinsters. Presence or absence of minor children was sometimes decisive. See Teodor Shanin, *The Awkward Class*, pp. 222-23.

15. *PM 1902*, pt. 1, sec. 1, table 1, pp. 2-4; sec. 2, table 1, pp. 54-56.

16. Ibid., pt. 1, sec. 1, table 4, pp. 9-10.

17. Hajnal, "European Marriage," p. 102.

18. A study of marital patterns in rural England in the seventeenth and eighteenth centuries reached a similar conclusion: "Since marriage was conditioned upon economic independence, the stagnancy of the pre-industrial economy created conditions which led to late marriage. This customary restraint to population growth was broken down by a series of economic changes which transformed peasants and artisans into agricultural and industrial proletarians. . . . When employment became available to all who were willing to sell their labour, it was no longer possible to maintain the equilibrating mechanism of postponed marriage because . . . there was no longer any reason to defer marriage" (David Levine, "The Demographic Implications of Rural Industrialization," pp. 191-92).

19. I. I. Kurkin, *Statistika dvizheniia naseleniia v Moskovskoi gubernii v 1883-1897 gg*, pp. 31-32 ff.

20. Robert Eugene Johnson, "Family Relations and the Rural-Urban Nexus," in *The Family in Imperial Russia*, ed. David Ransel, p. 273 ff.

21. Shestakov, *Rabochie*, pp. 36-37.

22. Anderson, "Internal Migration," pp. 67-68.

23. *SSSMG*, 4:1, pp. 273, 279; similar results were found by Peskov in his 1881 study of Moscow city workers (*Sanitarnoe issledovanie*, pt. 1, pp. 140-46).

24. I. M. Koz'minykh-Lanin, *Semeinyi sostav fabrichno-zavodskikh rabochikh Moskovskoi gubernii*, table I, pp. 2-11. Data refer to 69,000 workers and were collected in 1908. A study of female workers in Saint Petersburg (1905-14) found that the percentage married was higher in more backward industries and enterprises (E. E. Kruze, *Peterburgskie rabochie v 1912-1914 gg.*, p. 84).

25. The most recent and comprehensive treatment of this question is that of L. M. Ivanov, "Preemstvennost' fabrichno-zavodskogo truda i formirovanie proletariata v Rossii," in *Rabochii klass i rabochee dvizhenie (1861-1917)*, ed. L. M. Ivanov, pp. 58-140.

26. Peskov, *Sanitarnoe issledovanie*, pt. 1, p. 134.

27. *SSSMG*, 4:2, pp. 298-99. These counties, as noted in Chapter One, were among the five most industrial in Moscow province.
28. Shestakov, *Rabochie*, pp. 24-25.
29. According to Shestakov's findings, workers who entered the factory before age sixteen were 80 percent second generation; those who began factory work after age twenty-one were 78 percent first generation (ibid., p. 24).
30. Dement'ev, *Fabrika*, p. 46.
31. On this point, see Reginald Zelnik, "Russian Workers and the Revolutionary Movement," pp. 217-19.
32. Shestakov, *Rabochie*, p. 26.
33. "Otchet fabrichnoi inspektsii Vladimirskoi gubernii 1894-1897," as cited by Ivanov, "Preemstvennost'," p. 81.
34. Peskov, *Sanitarnoe issledovanie*, pt. 1, p. 134. Dement'ev did not publish a detailed breakdown of occupations but indicated that several groups with above-average proportions of hereditary workers (handweavers and warpers) were also "half-proletarians," i.e., sons would work beside their fathers in the factories and then return with them to the countryside in the summer (*SSSMG*, 4:2, p. 300).
35. *SSSMG*, 4:2, pp. 298-99. The same pattern appeared among dyers and dye printers, but to a lesser degree.
36. Ibid., p. 300.
37. Peskov, *Sanitarnoe issledovanie*, pt. 1, pp. 137-41.
38. On the operation of such a system in post-Petrine Russia, see Arcadius Kahan, "The 'Hereditary Workers' Hypothesis and the Development of a Factory Labor force in 18th and 19th Century Russia," pp. 291-97.
39. "Materialy dlia otsenki zemli Vladimirskoi gubernii," as quoted in Ivanov, "Preemstvennost'," p. 103.
40. For an explanation of this term, see Chapter One, p. 12.
41. A. V. Pogozhev, factory sanitation inspector in Vereiskii county, in *SSSMG*, 3:3, p. 14.
42. M. K. Rozhkova reached a strikingly similar conclusion in her study of textile workers in Bogorodskii county ("Fabrichnaia promyshlennost' i promysly krest'ian v 60-70kh godakh XIX veka," p. 217).

Chapter Four

1. Arthur A. Goren, *New York Jews and the Quest for Community*, pp. 20-21; Phyllis H. Williams, *South Italian Folkways in Europe and America*, pp. 9-17; Paul L. Doughty, "Behind the Back of the City," pp. 30-45; Leonard Plotnicov, "Rural-Urban Communications in Contemporary Nigeria," p. 81.
2. On the absence of territorial loyalties, see Marc Raeff, *Origins of the Russian Intelligentsia*, p. 73 ff., and Terrence Emmons, *The Russian Landed Gentry and the Peasant Emancipation of 1861*, p. 7, both referring to Russia's privileged classes. Cf. Donald Treadgold, *The Great Siberian Migration*, pp. 241-42, on the apparent lack of territorial loyalties among peasants who migrated to Siberia.
3. Vladimir Soloukhin, *A Walk in Rural Russia*, p. 12.
4. On student *zemliachestva*, see P. S. Tkachenko, *Moskovskoe studen-*

chestvo v obshchestvenno-politicheskoi zhizni Rossii vtoroi poloviny XIX veka, p. 178 ff.

5. T. S. Vlasenko et al., "K voprosu o formirovanii proletariata v Rossii v kontse XIX-nachale XX v." [On the question of the formation of the proletariat in Russia at the end of the nineteenth and beginning of the twentieth centuries], in *Iz istorii rabochego klassa i revoliutsionnogo dvizheniia*, ed. M. V. Nechkina, p. 282.

6. I. I. Ianzhul, *Fabrichnyi byt Moskovskoi gubernii*, p. 89. He specifically mentions the Prokhorovskaia Trekhgornaia factory as one at which this pattern was observed. The experience of V. V. Morozkin, reared in the village by *zemliaki* while his parents, who had both been factory workers since their early teens, stayed in Moscow, suggests that village–factory ties could work in both directions: unpublished memoirs in TsGAOR, f. 7952, quoted by V. I. Romashova, "Obrazovanie postoiannykh kadrov v poreformennoi promyshlennosti Moskvy" [The formation of permanent cadres in post-reform industry of Moscow], in *Rabochii klass i rabochee dvizhenie (1861-1917)*, ed. L. M. Ivanov, p. 155.

7. F. P. Pavlov, *Za desiat' let praktiki*, p. 55.

8. Fyodor Dostoyevsky [Dostoevski], *Crime and Punishment*, pp. 135-36. "I've known this peasant, Nikolai Dementyev, from a child; he comes from the same province and district of Zaraisk, we are both Riazan men . . . he had a job in that house-painting work with Dmitri, who comes from the same village."

9. Maksim Gor'kii [Gorki] *Mat'*, p. 130.

10. The word *zemliachestvo* is used in Russian to describe either a formal organization or a feeling of regional identification (*"zemliak-ness"*).

11. Shestakov, *Rabochie*, pp. 21, 25.

12. *PM 1902*, pt. 2, table 5, pp. 39-45.

13. At another giant textile enterprise, the Prokhorovskaia Trekhgornaia, workers from Riazan' were 25 percent of the work force; migrants from other provinces were present in very different proportions from their numbers in the city's population. Those from Smolensk province, for example, were 4.4 percent of the city's population but 9.6 percent of the factory's (*Prokhorovskaia Trekhgornaia manufaktura*, p. 48).

14. A. M. Pankratova, "Proletarizatsiia krest'ianstva i ee rol' v formirovanii promyshlennogo proletariata Rossii (60-90e gg. XIX v.)," pp. 218-19.

15. *SSSMG*, 3:2, app., pp. 1-17. In those few cases where workers from other localities were present, a clear division of labor occurred. An example was the D. T. Romanov factory, which employed fifteen workers from Zhizdrinskii county as diggers of clay, forty from Suzdal'skii county (Vladimir province) as shapers of bricks, and fifteen from Venevskii county (Tula province) as firers. Ibid., p. 85.

16. Peskov, *Sanitarnoe issledovanie*, pt. 1, pp. 78-81.

17. Moscow, Statisticheskii komitet, *Statisticheskie svedeniia o zhiteliakh*, pp. 78-81.

18. For example, 21 percent of all migrants from Bronnitskii county were in Rogozhskaia precinct compared to only 5.7 percent from Zvenigorodskii county (*PM 1882*, pt. 2, sec. 1, pp. 69-74).

19. M. Balabanov, *Ocherki po istorii rabochego klassa v Rossii*, vol. 2, p. 62.

20. Dement'ev, *Fabrika*, p. 3.

21. *SSSMG*, 3:13, p, 123; app., pp. 1-45. These migrants, a small minority

at the Kolomna factory, were generally found in the better-paying occupational categories, though not all of them could be counted as skilled veterans.

22. Peskov, *Sanitarnoe issledovanie*, pt. 1, p. 115.
23. Ibid., p. 121. Peskov concluded that skilled workers were almost exclusively "local," i.e., had traveled from no further than Moscow province, whereas unskilled workers had come greater distances from other provinces.
24. My calculation, from ibid., p. 117; and *SSSMG*, 3:4, pp. 132-33. Note that the two sets of statistics were compiled within one year of one another. The city and county were both almost equidistant from all neighboring provinces and were far enough from all of them that migrating workers must have had some reason other than proximity for settling in a particular factory.
25. This conclusion comes from a comparison of Peskov's tables on workers' places of origin (*Sanitarnoe issledovanie*, pt. 1, pp. 103-12, 117) with tables presented by F. F. Erisman (*SSSMG*, 4:1, pp. 130-31) on the distribution of industry through Moscow province. As noted above, Peskov presents a detailed breakdown only of male workers; his aggregate data on female workers do indicate, however, that the least industrial counties of Moscow province surpassed all others as suppliers of labor for the city's textile factories.
26. On the numerous meanings of the term *artel'* see Chapter Five, pp. 91-92. The meaning here is a group of individuals who joined together before leaving their native village.
27. Ianzhul, *Fabrichnyi byt*, pp. 86-88.
28. Contracts, passbooks, and other records are preserved in certain Soviet archives but have rarely been studied. See, however, B. F. Borzunov, "Dogovory podriadchikov s rabochimi kak istoricheskii istochnik," for a description of the records of railway-construction workers.
29. Those who went home in the winter were not of course working the soil; instead they hauled timber, engaged in such cottage industry as the squeezing of oil from hempseed, or simply stayed at home waiting for the spring (*SSSMG*, 3:2, p. 189). Bast-rug weavers returned home in the spring and hired themselves out almost immediately as agricultural laborers in other provinces (ibid., 4:2, p. 292).
30. On this system and its abuses, see Iu. Kharitonova and D. Shcherbakov, *Krest'ianskoe dvizhenie v Kaluzhskoi gubernii (1861-1917 gg.)*, pp. 69-72.
31. This system was not unique to Russia. Among Italian immigrants in North America, the *padrone* system operated in almost identical fashion; the *padrone*, like the *podriadchik*, relied on the workers' loyalty to fellow villagers (Lawrence Frank Pisani, *The Italian in America*, pp. 81-88). On comparable practices in England at the beginning of the nineteenth century, see Reinhard Bendix, *Work and Authority in Industry*, pp. 54-56.
32. *SSSMG*, 3:2, p. 187. Individual examples of such departures can be found in TsGAOR, f. 102, 2 del-vo, d. 61:8 (1893); TsGAM, f. 16, op. 76, d. 132 (1886), pp. 26, 60-77.
33. I. M. Lukomskaia, "Formirovanie promyshlennogo proletariata Donbassa 70-80kh godov XIX v." [Formation of the industrial proletariat

of the Donbas in the 1870s and 1880s] in *Iz istorii rabochego klassa,* ed. Nechkina, pp. 297-300.

34. D. N. Zhbankov, *Bab'ia storona,* pp. 10, 22-23. According to this author, who studied out-migration from Kostroma province in the 1880s, *arteli* were used in the time of serfdom as a device for collecting the migrant serfs' quitrent (*obrok*). The *starosta* who collected these payments was sometimes able to line his own pockets in the process, and this was the origin of several private fortunes in the region Zhbankov studied.

35. Vlasenko, "K voprosu o formirovanii," p. 279.

36. P. A. Moiseenko, *Vospominaniia starogo revoliutsionera,* p. 17. An almost identical account is given by Ivan Gudov, who first traveled to Moscow in the 1930s looking for work (*Sud'ba rabochego,* pp. 5-6).

37. For example, I. V. Babushkin, *Recollections of I. V. Babushkin,* p. 93. Cf. Zhbankov, *Bab'ia storona,* pp. 48-49. After 1905, with the partial legalization of trade-union activity, union leaders complained that this practice was an obstacle to worker solidarity because it put the interests of *zemliaki* ahead of those of fellow unionists; see K. Dmitriev, *Professional'noe dvizhenie i soiuzy v Rossii,* p. 69.

38. Zhbankov, *Bab'ia Storona,* p. 84, notes that a certain proportion of villagers made their living by carrying parcels and messages back and forth; in Moscow city, one experienced radical agitator used to pose as a worker's visiting *zemliak* in order to slip past the factory guards (S. I. Mitskevich, ed., *Na zare rabochego dvizheniia v Moskve,* p. 16n).

39. *Statisticheskii ezhegodnik Moskovskogo gubernskogo zemstva za 1885 g.,* sec. VI ("Vidy na zhitel'stvo" [Residence permits]), p. 13.

40. V. N. Grigor'ev, *Pereselenie krest'ian Riazanskoi gubernii,* pp. 76-77, 82-83, 146-92.

41. I. Martynov, *Gosudarstvennyi russkii narodnyi khor imeni Piatnitskogo,* p. 9 ff. In time the local traditions were blended into a common repertoire and the Piatnitskii chorus became famous as one of the Soviet Union's outstanding folk music ensembles.

42. I observed impromptu singing and dancing in Moscow's Izmailovskii park on Sunday afternoons in 1969 and was told by native Muscovites that this was a tradition among "country people." Those who took part were not performers or semiprofessionals but picnickers who sang or danced for their own pleasure. Soloukhin, *A Walk,* presents numerous examples of surviving regional traditions, e.g., pp. 185-86 on the horn blowers of Kobelikha.

43. Moiseenko, *Vospominaniia,* p. 72.

44. For example, Moscow province provided 27.3 percent of all male migrants to Moscow city in 1902 and 26.9 percent of females; Kaluga sent 8.6 percent of males and 8.4 percent of females; and so forth. Of the eight surrounding provinces, there was only one case (Tula: males, 11.8 percent; females, 13.7 percent) in which the two figures differed by more than 1 percent (*PM 1902,* pt. 2, table 5, pp. 28-45, my calculation). For residence patterns, see *PM 1882,* pt. 3, table 10, pp. 220-32.

45. Zhbankov, *Bab'ia storona,* p. 80.

46. TsGAOR, f. 102, 4 del-vo, d. 121:2 (1908), pp. 209-45.

47. My calculation, from ibid.

48. The list does not always explain leaders' positions. In only a few cases

are the persons listed specifically identified as founders, but when they are they often turn out to be the chairmen or treasurers as well.

49. Factory inspectors were also required to submit reports on strikes, but the prescribed form gave only summary information: number of strikers, duration, etc. These records, preserved in TsGIA f. 23 op. 17, were summarized in V. E. Varzar, *Statisticheskie svedeniia o stachkakh na fabrikakh i zavodakh za desiatiletie 1895-1904 g.* Unfortunately this file has suffered from the ravages of time and contains only twenty-two reports for Moscow province for all years before 1905. More detailed strike reports from inspectors have survived in a few instances, but I have not used them in this study.

50. A county (*uezd*) was divided into ten-to-fifteeen townships (*volosti*).

51. TsGAM, f. 46, op. 2, d. 1472 (1884-85), p. 78. Of the remaining five, three were from one village in Riazan'.

52. TsGAOR, f. 102, 3 del-vo, d. 606:3 (1896), p. 144.

53. Ibid., f. 102, 2 del-vo, d. 26:28 (1895), p. 11 ff.; ibid., f. 63, op. 7, d. 256 (1894), p. 10; ibid., f. 102, 2 del-vo, d. 15:16 (1896), pp. 41-42; ibid., f. 63, op. 7, d. 124 (1893), pp. 21-23.

54. A. Markov, *Na Presne 30 let tomu nazad*, app.

55. The police archives also include a number of collective protests from village-based *arteli*. These took the form of petitions or formal complaints more often than work stoppages, but when strikes did occur they were unanimously supported. Examples were found in the following archives: TsGAM, f. 16, op. 76, d. 132 (1886), pp. 26-28, 29, 31-32; ibid., f. 46, op. 2, d. 1472 (1884-85), pp. 18, 46; TsGAOR, f. 102, 2 del-vo, d. 61:8 (1893), pp. 1-3; ibid., f. 63, op. 7, d. 126 (1894), pp. 26-30.

56. TsGAOR, f. 102, 3 del-vo, d. 606:3 (1896), pp. 45-52. In a separate incident in 1896, a peasant from Tula province was thought by police to have triggered disorders among workers at the Gerasimov brickworks (Moscow county). He was not himself employed at the brick factory and had come there only to visit his *zemliaki* (ibid., f. 102, 2 del-vo, d. 15:16 [1896] pp. 7-8).

57. The reports of the local police and factory inspector are reprinted in *RD*, vol. 4, pt. 1, docs. 236, 239, pp. 642, 649.

58. Vlasenko, "K voprosu o formirovanii," p. 286.

59. Ibid., p. 286; for examples of employers who followed this practice, see A. S. Trofimov, *Rabochee dvizhenie v Rossii, 1861-1894 gg.*, pp. 114, 117.

60. This subject is discussed in greater detail in Chapters Six and Seven.

61. Moiseenko, *Vospominaniia*, pp. 90, 93.

Chapter Five

1. The fullest survey of this subject is K. A. Pazhitnov, *Polozhenie rabochego klassa v Rossii*, of which volume 2 deals with the period 1861-1905. The vast literature on this subject is outlined in Iu. N. Kirianov and P. V. Pronina, eds., *Oblik proletariata Rossii*, especially pp. 55-80.

2. For a general discussion of this question in early stages of industrialization, see Sidney Pollard, "Factory Discipline in the Industrial Revolu-

tion"; E. P. Thompson, *The Making of the English Working Class,* especially pp. 394-96; and Reinhard Bendix, *Work and Authority in Industry,* pp. 60-116.

3. M. I. Tugan-Baranovskii, *The Russian Factory in the 19th Century,* pp. 322-23 ff.

4. Balabanov, *Ocherki,* vol. 2, p. 94.

5. The Prokhorovskaia Trekhgornaia cotton mill in Moscow city was able to renovate its factories in the early 1870s only because its older facilities had been destroyed by fire; other factories normally grew in piecemeal fashion, adding new buildings or sections while retaining older ones.

6. I. F. Gindin, "Russkaia burzhuaziia v period kapitalizma," pt. 1, pp. 64, 66-67; for a comparison between Moscow's wage levels and those of other Russian centers, see Ministerstvo Finansov, Departament Torgovli i Manufaktur, *Prodolzhitel'nost' rabochego dnia i zarabotnaia plata rabochikh,* pp. 91-116.

7. Viz, the comments of a police inspector in Bogorodskii county: "Owners send their agents to the country in the winter, they reach an agreement with the village elder [*starshina*] who in turn is concerned to pay off the taxes levied on the village peasants, and hire their workers in whole groups, giving big advances. They indicate neither the work to be performed nor the wage." TsGAOR, f. 102, 3 del-vo, d. 88:35 (1884), p. 53. On debt bondage [*kabal'nye*] contracts throughout central Russia, see Balabanov, *Ocherki,* vol. 2, pp. 104-7.

8. TsGIA, f. 22, op. 1, d. 249, pp. 7-9. Cf. Bendix, *Work and Authority,* p. 183, for a case in which the employer used the opposite argument to justify withholding of wages. The employer's object in both cases was to keep the workers in a dependent condition.

9. At one unnamed central Russian factory, 590 out of 2,200 workers were fired in a single year (S. Gvozdev, *Zapiski fabrichnogo inspektora, 1894-1906,* pp. 96-98). Employers in other regions of the Russian empire are quoted as preferring to hire long-distance migrants for the same reason: cut off from familiar surroundings, workers were less likely to cause trouble or quit before the expiration of their contracts (Balabanov, *Ocherki,* vol. 2, p. 65). In central Russia, on the other hand, as indicated in Chapter Two, the factory surroundings were familiar to the workers, who were mostly short-distance migrants; employers in this region were more suspicious of the long-distance migrant, who was considered turbulent and unpredictable (Gvozdev, *Zapiski,* p. 36).

10. Shestakov, *Rabochie,* p. 12; G. F. Semeniuk, "Polozhenie rabochego klassa v tekstil'noi promyshlennosti Moskovskoi gubernii v 90e gody XIX v.," pp. 125-26.

11. At the Danilovskaia cotton-spinning mill, factory guards are said to have confiscated and destroyed goods purchased outside the factory by workers (Semeniuk, "Polozhenie," pp. 128-29, citing workers' recollections as recorded by the "Istoriia zavodov" project in the 1930s).

12. Ianzhul, *Fabrichnyi byt,* p. 81; deductions for food and lodging were limited by the Factory Law of 1886, but evidence from the 1890s suggests that abuses continued (see below, p. 90); for comparable cases in Saint Petersburg in the 1880s and 1890s, see D.G. Kutsentov, "Peterburgskii proletariat v 90kh godakh XIX veka" [The Petersburg pro-

letariat in the 1890s], in *Istoriia rabochego klassa Leningrada*, ed. V. A. Ovsiankin, p. 39.

13. Shestakov, *Rabochie*, p. 25; at another factory, the Troitskii broadcloth mill in Podol'skii county, a local police official reported that almost all of the workers had lived there for twenty years (*RD*, vol. 3, pt. 2, supp. doc. 13, p. 590).

14. Markov, *Na Presne*, pp. 19-21.

15. An analysis of payroll records at the Prokhorovskaia Trekhgornaia factory for a somewhat later period (1913-14) offers indirect support for this suggestion. At that time the work force had grown to 7,392, but wage records show a total of 8,348 workers on the payroll between the spring of 1913 and the spring of 1914. The difference between the two figures represents the total turnover in the work force in one year—roughly 11 percent of the total force. (M. K. Rozhkova, "Zarabotnaia plata rabochikh Trekhgornoi manufaktury" [The wages of workers at the Trekhgornaia Factory], in *Iz istorii rabochego klassa*, ed. M. V. Nechkina, pp. 333-34).

16. Some such records have been preserved in TsGAM and are described in some detail in the archive's publication, *Iz istorii fabrik i zavodov Moskvy i Moskovskoi gubernii*, ed. V. A. Kondrat'ev and V. I. Nevzorov. These collections were not available to me for this study.

17. *SSSMG*, 4:2, p. 218; 18 percent of all workers lived in rented quarters, and 25 percent were locally born peasants who lived at home. For a more detailed survey of factory living quarters in one outlying county in 1899, see A. I. Skibnevskii, *Zhilishcha fabrichno-zavodskikh rabochikh Bogorodskogo uezda*, especially pp. 9, 34. Half of the workers in Skibnevskii's study lived at the factory, and the number of occupants of such quarters had grown at the same rate as the work force for the preceding fifteen years.

18. Pazhitnov, *Polozhenie*, vol. 2, pp. 112-13; Gvozdev, *Zapiski*, p. 134; S. N. Semanov, *Peterburgskie rabochie nakanune pervoi russkoi revoliutsii*, pp. 144-56.

19. In 1899 there were sixteen thousand such establishments in the city, with 180,000 inhabitants. Results of a general survey of these quarters were reported by I. Verner, "Zhilishcha bedneishego naseleniia Moskvy"; cf. "Neskol'ko dannykh o moskovskikh koechno-kamorochnykh kvartirakh."

20. S. Lapitskaia, *Byt rabochikh Trekhgornoi manufaktury*, p. 40 ff.

21. I. Kh. Ozerov, *Politika po rabochemu voprosu*, p. 21.

22. At the Tsindel' factory, for example, no one could leave the premises after nine o'clock in the summer or after eight o'clock in winter; the work day ended at seven o'clock throughout the year (Shestakov, *Rabochie*, app.). Rules at other Moscow city factories are surveyed in Peskov, *Sanitarnoe issledovanie*, pt. 2, especially pp. 14-15.

23. These examples are drawn from Shestakov, *Rabochie*, pp. 1-14 (Rules at Tsindel', 1885, 1886, and 1899), and *RD*, vol. 2, pt. 2, supp. docs. 3, 11, pp. 590, 596-97 (Rules at Troitskii broadcloth factory, 1876, and Danilovskaia cotton mill, 1881). Not all the rules were arbitrary or oppressive: at the Danilovskaia factory workers were required to innoculate their children against smallpox.

24. Lapitskaia, *Byt rabochikh*, p. 56.

25. TsGAOR, f. 63, op. 7, d. 256 (1894), p. 6.

26. Evidence gathered by factory inspectors in Moscow province in 1887–88 indicates that a majority of employers continued to impose fines and that, of those who did, smaller factories tended to impose higher fines (TsGIA, f. 20, op. 15, d. 132 [1886-88], pp. 1-10); this file is alphabetically incomplete, but not in ways that would distort the trend of the evidence. Of the fines recorded, 28 percent were for absenteeism or tardiness, 13 percent for violations of order, and 59 percent for breakage or defective workmanship.

27. TsGAOR, f. 63, op. 7, d. 256 (1894), p. 9.

28. Lapitskaia, *Byt rabochikh*, p. 43; one was fired for allegedly wanting to hang himself in the sleeping quarters.

29. Markov, *Na Presne*, p. 19.

30. Semeniuk, "Polozhenie", p. 136.

31. According to statistics compiled by the department of Trade and Manufactures in 1886-87, only 1,471 out of 21,000 factory *managers* had received higher education or specialized training, and of those who did, 492 were foreigners (*Prakticheskaia zhizn'*, 1891, no. 2, p. 45). Among lower-level supervisors the proportion with specialized training was undoubtedly lower. On the unpopularity of foreign supervisors, see Gerald Norman, *All the Russias*, p. 30.

32. In that same company's calico division, more than half of the supervisory personnel (29 out of 55 persons) had been employed there for more than ten years (*Prokhorovskaia Trekhgornaia manufaktura*, pp. 66-69, my computation).

33. Pazhitnov, *Polozhenie*, vol. 2, pp. 179-80; Gvozdev, *Zapiski*, pp. 106-10; Lapitskaia, *Byt rabochikh*, pp. 38, 44. Favoritism was especially widespread in the textile industry, where a single factory produced many different grades of yarn or fabric. Not only were the wage rates higher for certain products, but the quality of raw material also varied in ways that made it easier or harder to work with, e.g., warp strings could snap, causing costly delays.

34. Thompson, *Making of the Working Class*, pp. 456-69; cf. Arnold Bonner, *British Cooperation*, chaps. 1-3.

35. C. R. Fay, *Cooperation at Home and Abroad*, pp. 51-76; R. E. Bedi, *Theory, History and Practice of Cooperation*, pp. 71-79.

36. Immanuel Wallerstein, *The Road to Independence*, pp. 83-87 ff., provides theoretical discussion and bibliography on this question, followed by a detailed account of associations' roles in two West African nations.

37. Before 1897, the minister of internal affairs had to give personal assent, after consultation with "other affected departments" (*Polnoe sobranie zakonov Rossiiskoi imperii*, 2d ser., vol. 37, no. 37852 [12 January 1862]); this responsibility was then shifted to the provincial governors (ibid., 3rd ser., vol. 17, no. 13736 [15 February 1897], arts. 5, 7).

38. An extreme but revealing example was the proposal of a group of Moscow textile engravers to establish a mutual-aid society (1900). The head of the Moscow secret police (*Okhranka*), Sergei Zubatov, proposed to revise the charter in ways objectionable to the minister of finance. The final decision was left to the minister of internal affairs, who was reluctant to offend either party and compromised by neither approving nor rejecting the charter, so that the aid society never came

into existence (Jeremiah Schneiderman, "The Tsarist Government and the Labor Movement," pp. 178–80). Cf. the experience of the savings-and-loan fund of the senior workers and supervisory personnel (*sluzha-shchie, masterovye*) of the Riabovskaia factory in Moscow, who waited from 1902 to 1905 for approval (TsGIA, f. 1288, op. 15:7, d. 75 [1904], p. 10).

39. TsGIA, f. 1287, op. 9, d. 2555, p. 2.

40. Ibid., d. 2643, p. 14; ibid., d. 2555, p. 12. The original charter of a cooperative at Prokhorov Trekhgornaia factory proposed a triennial general meeting whose only purpose would have been the election of delegates; this clause was eliminated by the Ministry of Internal Affairs.

41. In the case of the Moscow textile engravers' proposal, "Membership requirements were to be [re]defined in such a way as to inhibit the penetration of subversive elements, the chairman of the society was to keep the police informed on its personnel . . . and the Moscow authorities were to exercise broad control over the society, which could never meet without their approval" (Schneiderman, "Tsarist Government," pp. 179–80). There are other examples of administrative intervention in TsGIA, f. 20, op. 5, d. 760 (1897–1900); f. 1288, op. 15:7, d. 75 (1904), p. 6; f. 1287, op. 9, d. 2555, p. 10.

42. TsGIA, f. 22, op. 1, d. 352, pp. 1, 3.

43. Ibid., f. 1287, op. 9, d. 2671. Here, a society's charter permitted a total of four musical, literary, or dance gatherings per year, but required that each be approved by the chief of police.

44. *Svod zakonov Rossiiskoi imperii* (1892), vol. 2, arts. 321, 863.

45. The only exception to this pattern in the Moscow region seems to have been the stillborn association of textile engravers (described in notes 38 and 41). Even in that case, the would-be founders were a highly paid and unrepresentative minority among textile workers. Informal associations founded by rank-and-file workers may have existed for short periods without official approval, but without support from government or employers they soon collapsed. One such example is related by I. V. Babushkin, a worker–Social Democrat who was exiled to Ekaterinoslav in the late 1890s (*Recollections of I. V. Babushkin*, pp. 120–24, 163–68).

46. I. Kh. Ozerov, *Obshchestva potrebitelei*, pp. 164–66; TsGAOR, f. 102, 4 del-vo, d. 121:2 (1908), p. 235.

47. I. Kh. Ozerov, an advocate of close worker involvement in cooperative associations, gave the following examples of outstanding Moscow associations: the Prokhorovskaia Trekhgornaia factory, where supervisory personnel directed the cooperative; the Kolomna machine works, whose directorate consisted of two office workers and one machinist; and the Moscow-Riazan' railwaymen's cooperative, whose assembly of delegates was limited to members who earned over 600 rubles per year (Ozerov, *Obshchestva*, p. 166).

48. Ibid., pp. 164, 166.

49. The records of some societies have been preserved in the archives of individual factories at the Moscow city archive (TsGAM), but my request to examine them was denied in April 1970.

50. The model statute approved by the minister of internal affairs in 1897 made 10 rubles the maximum cost of a share but allowed an additional

entrance fee of 3 rubles. Ozerov, *Obshchestva*, app., pp. 291-309, art. 13.

51. Members of the aid society of Moscow printers paid from 60 kopecks to 1 ruble and 20 kopecks per month, plus an entrance fee ranging from 2 to 4 rubles (V. V. Sher, *Istoriia professional'nogo dvizheniia rabochikh pechatnogo dela v Moskve*, pp. 78-79). At the Zimin textile factory, monthly dues ranged from 1 to 5 rubles, depending on the member's wages (TsGIA, f. 1288, op. 15:5, d. 90 [1903], p. 8); membership was restricted to supervisory personnel.

52. A. Svavitskii and V. Sher, *Ocherk polozheniia rabochikh pechatnogo dela v Moskve*, p. 20.

53. Sher, *Istoriia professional'nogo dvizheniia*, p. 79; Svavitskii and Sher, *Ocherk polozheniia*, p. 20. Barely 4 percent of all Moscow printers were members of the society.

54. Ozerov, *Obshchestva*, pp. 166, 174.

55. At the Prokhorov factory, 15 percent of the workers were members; at the Moscow metal works, 34 percent were.

56. In one instance, workers who had no cash before payday were reportedly buying unwanted goods at the cooperative store in order to exchange them for vodka in private shops or taverns (TsGIA, f. 22, op. 1, d. 249, pp. 9-10).

57. Babushkin, *Recollections*, p. 222 (describing the cooperative at the Morozov Nikol'skaia factory in Orekhovo).

58. At the Moscow metal works, the administration acknowledged that workers had received goods valued at 49.5 thousand rubles in February 1899 against anticipated earnings of 60 thousand rubles. In other months, the total of goods received on credit was never less than four-sevenths of anticipated wages. The management presented these figures to justify its practice of paying wages at longer intervals than the Factory Law of 1886 specified; workers, it argued, has less need of wages because they could get all that they needed from the cooperative (TsGIA, f. 22, op. 1, d. 249, pp. 5-8).

59. Sher, *Istoriia professional'nogo dvizheniia*, pp. 78, 89-90.

60. V. P. Litvinov-Falinskii, *Fabrichnoe zakonodatel'stvo i fabrichnaia inspektsiia v Rossii*, p. 136.

61. TsGAOR, f. 63, op. 7, d. 126 (1894), p. 17.

62. For a detailed description of one such arrangement, see Ozerov, *Obshchestva*, pp. 164-65.

63. TsGAOR, f. 63, op. 7, d. 276 (1894), pp. 1-10 (an anonymous complaint about an *artel'* whose assistant director doubled as a factory guard); cf. Lapitskaia, *Byt rabochikh*, pp. 4-5.

64. *SSSMG*, 4:2, pp. 465-66, 469.

65. Gvozdev, *Zapiski*, pp. 189-90. In 1903, the Russian government introduced a law that gave limited expression to this principle, but it was strongly opposed by employers and was never fully implemented (ibid., pp. 215-16).

66. Erving Goffman, *Asylums*, pp. 4-6.

67. Babushkin, *Recollections*, pp. 39-43. Another worker-radical was able to approach Moscow textile workers because of his Old Believer style of dress—a caftan, a long beard, and the haircut of a peasant *muzhik* (S. I. Mitskevich, *Na grani dvukh epokh*, p. 178.)

68. Shestakov, *Rabochie*, pp. 70-71.
69. Bendix, *Work and Authority*, p. 183.
70. Ibid., p. 206.
71. Goffman, *Asylums*, p. 304.
72. I. I. Ianzhul, *Moskovskii fabrichnyi okrug*, pp. 74-76, 36.
73. Gvozdev, *Zapiski*, pp. 160, 207.
74. Ibid., pp. 203-4. Cf. Goffman, *Asylums*, p. 114. "[Lower-level staff] must personally present the demands of the institution to the inmates. They can come, then, to deflect the hate of inmates from higher staff persons . . . inmates very generally obtain some sense of security from the feeling, however illusory, that although most staff persons are bad, the man at the top is really good."
75. Daniel Field, *Rebels in the Name of the Tsar*, pp. 17-26.
76. A classic example is provided by Moiseenko from his experience in a Saint Petersburg textile factory (*Vospominaniia*, pp. 24-27).
77. On this point see Gatson V. Rimlinger, "Autocracy and the Factory Order in Early Russian Industrialization."
78. TsGAOR, f. 63, op. 7, d. 124 (1893), p. 28; ibid., d. 126 (1894), pp. 8-12; ibid., d. 363 (1893), p. 10. From the point of view of radical agitators, such narrow loyalties were an obstacle rather than an encouragement to collective action and were sometimes referred to as *tsekhovshchina*.
79. See for example the memoir of A. Markov, *Na presne*, passim. He belonged to a loosely grouped *kruzhok* of unmarried young men who shared a distaste for drunkenness and an interest in radical ideas. They shared and discussed books, including many legal ones. Although the group functioned at the Prokhorovskaia factory for more than three years, it became involved in agitation and strikes only in its later stages, and it played no part at all in the factory's first major strike.
80. David Ransel, "Abandonment and Fosterage of Unwanted Children," in *The Family in Imperial Russia*, ed. David Ransel.
81. Zhbankov, *Bab'ia storona*, p. 27; cf. Sula Benet, ed., *The Village of Viriatino*, pp. 84-88; Pazhitnov, *Polozhenie*, vol. 2, p. 86.
82. Shestakov, *Rabochie*, p. 45; Tsentral'nyi Statisticheskii Komitet, *Obshchii svod po imperii rezul'tatov razrabotki dannykh pervoi vseobshchei perepisi naseleniia proizvedennoi 28 ianvaria 1897 g.*, pt. 1, table 3a, pp. 40-41. Of all males of ages twenty to twenty-nine in European Russia, 35 percent were literate.
83. Zhbankov, *Bab'ia storona*, pp. 93-98.
84. Babushkin, *Recollections*, p. 192.
85. For fuller discussion of this minority and its place in the labor movement and the radical underground, see Reginald Zelnik, "Russian Bebels."
86. E.g., Otto Goebel, *Entwicklungsgang der russischen Industriearbeiter bis zur ersten Revolution* (Leipzig, 1920, p. 13), as cited by Bendix, *Work and Authority*, p. 177.
87. Babushkin, *Recollections*, pp. 182-83; for a similar assessment of Moscow and central Russia in the years before 1905, see V. I. Lenin, "Days of Bloodshed in Moscow," p. 336.
88. For specific examples see A. S. Trofimov, *Rabochee dvizhenie v Rossii*,

1861-1894 gg., pp. 137, 145, 150, 156; cf. Lapitskaia, *Byt rabochikh,* p. 83.

Chapter Six

1. On the earliest revolutionary propaganda, see E. E. Vilenskaia, *Revoliutsionnoe podpol'e v Rossii (60-e gody XIX veka),* especially pp. 261-95; O. D. Sokolov, "Revoliutsionnaia propaganda sredi fabrichnykh i zavodskikh rabochikh v 70kh godakh XIX veka," pp. 12-14.
2. For a fuller discussion of the Saint Petersburg circles, see Reginald E. Zelnik, "Populists and workers."
3. Sokolov, "Revoliutsionnaia propaganda," pp. 15-18; E. K. Pekarskii, "Rabochii P. Alekseev (iz vospominanii)," pp. 80-86.
4. A contemporary described Alekseev as having "the practicality of a peasant *muzhik* and a factory worker, knowing from which side to approach someone of his own milieu, and how to speak with him" (N. Volkhovskii, quoted in N. S. Karzhanskii, *Moskovskii tkach Petr Alekseev,* pp. 24, 34).
5. Zelnik, "Populists," pp. 264-66; nonetheless, the Saint Petersburg workers established a library fund based on monthly contributions from each worker, which later was used to provide mutual aid.
6. V. Burtsev, "Severnyi Soiuz Russkikh Rabochikh," pp. 174-93; cf. A. E. El'nitskii, *Pervye shagi rabochego dvizheniia v Rossii,* pp. 54-66. On the Union's activities in Moscow, see Sh. M. Levin, "Obshchestvennoe dvizhenie v Moskve v 1868-1882" [The social movement in Moscow in 1868-1882], in Akademiia nauk SSSR, *Istoriia Moskvy,* vol. 4, pp. 355-64.
7. In one instance, the group reestablished ties with a *kruzhok* that had been founded by Dolgushin's circle in 1874; its worker members had been meeting on their own, with no contact with the intelligentsia or revolutionary movement, for six years (N. Volkov, "Narodnicheskaia propaganda sredi moskovskikh rabochikh v 1881 g.," pp. 178-79).
8. G. V. Plekhanov, "Our Differences," in his *Selected Philosophical Works,* vol. 1, pp. 309-10.
9. The activities of this group are discussed in Iu. Z. Polevoi, *Zarozhdenie marksizma v Rossii,* pp. 337-49, and in P. S. Tkachenko, *Moskovskoe studenchestvo v obshchestvenno-politicheskoi zhizni Rossii vtoroi poloviny XIX veka,* pp. 264-68.
10. Polevoi, *Zarozhdenie,* pp. 343-44. The proclamation is thought to have been written by Ianovich, who was influenced by the Polish Social-Democratic organization "Proletariat"; that group had been especially successful in establishing ties between workers and intelligentsia and in organizing *kassy.*
11. Moiseenko, *Vospominaniia,* pp. 67-68. The ease with which Moiseenko and other known worker-agitators resumed revolutionary activity after arrest or exile is one of the remarkable features of this period. Cf. Zelnik, "Russian Bebels," p. 270.
12. S. I. Mitskevich, *Na grani dvukh epokh,* p. 154.

13. Report of police constable Nosov, Presnenskaia precinct, to Moscow Okhranka, April 1890, reprinted in *RD*, vol. 3, pt. 2, doc. 6, pp. 18-19.

14. R. A. Kazakevich, *Sotsial-demokraticheskie organizatsii Peterburga kontsa 80kh-nachala 90kh godov*, pp. 62-75.

15. Tochisskii himself, the son of a Polish officer in the Russian army, had worked in a metal plant and a railroad workshop before coming to Saint Petersburg, where he enrolled in the industrial academy of the Russian Technical Society (ibid., pp. 38-40).

16. TsGAOR, f. 102, op. 252, d. 13 (1892), pp. 17-33.

17. The fullest account of this period is that of S. I. Mitskevich, first published in 1906 as "Na zare rabochego dvizheniia v Moskve," in the confiscated *Tekushchii moment*, reprinted in Mitskevich, ed., *Na zare rabochego dvizheniia v Moskve*, pp. 1-28. A greatly expanded but perhaps less reliable version is Mitskevich's *Na grani dvukh epokh*.

18. S. I. Prokof'ev, "Iz perezhitogo" [From my past], in Mitskevich, *Na zare*, pp. 106-9.

19. Mitskevich, *Na zare*, p. 17. For an account of a far more ambitious and detailed program of study, cf. the outline compiled by Brusnev, which extended from reading and counting to chemistry, physics, Darwin's theory, the history of civilization, political economy, the history of social movements in Europe and Russia, etc. (reprinted in Richard Pipes, *Social Democracy and the St. Petersburg Labor Movement, 1885-1897*, pp. 29-30).

20. Mitskevich, *Na grani*, pp. 121, 137.

21. M. Liadov, "Kak zarodilas' Moskovskaia rabochaia organizatsiia" [How the Moscow workers' organization came into existence], in Mitskevich, *Na zare*, p. 45. The quotation is Liadov's paraphrase of a conversation he had with Krukovskii, who at the time was working as manager of a typical, and to Liadov shockingly exploitative, chemical plant.

22. Mitskevich, *Na grani*, pp. 193-94. Perhaps paradoxically, the Mitskevich group owed some of its earliest success to the fact that the police were preoccupied with populists in 1893-94 and paid little attention to Marxists (ibid., p. 136).

23. Ibid., p. 161.

24. M. P. Petrov, "Moi vospominaniia" [My recollections], in Mitskevich, *Na zare*, p. 184.´

25. Ia. G. Turkin, "Vospominaniia" [Recollections], in ibid. p. 201 (describing the mid-1880s).

26. Petrov, "Moi vospominaniia," p. 186.

27. Markov, *Na Presne*, pp. 5-8; Volynkin, "Iz vospominanii rabochego" [From the recollections of a worker], in Mitskevich, *Na zare*, p. 209.

28. See for example the recollections of Nemchinov, Volynkin, and Petrov, in Mitskevich, *Na zare*, pp. 159-60, 188, 209-10.

29. When Brusnev and several members of his group were arrested, populists at the Brest railroad helped to organize a collection for their families (E. Nemchinov, "Vospominaniia starogo rabochego" [Recollections of an old worker], in ibid., p. 160).

30. Liadov, in ibid., p. 57.

31. Mitskevich, *Na grani*, pp. 160-61. The other participants in this dispute have not commented on this aspect of the Central Workers' Circle (see

memoirs of A. Vinokurov, Sponti, Liadov, and Prokof'ev, in Mitskevich, *Na zare)*. On analogous disputes within newly formed Social-Democratic organizations in Saint Petersburg and other Russian cities, see Pipes, *Social Democracy*, pp. 90-91, 111-15, and Allan Wildman, *The Making of a Workers' Revolution*, chap. 4.

32. Mitskevich, *Na grani*, pp. 161-62.
33. TsGAOR, f. 102, op. 102, d. 12 (1891-95), pp. 131-33; cf. *RD*, vol. 4, pt. 1, doc. 32, pp. 90-101.
34. Mitskevich, *Na zare*, p. 21. In the 1937 version of his memoirs, Mitskevich omits mention of his own role in the preparation of "Ob agitatsii" and of the discussions he had with leaders of the Jewish agitation (*Na grani*, pp. 145-46, 163-65).
35. Wildman, *Workers' Revolution*, p. 28, describes the conversion to agitation as "a fundamental reorientation in outlook, habit of mind, and practical endeavor every bit as cataclysmic as the original conversion to Marxism itself."
36. Both leaflets are reprinted in Mitskevich, *Na grani*, pp. 146-47, 239. A much fuller compilation of the group's pamphlets and leaflets is *Literatura Moskovskogo Rabochego Soiuza*, ed. S. I. Mitskevich and N. P. Miliutin.
37. Mitskevich, *Na grani*, pp. 147-48. The Veikhelt works experienced a strike in April 1894, but available sources, though they attribute the strike to agitation, are unclear about the timing of Liadov's leaflet and do not indicate whether it played any part in the strike (see in particular the memoir of A. D. Karpuzi, a worker Social Democrat who was employed at Veikhelt at the time of the strike, in Mitskevich, *Na zare*, p. 198).
38. Reprinted in *RD*, vol. 4, pt. 1, doc. 22, pp. 56-59.
39. At the time of their arrest, Mitskevich and Sponti were preparing a brochure that spoke favorably of the two million votes received by the German Social Democrats. In his memoirs, Mitskevich rejects the suggestion that this implied approval of electoral tactics, and he notes that Engels had predicted that German workers would achieve power only through armed struggle; the Russian pamphlet, however, made no direct mention of such struggle (Mitskevich, *Na grani*, p. 190).
40. Ibid., p. 162.
41. TsGAOR, f. 102, op. 102, d. 12 (1891-95), p. 133; ibid., op. 252, d. 15 (1894), pp. 135-36. At Mitskevich's apartment the police found two pamphlets—Lenin's "Who are the 'Friends of the People'?" and Tolstoi's "The Kingdom of God is Within You"—both of them supposedly being prepared for publication.
42. *RD*, vol. 4, pt. 1, doc. 31, pp. 72-73.
43. Iu. Z. Polevoi, *Iz istorii Moskovskoi organizatsii VKP(b), 1894-1904*, p. 41. Sponti, who had been traveling in Western Europe at the time of the summer arrests, returned to Moscow in September and participated in the new union's activities until his arrest in December.
44. The pamphlet is reprinted in *RD*, vol. 4, pt. 1, doc. 31, pp. 72-89.
45. Reprinted in ibid., doc. 30, pp. 71-72.
46. Ibid., doc. 119, pp. 338-40, 844; at the same time a leaflet was issued explaining the significance of the commune and sketching (in a few

sentences) the history of European revolutionary movements since 1789. It stated that Russian workers were ready to respond whenever their foreign comrades should issue the call to revolution (ibid., pp. 340-41).

47. Ibid., docs. 123-25, pp. 343-48.

48. TsGAOR, f. 102, op. 252, d. 16 (1895-96), pp. 49-61; "Rabochee dvizhenie v Moskve," in the émigré journal *Rabotnik*, no. 3-4 (Geneva, 1897), reprinted in *RD*, vol. 4, pt. 1, doc. 152, pp. 399-404.

49. *RD*, vol. 4, pt. 1, doc. 152, p. 403.

50. Wildman, *Workers' Revolution*, pp. 102, 54-55, cites as evidence of "hostility to intelligentsia leadership" the fact that members of Prokof'-ev's *kruzhok* expressed unwillingness to participate in a mass meeting on May Day. They feared that such a public manifestation would lead to arrests and destruction of the union, and one month later their fears were realized.

51. Markov, *Na Presne*, is the history of one such *kruzhok* at the Prokhorov-skaia factory, whose activities lasted from 1895 to 1900.

52. Quoted by S. I. Chernomordik, "Osobennosti Moskovskogo sotsial-demokraticheskogo dvizheniia pered vtorym s'ezdom," p. 81.

53. TsGAOR, f. 102, op. 252, d. 16, pp. 53-59.

54. A police report of 12 March 1898 listed seven active members and twelve sympathizers. All were *intelligenty*, and only two of them, the brothers Aleksandr and Viktor Vanovskii, had been active in any previous propaganda organization (*RD*, vol. 4, pt. 2, doc. 14, pp. 62-66).

55. Ibid., doc. 17, pp. 70-72.

56. See the police report of June 1900 and the report published in the émigré journal *Rabochee delo*, April 1900, both reprinted in ibid., docs. 88-89, pp. 287-94.

57. L. S. Tsetlin, "V Moskve pered II s'ezdom RSDRP," pp. 89-90.

58. S. Bleklov, "Obrazovatel'nye uchrezhdeniia dlia rabochikh goroda Moskvy," p. 125 ff. On radical influence in one school program, the "Prechistenskii courses," see Jeremiah Schneiderman, *Sergei Zubatov and Revolutionary Marxism*, pp. 91-92.

59. Mitskevich, *Na grani*, pp. 152, 102-3; in contrast to these "advanced" workers, Mitskevich describes F. I. Poliakov as the son of a weaver, with a weakness for drink and a tendency to get into fights and scandals—a typical factory hand who enjoyed great popularity among the textile workers (ibid., p. 153).

60. On Zubatov's activities in Moscow, see Schneiderman, *Sergei Zubatov*, expecially pp. 51-55, 77-82.

61. One example of this phenomenon was the metalworker Z. Ia. Litvin (Sedov), who helped to establish a Social-Democratic organization in Kolomna after being banished from Moscow (V. Maksimovskii, "Nach-alo Kolomenskoi organizatsii [RSDRP]," in *Rabochie o 1905 gode v Moskovskoi gubernii*, ed. E. Popova, pp. 107-9). Cf. F. M. Suslova, "Peterburgskie stachki 1895-96 gg: ikh vliianie na razvitie massovogo rabochego dvizheniia" [The Petersburg strikes of 1895-96: Their influence on the development of a mass workers' movement], in *Istoriia rabochego klassa Leningrada*, ed. V. A. Ovsiankin, vol. 2, pp. 85-91.

Chapter Seven

1. The work was published under the joint auspices of the Central Archival Administration and the Academy of Sciences of the USSR. It consists of four volumes, each in two parts. The editor in chief of volumes 1–3 was A. M. Pankratova; of volume 4, L. M. Ivanov.

2. *RD*, vol. 4, pt. 1, p. xxi: "The work is intended for scholars, teachers in higher and secondary schools, university students in history, lecturers, propagandists. . . ."

3. I examined the archival documents for approximately 10 percent of the incidents listed in Moscow city and province in the period from 1880 to 1900. Reginald Zelnik, who has worked more extensively in the archives from which the *Rabochee dvizhenie* series was compiled, reports finding "no substantial differences" between the picture of the labor movement in the published documents and that found in unpublished records ("Soviet Materials on Industrial Workers and the Labor Question in the 1870's and 1880's," p. 13).

4. On the tendency of some police officials to exaggerate subversion in order to inflate their own role of surveillance, see E. K. Barshtein, "Istochniki TsGIAM po istorii rabochego dvizheniia i metody ikh ispol'-zovaniia," pp. 38-50.

5. *RD*, vol. 4, pt. 1, pp. xxvii, xxix-xxx.

6. D. P. Poida, "Krest'ianskoe dvizhenie v Rossii v 1881-1889 gg.," pp. 119-20; B. G. Litvak, "Krest'ianskoe dvizhenie v Rossii v 1861-1869 gg.," pp. 166-69.

7. Roughly half of all chronicle entries for Moscow for the period from 1880 to 1890 were drawn from the Gosudarstvennyi Arkhiv Moskovskoi Oblasti (now known as the Tsentral'nyi Gosudarstvennyi Arkhiv goroda Moskvy).

8. S. Gvozdev, *Zapiski fabrichnogo inspektora, 1894-1906*, pp. 180-85.

9. This problem is discussed with reference to a somewhat later period by L. I. Leskova, "K voprosu o metodike statisticheskogo izucheniia rabochego dvizheniia v Rossii na primere Urala 1910-1914 gg.," in *Bol'shevistskaia pechat' i rabochii klass Rossii v gody revoliutsionnogo pod'ema 1910-1914*, ed. L. M. Ivanov, pp. 341-46.

10. For many cases the information in the chronicle is incomplete. For this reason, the number of cases in my statistical computations is not always 452. The chronicle also provides detailed information about conspiratorial activities of the Social-Democratic underground. Such cases (secret meetings, leaflets, and publications) have been included in the data file only when they were shown to involve workers from a specific factory.

11. Two other chronicles were prepared in prerevolutionary times: V. E. Varzar, *Statisticheskie svedeniia o stachkakh na fabrikakh i zavodakh za desiatiletie 1895-1904 g.*, and S. N. Prokopovich, "K bibliografii stachechnogo dvizheniia v Rossii." The former work is based on evidence supplied to the Ministry of Trade and Industry by factory inspectors; the latter publication lists contemporary accounts that appeared in the legal press. Varzar identified 74 strikes in Moscow in the years 1885-

1900, compared to 147 in the *Rabochee dvizhenie* and 15 listed by Prokopovich.

12. On unrest in the time of serfdom, see A. M. Pankratova's introductory article in *RD*, vol. 1, pt. 1; cf. M. I. Tugan-Baranovskii, *The Russian Factory in the 19th Century*, pp. 111-31. One of the greatest disturbances in Moscow in preemancipation times took place at the Kupavna silk factory in Bogorodskii county in 1794, when workers, protesting against the imposition of nonindustrial (agricultural) tasks, sent written petitions to the Moscow procurator-general, elected delegates to deal with authorities, and kept up a united front in the face of military intervention (V. A. Kondrat'ev and V. I. Nevzorov, eds., *Iz istorii fabrik i zavodov Moskvy*, p. 21).

13. A. S. Trofimov, *Rabochee dvizhenie v Rossii, 1861-1894 gg.*, pp. 57, 72, 102.

14. Varzar, *Statisticheskie Svendeniia*, app., tables 1, 3.

15. The Russian language has two terms for work stoppages: *stachka* and *zabastovka*. In the original coding, I made a distinction between the two, but an examination of the data disclosed no differences between them, so the categories were merged.

16. The Konshin strike in Serpukhov in January 1897 was one in which such pressure was important (*RD*, vol. 4, pt. 1, doc. 230, pp. 625-32).

17. E.g., TsGAOR, f. 102, 2 del-vo, op. 52, d. 26:5 (1895), pp. 10-12.

18. Indirect support for this suggestion can be found in vital statistics for Moscow province. Local officials noted that the rate of marriage rose and fell as the national economy prospered or declined; unlike other provinces, where agricultural prices were the best predictor of marriage trends, Moscow recorded more marriages in years of full employment and fewer marriages in years when the factories were laying off workers. The rate of marriage was extremely low in the first seven months of 1885 but rose significantly from August to November (I. I. Kurkin, *Statistika dvizheniia naseleniia v Moskovskoi gubernii v 1883-1897 gg.*, pp. 32-34, 45.

19. Unfortunately, most available year-to-year indexes describe nationwide trends, and these may not always reflect the local patterns of a city or province such as Moscow. The only exception I have been able to locate is Gil'bert's statistics on the work force at the Tsindel' mill, which suggest that economic recovery began a little earlier there than in Russia as a whole.

20. Richard Robbins, *Famine in Russia, 1891-92*, pp. 185, 195.

21. Possibly, too, the Moscow police were being especially attentive to the workers' moods in the aftermath of the Morozov incident. Note that the years 1885-86 saw the greatest concentration of *volneniia* in the entire twenty-one-year period. This may mean that local officials were reporting rumors and rumblings among the workers that would have been ignored in earlier years.

22. The difficulties presented by the sources are illustrated by the documents in *RD*, vol. 4, pt. 1, docs. 230-32, pp. 625-34, dealing with the Konshin strike in Serpukhov, 1897. A small group of workers began by demanding that wages be restored to their earlier levels. When members of this group were arrested (charged with drunkenness and disorderly conduct), the entire work force of six thousand went on strike. A fac-

tory inspector spoke with the crowd at the factory gates and took down a list of twelve complaints; after investigating these, he found most to be unfounded. The most serious and justified complaints, according to the inspector, were those dealing with wage reductions, but the basic cause of these—dislocations caused by the introduction of a shorter work day with two shifts—was not mentioned by the workers at any time.

23. The end of a strike is often harder to pinpoint. During the Morozov strike of 1885, workers began to return to the factory after seven days, but two more weeks elapsed before the work force was back to full strength (Trofimov, *Rabochee dvizhenie v Rossii*, pp. 139–41).

24. In strikes where offensive demands were mentioned, the average number of participants was 485; when defensive ones appeared, the average was 556.

25. In the years 1880-94, 11 percent of all strikes lasted three days or more; in the years 1895-1900, the figure was 22 percent.

26. For all strikes lasting one full day or less, the ratio of defensive to offensive demands was 0.57:1; for those of more than one day's duration, it was 0.74:1.

27. Varzar, *Statisticheskie svedeniia*, p. 40. Comparing my data file to Varzar's figures, Moscow's strikes appear to be of much shorter duration than those in other localities. By his computations, 19 percent of all strikes in Russia (1895-1900) lasted ten days or more, whereas the Moscow data file shows only 1.5 percent of cases lasting that number of days. The discrepancy is partially explained by the fact that Varzar's figures came from reports of the factory inspectors and are therefore more likely to exclude shorter strikes and small, out-of-the-way enterprises. It is also possible that, because they had had more experience dealing with labor unrest, Moscow employers and officials were able to deal with them more expeditiously. Even so, the Moscow workers appear to have shown less perseverence than those in other parts of Russia.

28. My calculation, from *RD*, vol. 4, pt. 2, pp. 695-842 (chronicle of events, 1895-1900).

29. Varzar, *Statisticheskie svedeniia* app., pp. 10-11, concluded that there were twenty-four "collective" strikes in Moscow in the years 1895-1900, including twenty-one in the cotton industry and three in metals. His only criterion seems to have been simultaneity; by this criterion, 60 percent of all the strikes in Russia in the years 1895-1904 were collective (ibid., pp. 21-24). Only rarely, as in the case of the Saint Petersburg textile strike of 1896, did workers from separate enterprises present a united front and common demands. Moscow experienced no collective strikes of this kind in the years under consideration.

30. Trofimov, *Rabochee dvizhenie v Rossii*, pp. 111-13.

31. TsGAM, f. 16, op. 76, d. 132 (1886), pp. 26-28, 31-32.

32. For example, a threatening letter was sent to the manager of the Butiugin textile mill in Moscow, threatening a repetition of worker violence "as at Tsindel'," a neighboring factory where a recent strike had caused considerable property damage (TsGAOR, f. 63, op. 7, d. 276, [1894], p. 1).

33. *RD*, vol. 4, pt. 1, docs. 122, 235, pp. 343, 642.

34. In a strike at the Reutovskaia cotton mill in Moskovskii county, June 1895,

the police arrested at least ten workers from five major textile factories in Moscow and Vladimir provinces (ibid., doc. 25, p. 65).

35. A. S. Trofimov, "Rabochee dvizhenie v Moskve i Moskovskoi gubernii vo vtoroi polovine 80kh godov," pp. 106, 108.
36. TsGAM, f. 16, op. 76, d. 132 (1886), especially pp. 68–69; cf. Gvozdev, *Zapiski*, p. 217.
37. *RD*, vol. 4, pt. 1, doc. 31, pp. 87–88.
38. A. N. Bykov, *Fabrichnoe zakonodatel'stvo i razvitie ego v Rossii*, p. 173; cf. Theodore Von Laue, "Russian Peasants in the Factory," p. 72 ff. Von Laue used the Tsindel' strike of 1894, one of the few violent episodes in Moscow, as a basis for generalization about the nature of the workers' movement and outlook.
39. TsGAOR, f. 102, 3 del-vo, d. 89: 19 (1888), p. 10.
40. Trofimov, *Rabochee dvizhenie v Rossii*, p. 154.
41. *RD*, vol. 3, pt. 1, doc. 77, pp. 308–9; vol. 4, pt. 1, docs. 21, 139, 236, pp. 53–56, 367–70, 640–43; vol. 4, pt. 2, doc. 154, p. 488; Trofimov, "Rabochee dvizhenie v Moskve," p. 108; Gvozdev, *Zapiski*, pp. 196–98 (Gvozdev reports that he never encountered violence in fifteen years as a factory inspector in central Russia).
42. A typical example of official thinking was a circular letter of the Moscow chief of police (*ober-politseimeister*), July 1884, which advised local police to keep track of the mood at factories; if unrest appeared to be brewing, they should intervene at once to remove ("by explanations and suggestions") the cause of discontent and "eliminate every effort toward corporate action by the workers" (TsGAM, f. 46, op. 2, d. 1472 [1884–85], p. 66). Cf. Gaston V. Rimlinger, "The Management of Labor Protest in Tsarist Russia, 1870–1905."
43. TsGAM, f. 46, op. 2, d. 1472 (1884–85), p. 8.
44. Trofimov, *Rabochee dvizhenie v Rossii*, p. 146 (citing the strike at the Izmailovskaia cotton-spinning mill, January 1885).
45. Ibid., p. 158; *RD*, vol. 3, pt. 2, doc. 77, pp. 308–9; vol. 4, pt. 1, docs. 152, 230, 234, pp. 396–415, 625–32, 636–37; vol. 4, pt. 2, doc. 84, pp. 280–83.
46. G. V. Pronina, "Iz istorii rabochego dvizheniia v Moskve i Moskovskoi gubernii v pervoi polovine 90kh godov XIX veka," p. 178.
47. *RD*, vol. 2, pt. 2, doc. 298, p. 563; vol. 3, pt. 1, doc. 77, p. 310; vol. 4, pt. 1, docs. 21, 122, 132, 230, pp. 53–56, 343, 356–58, 625–32.

Conclusion

1. An interesting intermediate case between the Western and Russian patterns of industrialization was Upper Silesia, whose labor-recruitment patterns are analyzed by Lawrence Schofer, *The Formation of a Modern Labor Force;* especially chap. 4.
2. L. Comitas, "Occupational Multiplicity in Rural Jamaica," pp. 157–73.
3. For specific examples, see Paul L. Doughty, "Behind the Back of the City: Provincial Life in Lima, Peru"; Leonard Plotnicov, "Rural-Urban Communications in Contemporary Nigeria," p. 81.

4. Frantz Fanon, *The Wretched of the Earth*, pp. 101–7.
5. Amilcar Cabral, "Brief Analysis of the Social Structure in Guinea," pp. 46–61.
6. Eric Wolf, *Peasant Wars of the 20th Century*, p. 291 ff.
7. Ibid., p. 292. Cf. Anthony Giddens, *The Class Structure of Advanced Societies*, pp. 116–17. Giddens, attempting to explain the sources of revolutionary consciousness, emphasizes "relativity of experience within a given system of production . . . a framework by reference to which individuals can distance their experience from the here-and-now." Workers whose labor conditions remain unchanged over long periods of time, he argues, are less likely to attain such consciousness, which is more likely to be linked to "groupings on the fringes of 'incorporation' . . . (e.g., peasants whose traditional mode of production has been undermined). . . ."
8. See for example Iu. Kharitonova and D. Shcherbakov, *Krest'ianskoe dvizhenie v Kaluzhskoi gubernii (1861–1917 gg.)*, pp. 64, 72, 80, 82, 90, 106, 116.
9. S. I. Antonova, *Vliianie Stolypinskoi agrarnoi reformy na izmeneniia v sostave rabochego klassa*, p. 194.
10. Allan Wildman concludes his study of Russian social democracy and the labor movement in the 1890s by describing the "Marxist intelligentsia's alienation from the class it purported to lead" (Allan Wildman, *The Making of a Workers' Revolution*, p. 251). Leopold Haimson has suggested that the gap between workers and educated society widened significantly in the years 1905–14 (Leopold Haimson, "The Problem of Social Stability in Urban Russia, 1905–1914," pp. 16–17).

Bibliography

Of all the sources I consulted for this study, a few deserve particular mention. First in importance were statistical publications: the national census of 1897 (Tsentral'nyi Statisticheskii Komitet [Central Statistical Committee], *Pervaia Vseobshchaia perepis' naseleniia Rossiiskoi imperii* [First general census of the population of the Russian empire]); the municipal censuses of Moscow for the years 1871 (Moscow, Stolichnyi i gubernskii statisticheskii komitet [Metropolitan and provincial statistical committee], *Statisticheskie svendeniia o zhiteliakh goroda Moskvy: Po perepisi 12 dekabria 1871 g.* [Statistical data on the occupants of the city of Moscow: According to the census of December 12, 1871]), 1882 (*Perepis' Moskvy 1882 goda* [Census of Moscow, 1882]), and 1902 (*Perepis' Moskvy 1902 goda* [Census of Moscow, 1902]); and the factory statistics published by the Moscow provincial zemstvo in the early 1880s (*Sbornik statisticheskikh svedenii* [Collection of statistical information], vols. 3, 4). The latter were compiled through firsthand investigations of almost all major industrial enterprises in the province; the results were published county-by-county in seventeen lengthy installments and summarized in two thick tomes, making a total of more than five thousand pages of information. Some of the statisticians' conclusions can be disputed, and some of their methods can be questioned, but the value of their evidence is indisputable; where defects exist, simple statistical manipulations can often be devised to overcome them.

A second major source of information was the records of the tsarist government, especially the police and the factory inspectorate. I was fortunate to be able to examine some of these records in the archives, but I have also relied on Soviet documentary publications. The multivolume *Rabochee dvizhenie v Rossii v XIX veke* [The workers' movement in Russia in the 19th century], edited by Pankratova and Ivanov, was especially useful; its strengths and weaknesses I have discussed in Chapter Seven.

Memoir literature is another important source of information, though far less abundant than the others. Few workers left written records of their lives, and of these, only a handful wrote in any detail about their experiences. In this category, the publications edited by S. I. Mitskevich in the early 1930s (*Na zare rabochego dvizheniia v Moskve* [On the eve of the workers' movement in Moscow] and *Literatura Moskovskogo Rabochego Soiuza* [Literature of the Moscow Workers' Union]) are especially useful, as they offer a wide range of memoirs and documents from the 1890s.

The list that follows includes all works cited in the text, as well as a selection of specialized works dealing with aspects of factory life and the workers' movement. This is in no sense a comprehensive list; a more comprehensive bibliography on the topic is *Oblik proletariata Rossii: Bibliografiia* [The outlook of the Russian proletariat: A bibliography], edited by Iu. N. Kirianov and P. V. Pronina.

For the convenience of the nonspecialist, English translations of Russian works have been cited in the bibliography and notes whenever possible.

Archival Sources

Tsentral'nyi Gosudarstvennyi Arkhiv goroda Moskvy
[Central State Archive of the city of Moscow]

Fond 16, Kantseliariia Moskovskogo General-Gubernatora [Office of the Moscow Governor-General]. Opis' 76, delo 132 (1886), "Po prosheniiam rabochikh fabrik i zavodov, s zhaloboiu na nepravil'nye deistviia ikh khoziaev . . ." [Workers' petitions, with complaints against improper actions of their employers].

Fond 17, Kantseliariia Moskovskogo Gubernatora [Office of the Governor of Moscow]. Opis' 77, delo 125 (1895), "Po otnosheniiu Nachal'nika Moskovskogo Gubernskogo Zhandarmskogo Upravleniia ob antisanitarnom sostoianii pomeshchenii na fabrikakh Zavodskogo i Popova [Report of the Chief of Moscow Gendarmes on the unsanitary condition of the premises of the Zavodskii-Popov factory]; opis' 77, delo 569 (1898), "Po predstavleniiu Dmitrovskogo Zemskogo Upravleniia o nepravomernom prieme maloletnikh na rabotu" [Representations of the Dmitrovskii Zemstvo Directorate on improper hiring of minors]; opis' 77, delo 864 (1901), "Po otnosheniiu Starshego Fabrichnogo Inspektora o nedorazumenii na fabrike Danilovskoi manufaktury" [Senior Factory Inspector's memorandum on misunderstanding at the Danilov factory].

Fond 46, Kantseliariia Moskovskogo Ober-Politsei–meistera [Office of Mos-

196 Bibliography

cow Police Chief]. Opis' 2, delo 1511 (1894), "O nakazanii rabochikh na fabrike Torgovogo Doma Karl Til' i Ko" [On punishment of workers at the Karl Til' firm]; opis' 2, delo 1472 (1884-85), "Perepiska Moskovskogo General-Gubernatora s politsei-meisterami 2-go i 3-go otdelenii i chastnymi pristavami o zabastovkakh . . . na fabrikakh Giubnera, Ganeshinykh, na zavode Malkievykh i dr" [Correspondence between Moscow Governor-General and local police officials concerning strikes at various factories].

Tsentral'nyi Gosudarstvennyi Arkhiv Oktiabr'skoi Revoliutsii [Central State Archive of the October Revolution]

Fond 63, Moskovskoe Okhrannoe Otdelenie [Moscow secret police (Okhranka)]. Opis' 7, delo 363 (1893), "O stachke rabochikh na Moskovsko-Kurskoi zheleznoi doroge" [On a strike by workers of the Moscow-Kursk railroad]; opis' 7, delo 124 (1893) and 126 (1894), "O litsakh uvolennykh s fabrik i zavodov za raznye prostupki" [On persons dismissed from factories and plants for various offenses]; opis' 7, delo 256 (1894), "O besporiadkakh uchrezhdennykh v 1894 g. rabochimi na fabrike Tsindel' v Moskve" [On disorders at the Tsindel' factory in Moscow in 1894]; opis' 7, delo 276 (1894), "O besporiadkakh na fabrike Butiugina" [On disorders at the Butiugin factory]; opis' 7, delo 121 (1893), "O byvshem artel'shchike Liapinskoi birzhevoi arteli D. M. Andreeve" [On the former head of the Liapin artel]; opis' 7, delo 774 (1890), "O stachke arteli rabochikh podriadchika Girsha" [On a strike by an artel of workers against the contractor Girsh].

Fond 102, Departament Politsii [Police Department]. 2-e deloproizvodstvo, delo 34:5 (1892), 61:8 (1893), 51:2 (1894), 26:2 (1895), 15:16 (1896), "O besporiadkakh i zabastovkakh po Moskovskoi gubernii" [On strikes and disorders in Moscow province]; opis' 52, delo 26:5, "O besporiadkakh sredi rabochikh v masterskikh Moskovsko-Riazanskoi zheleznoi dorogi v Moskve, II/95" [On disorders among workers in the workshops of the Moscow-Riazan' railroad in Moscow, February 1895]; 3-e deloproizvodstvo, delo 21:5 (1887), "O besporiadkakh sredi rabochikh na Reutovskoi manufakture (Mazurina), Moskovskii uezd" [On disorders among workers at the Reutov factory in Moskovskii county]; 3-e deloproizvodstvo, delo 88:35 (1888), 59:45 (1885), 9:46 (1887), 89:19 (1888), 47:12 (1890), 44:26 (1891), 152:35 (1893), 121:1A (1900), "Ezhegodnyi politicheskii obzor Moskovskoi gubernii" [Annual political review of Moscow province for 1883, 1884, 1886, 1887, 1889, 1890, 1892, 1899]; 3-e deloproizvodstvo, delo 606:2 and 606:3 (1896), "O volneniiakh i stachkakh sredi fabrichnykh rabochikh v raznykh mestnostiakh" [On disturbances and strikes among factory workers in various localities]; 4-e deloproizvodstvo, delo 121:1 (1908), "O kooperativnom dvizhenii" [On the cooperative movement]; 4-e deloproizvodstvo, delo 121:2 (1908), "Spisok potrebitel'nykh obshchestv, artelei . . . i drugikh uchrezhdenii etogo tipa" [List of consumer societies, artels . . . and other organizations of this type]; 4-e deloproizvodstvo, delo 42:2 (1913), "Po Moskovskoi gubernii: Rabochee dvizhenie na fabrikakh, zavodakh, masterskikh. . ." [Around Moscow province: The workers' movement at factories, plants, workshops . . .]; opis' 102, delo 11 (1890), 12 (1891-95), "Vsepoddanneishie doklady Ministra Vnutrennikh Del" [Confidential reports of Minister of Internal Affairs]; opis' 168, delo 29 (1896), "Ezhenedel'nye zapiski" [Weekly memoranda]; opis' 252, delo 11 (1890), 12 (1891), 13 (1892), 15 (1894), 16 (1895-96), "Obzor i vedomost' doznanii, proizvodivshikhsia v Zhandarmskikh Upravleniiakh Imperii po gosudarstvennym prestupleniiam" [Annual summary and register of Gendarme Departments' investigations of treasonous crimes].

Tsentral'nyi Gosudarstvennyi Istoricheskii Arkhiv,
Leningrad [Central State Historical Archive,
Leningrad]

Fond 20, Ministerstvo Finansov, Departament Torgovli i Manufaktur [Ministry of Finance, Department of Trade and Manufactures]. Opis' 3, delo 1914 (1899-1903), "O peredache v vendenie Ministerstva Finansov shtrafnogo kapitala dlia vspomoshchestvovaniia rabochim" [On the transfer to the Ministry of Finance of capital from fines (levied by employers) for assistance to workers]; opis' 5, delo 760, "Po khodataistvam ob utverzhdenii obshchestv vzaimopomoshchi (1897-1900)" [Petitions for approval of mutual aid societies]; opis' 13, delo 113 ". . . o nepreryvnosti rabot. . . na zavode Tovarishchestva Moskovskogo Metallicheskogo Zavoda, 1899" [On the round-the-clock operation of the Moscow Metal Company plant]; opis' 13A, delo 26, "O Samsonevskoi manufakture, 1891-93" [On the Samson factory, 1891-93]; opis' 13A, delo 80, "Kopii zhurnal'nykh postanovlenii Moskovskogo Stolichnogo Prisutstviia, 1900-1901" [Copies of the decisions of the Moscow Office of Factory-and-Plant Affairs]; opis' 13A, delo 183, "Postanovleniia Moskovskogo prisutstviia o vrachebnoi pomoshchi rabochim" [Decisions of the Moscow Office on medical care for workers]; opis' 13A, delo 205, "Postanovleniia Moskovskogo prisutstviia po voprosam ob organizatsii vrachebnoi pomoshchi na raznykh fabrikakh i zavodakh" [Decisions of the Moscow Office on the organization of medical services at various factories and plants]; opis' 15, delo 132, "O shtrafakh, nalozhennykh fabrikantami Moskovskoi gubernii na rabochikh, 1886-88" [On fines, imposed on workers by factory owners, in Moscow province, 1886-88]; opis' 15, delo 135, "Otchety o deiatel'nosti fabrichnykh inspektorov Kievskoi i Vladimirskoi gubernii 1886-1891" [Reports on the activities of factory inspectors of Kiev and Vladimir provinces, 1886-91]; opis' 15, delo 860, "Raznaia perepiska s fabrichnymi inspektorami" [Miscellaneous correspondence with factory inspectors].

Fond 22, Ministerstvo Torgovli i Promyshlennosti, Departament Torgovli i Promyshlennosti [Ministry of Trade and Industry, Department of Trade and Industry]. Opis' 1, delo 219, ". . . o narushenii Ustava o Promyshlennosti na fabrike br. K. i P. Marinichevykh, 1899-1900. . ." [On violation of the Industrial Code at the factory of the brothers K. and P. Marinichev,

1899-1900]; opis' 1, delo 249, "Po prosheniiu t-va Moskovskogo Metal-licheskogo Zavoda o razreshenii proizvodit' raschet s rabochimi tem-zhe poriadkom, kak eto praktikovalos' do perekhoda zavoda v vedenie fabri-chnoi inspektsii" [Petition of the management of the Moscow Metal Works to continue paying workers in the same manner in which they were paid before the plant came under the supervision of the factor inspectorate]; opis' 1, delo 352, "O razreshenii Kolomenskomu mashinostroitel'nomu zavodu otpuskat' v kredit rabochim . . . obuv', rukovitsy, chulki" [On granting permission to the Kolomna machine-building works to sell various goods to workers on credit]; opis' 1, delo 912, "O narushenii Ustava o Promyshlennosti na fabrike kompanii Bogorodsko-Glukhovskoi manufak-tury" [On violation of the Industrial Code at the factory of the Bogorodsko-Glukhovskaia manufactory]; opis' 1, delo 1094, "O nalozhenii na zavedy-vaiushchikh fabrichnymi promyshlennymi zavedeniiami vzyskanii za narushenie Ustava o Promyshlennosti" [On levying of fines against opera-tors of industrial establishments for violation of the Industrial Code]; opis' 5, delo 232, "Glavnoe po Fabrichnym Delam Prisutstvie" [Central Board on Factory Affairs—untitled folder]; opis' 16, delo 59, "Svedenie o kolichestve rabochikh v Moskve, Sankt-Peterburge, 1908-1909" [Informa-tion of the number of workers in Moscow and Saint Petersburg, 1908-9].

Fond 23, Ministerstvo Torgovli i Promyshlennosti [Ministry of Trade and Industry]. Opis' 17, delo 311, "O zabastovkakh, stachkakh v Moskovskoi gubernii, 1895-1913" [On strikes and work stoppages in Moscow province, 1895-1913]; opis' 17, delo 528, "O tsenakh na glavneishie predmety potrebleniia fabrichnogo naseleniia" [On prices of main consumer items for the factory population]; opis' 24, delo 1171, "Ob ustroistve spalen dlia maloletnikh rabochikh na rogozhnoi fabrike Miasnitskogo" [On construc-tion of sleeping quarters for minors at the Miasnitskii bast-matting factory].

Fond 1284, Ministerstvo Vnutrennikh Del, Departament Obshchikh Del [Ministry of Internal Affairs, Department of General Affairs]. Opis' 188, delo 17, "O razreshenii sozyva raznykh s'ezdov" [On permission for holding various meetings].

Fond 1287, Ministerstvo Vnutrennikh Del, Khoziaistvennyi Departament [Ministry of Internal Affairs, Economic Department]. Opis' 9, delo 2555, "Po ustavu obshchestva potrebitelei pri fabrike Prokhorovskoi manufak-tury" [On the charter of the consumer society of the Prokhorov factory]; opis' 9, delo 2643, "Po ustavu obshchestva potrebitelei sluzhashchikh na Moskovsko-Riazanskoi zheleznoi doroge" [On the charter of the consumer society of clerks of the Moscow-Riazan railroad]; opis' 9, delo 2671, "Ob utverzhdenii ustava obshchestva vzaimopomoshchi Moskovsko-Nizhegorod-skoi zheleznoi dorogi" [On approval of the charter of the mutual-aid society of the Moscow-Nizhnii Novgorod railroad].

Fond 1288, Ministerstvo Vnutrennikh Del, Khoziaistvennyi Departament [Ministry of Internal Affairs, Economic Department]. Opis' 15:5, delo 90 (1903), "Ob utverzhdenii proekta ustava kassy na fabrikakh Zuevskoi manufaktury I. N. Zimina" [On approval of proposed charter of an aid society at the Zuevo factory of I. N. Zimin]; opis' 15:7, delo 75 (1904), "Ob utverzhdenii ustava sberegatel'noi i ssudo-sberegatel'noi kassy na fabrike Riabovskoi manufaktury" [On approval of the charter of the savings-and-loan association at the Riabov factory].

Published Sources

Ainzaft, S. "Byli li kassy vzaimopomoshchi odnim iz istochnikov rossiiskogo professional'nogo dvizheniia?" [Were mutual aid associations a source of the Russian trade-union movement?]. *Materialy po istorii professional'-nogo dvizheniia* [Materials on the history of the trade-union movement] 2 (1924):74-101.

Akademiia nauk SSSR, Institut istorii [Academy of sciences of the USSR, Institute of history]. *Istoriia Moskvy* [History of Moscow]. 6 vols. Moscow, 1952-59.

Alexander, John T. "Catherine II, Bubonic Plague, and Industry in Moscow." *American Historical Review* 79 (1974):637-71.

Anderson, Barbara Ann. "Internal Migration in a Modernizing Society: The Case of Late 19th Century Russia." Ph.D. dissertation, Princeton University, 1974.

Anfimov, A. M. *Zemel'naia arenda v Rossii v nachale XX veka* [Land rent in Russia at the beginning of the 20th century]. Moscow, 1961.

Antonova, S. I. *Vliianie Stolypinskoi agrarnoi reformy na izmeneniia v sostave rabochego klassa (po materialam Moskovskoi gubernii, 1906-1913 gg.)* [The influence of the Stolypin agrarian reform on changes in the composition of the working class (based on materials from Moscow province, 1906-1913)]. Moscow, 1951.

Artemenkov, M. N. "Naemnye rabochie Moskovskikh manufaktur v 40-70kh godakh XVIII veka" [Wage laborers of Moscow manufactories in the '40s-'70s of the 18th century]. *Istoriia SSSR*, March-April 1964, pp. 133-144.

Ashukin, N. S., comp. *Ushedshaia Moskva: Vospominaniia sovremennikov o Moskve vtoroi poloviny XIX veka* [Bygone Moscow: Recollections of contemporaries about Moscow in the second half of the 19th century]. Moscow, 1964.

Babushkin, I. V. *Recollections of I. V. Babushkin.* Moscow, 1958.

Baker, Anita B. "Deterioration or Development: The Peasant Economy of Moscow Province Prior to 1914." *Russian History* 5 (1978):1-23.

Balabanov, M. *Ocherki po istorii rabochego klassa v Rossii* [Essays on the history of the working class in Russia]. 3 vols. 2d rev. ed. Moscow, 1925.

Barshtein, E. K. "Istochniki TsGIAM po istorii rabochego dvizheniia i metody ikh ispolzovaniia" [Sources in TsGIAM on the history of the workers' movement and methods of using them]. *Voprosy arkhivovedeniia* [Questions of archival science], 1959, no. 1, pp. 38-50.

Baykov, Alexander. "The Economic Development of Russia." *Economic History Review*, 2d ser. 8 (1954):137-49.

Bedi, R. E. *Theory, History and Practice of Cooperation*. New Delhi: National Cooperative Printing Press, 1958.

Bendix, Reinhard. *Work and Authority in Industry*. 2d ed. Berkeley and Los Angeles: University of California Press, 1974.

Benet, Sula, ed. *The Village of Viriatino: An Ethnographic Study of a Russian Village from before the Revolution to the Present*. New York: Doubleday, 1970.

Bill, Valentine T. *The Forgotten Class: The Russian Bourgeoisie from the Earliest Beginnings to 1900*. New York: Praeger, 1959.

Blackwell, William. *The Beginnings of Russian Industrialization: 1800-1861*. Princeton: Princeton University Press, 1968.

Bleklov, S. "Obrazovatel'nye uchrezhdeniia dlia rabochikh goroda Moskvy" [Educational institutions for workers of Moscow city]. *Russkaia mysl'* [Russian thought], May 1904, pp. 121-45.

Bonner, Arnold. *British Cooperation*. 2d. ed., rev. Manchester: Cooperative Union, 1970.

Borzunov, B. F. "Dogovory podriadchikov s rabochimi kak istoricheskii istochnik" [Contractors' agreements with workers as a historical source]. *Istoricheskii arkhiv*, September-October 1962, pp. 189-97.

Burtsev, V. "Severnyi Soiuz Russkikh Rabochikh" [The Northern Union of Russian Workers]. *Byloe*, Saint Petersburg, 1906, no. 1, pp. 174-93.

Bykov, A. N. *Fabrichnoe zakonodatel'stvo i razvitie ego v Rossii* [Factory legislation and its development in Russia]. Saint Petersburg, 1909.

Cabral, Amilcar. "Brief Analysis of the Social Structure in Guinea." In *Revolution in Guinea: An African People's Struggle*. London: Stage 1, 1969.

Chekhov, Anton. "Peasants." In *The Oxford Chekhov*, translated by Ronald Hingley. London: Oxford University Press, 1965.

Chernomordik, S. I. "Osobennosti moskovskogo sotsial-demokraticheskogo dvizheniia pered vtorym s'ezdom" [Features of the Moscow Social-Democratic movement before the second congress]. *Katorga i ssylka* 114-15 (1935):80-88.

Comitas, L. "Occupational Multiplicity in Rural Jamaica." In *Work and Family Life: West Indian Perspectives*, edited by L. Comitas and D. Lowenthal. New York: Doubleday Anchor, 1974.

Dement'ev, E. M. *Fabrika, chto ona daet naseleniiu i chto ona u nego beret* [The factory: What it gives the population and what it takes from it]. Moscow, 1893.

Dmitriev, K. *Professional'noe dvizhenie i soiuzy v Rossii* [The labor movement and unions in Russia]. 2d ed. Saint Petersburg, 1909.

Dmitriev, S. S. "Ob izuchenii dokumentov po istorii rabochego dvizheniia Rossii v XIX v." [On studying documents on the history of the workers' movement in Russia in the 19th century]. *Voprosy istorii*, July 1953, pp. 131-37.

Dostoyevsky, Fyodor [Dostoevski, Fëdor]. *Crime and Punishment.* New York: Random House, Modern Library, 1950.

Doughty, Paul L. "Behind the Back of the City: Provincial Life in Lima, Peru." In *Peasants in Cities,* edited by William Mangin. Boston: Houghton Mifflin, 1970.

Druzhinin, N. K., ed. *Usloviia byta rabochikh v dorevoliutsionnoi Rossii* [Conditions of existence of workers in prerevolutionary Russia]. Moscow, 1958.

Dunn, Stephen, and Dunn, Ethyl. *The Peasants of Central Russia.* New York: Holt, Rinehart & Winston, 1967.

El'nitskii, A. E. *Pervye shagi rabochego dvizheniia v Rossii* [First steps of the workers' movement in Russia]. Berlin, n.d.

Emmons, Terrence. *The Russian Landed Gentry and the Peasant Emancipation of 1861.* Cambridge: Cambridge University Press, 1968.

Fanon, Frantz. *The Wretched of the Earth.* New York: Grove, 1966.

Fay, C. R. *Cooperation at Home and Abroad.* London, 1908.

Fenin, A. I. *Vospominaniia inzhenera: K istorii obshchestvennogo i khoziaistvennogo razvitiia Rossii, 1883-1906* [Reminiscences of an engineer: Toward a history of the social and economic development of Russia]. Prague, 1938.

Field, Daniel. *Rebels in the Name of the Tsar.* Boston: Houghton Mifflin, 1976.

Gavlin, M. L. "Rol' tsentra i okrain Rossiiskoi imperii v formirovanii krupnoi moskovskoi burzhuazii v poreformennyi period" [The role of the center and periphery of the Russian empire in the formation of the big bourgeoisie in the postreform period]. *Istoricheskie zapiski* 92 (1973):336-55.

Gerschenkron, Alexander. "The Rate of Industrial Growth in Russia Since 1885." *The Tasks of Economic History* 7 (1947):144-57.

Gerschenkron, Alexander. *Economic Backwardness in Historical Perspective.* Cambridge: Harvard University Press, 1962.

Gerschenkron, Alexander. "Agrarian Policies and Industrialization: Russia, 1861-1917." In *Cambridge Economic History of Europe,* vol. 6, pt. 2, edited by H. J. Habbakuk and M. Postan. Cambridge: Cambridge University Press, 1965.

Gerschenkron, Alexander. *Europe in the Russian Mirror.* Cambridge: Cambridge University Press, 1970.

Giddens, Anthony. *The Class Structure of Advanced Societies.* London: Hutchinson University Library, 1973.

Giffin, Frederick C. "The Prohibition of Night Work for Women and Young Persons: The Russian Factory Law of June 3, 1885." *Canadian Slavic Studies* 2 (1969): 208-18.

Gindin, I. F. "Russkaia burzhuaziia v period kapitalizma: Ee razvitie i osobennosti" [The Russian bourgeoisie in the period of capitalism: Its development and peculiarities]. *Istoriia SSSR,* part 1, March-April 1963, pp. 57-80; part 2, May-June 1963, pp. 37-60.

Gliksman, Jerzy G. "The Russian Urban Worker: From Serf to Proletarian."

In *The Transformation of Russian Society*, edited by Cyril Black. Cambridge: Harvard University Press, 1960, pp. 311-23.

Goffman, Erving, *Asylums*. Chicago: Aldine, 1962.

Golikov, A. G. "Obrazovanie monopolisticheskogo ob'edineniia 'Kolomna-Sormovo'" [The formation of the monopolistic amalgamation 'Kolomna-Sormovo']. *Vestnik Moskovskogo Universiteta, Seriia 9 (Istoriia)*, [Bulletin of Moscow University: Historical Series 9], 1971, no. 5, pp. 74-87.

Goren, Arthur A. *New York Jews and the Quest for Community*. New York: Columbia University Press, 1970.

Gorki, Maxim. *Fragments from My Diary*. Translated by Moura Budberg. New York: Praeger, 1972.

Gor'kii, Maksim [Gorki]. *Mat'* [Mother]. New York: M. Maizel', 1919.

Grigor'ev, V. N. *Pereselenie krest'ian Riazanskoi gubernii* [Resettlement of peasants from Riazan' province]. Moscow, 1886.

Grigor'ev, V. N., ed. *Smertnost' naseleniia goroda Moskvy, 1872-1889 g.* [Mortality of the population of the city of Moscow, 1872-1889]. Moscow, 1891.

Grinevich, V., and Kogan, M. *Professional'noe dvizhenie rabochikh v Rossii* [The trade-union movement in Russia]. Saint Petersburg, 1908.

Gudov, Ivan. *Sud'ba rabochego* [A worker's destiny]. 2d ed., rev. Moscow, 1974.

Gvozdev, S. *Zapiski fabrichnogo inspektora, 1894-1906* [Notes of a factory inspector]. 2d ed. Moscow and Leningrad, 1925.

Habbakuk, H. J. "Family Structure and Economic Change in Nineteenth-Century Europe." *Journal of Economic History* 15 (1955): 1-12.

Haimson, Leopold. "The Problem of Social Stability in Urban Russia, 1905-1914." *Slavic Review* 23 (1964): 619-42; 24 (1965):1-22.

Hajnal, J. "European Marriage Patterns in Perspective." In *Population in History*, edited by D. V. Glass and D. E. C. Eversley. London: Arnold, 1965.

Hamm, Michael, ed. *The City in Russian History*. Lexington: University of Kentucky Press, 1976.

Haxthausen, August von. *The Russian Empire: Its People, Institutions and Resources*. 2 vols. Translated by Robert Farie. 1856. Reprint. New York, Arno Press, 1970.

Ianzhul, I. I. *Fabrichnyi byt Moskovskoi gubernii: Otchet za 1882-1883 fabrichnogo inspektora nad zaniatiiami maloletnikh rabochikh Moskovskogo okruga* [Factory life in Moscow province: Report of a factory inspector on the employment of minors in Moscow district, 1882-1883]. Saint Petersburg, 1884.

Ianzhul, I. I. *Ocherki i issledovaniia: Sbornik statei po voprosam narodnogo khoziaistva, politiki, i zakonodatel'stva* [Essays and studies: A collection of articles on questions of economics, politics, and legislation]. 2 vols. Moscow, 1884.

Ianzhul, I. I. *Moskovskii fabrichnyi okrug: Otchet za 1885 g. fabrichnogo*

inspektora [Moscow factory district: Factory inspector's report for 1885].
Saint Petersburg, 1886.

"Istoki professional'nogo dvizheniia v Rossii" [Sources of the trade-union
movement in Russia]. *Materialy po istorii professional'nogo dvizheniia v
Rossii* [Materials on the history of the trade-union movement in Russia]
2 (1924):3-50.

Itkin, M. L. "Bibliografiia po istorii proletariata Rossii" [A bibliography
on the history of the proletariat of Russia]. *Istoriia SSSR*, September-
October 1961, pp. 182-87.

Ivanov, L. M. "Sostoianie i zadachi izucheniia istorii proletariata Rossii"
[The present state and tasks for studying the history of the proletariat
of Russia]. *Voprosy istorii*, March 1960, pp. 50-74.

Ivanov, L. M. "Izuchenie istorii proletariata Rossii—Vazhneishaia zadacha
sovetskikh istorikov" [Studying the history of the proletariat of Russia—
The most important task of Soviet historians]. In *Sovetskaia istoricheskaia
nauka ot XX k XXII s'ezdu KPSS: Sbornik statei* [Soviet historical science
from the 20th to the 22nd congress of the CPSU: A collection of articles],
edited by N. M. Druzhinin. Moscow, 1962.

Ivanov, L. M., ed. *Bol'shevistskaia pechat' i rabochii klass Rossii v gody
revoliutsionnogo pod'ema, 1910-1914* [The Bolshevik press and the
working class in the years of revolutionary upsurge]. Moscow, 1965.

Ivanov, L. M., ed. *Rabochii klass i rabochee dvizhenie (1861-1917): Sbornik*
[The working class and the worker's movement (1861-1917): A collec-
tion]. Moscow, 1966.

Ivanov, L. M., ed. *Rossiiskii proletariat: Oblik, bor'ba, gegemoniia* [The
Russian proletariat: Outlook, struggle, hegemony]. Moscow, 1970.

Jansen, C. J., ed. *Readings in the Sociology of Migration.* Oxford: Pergamon,
1970.

Johnson, Robert Eugene. "The Nature of the Russian Working Class: Social
Characteristics of the Moscow Industrial Region, 1880-1900." Ph.D. dissertation, Cornell University, 1975.

Johnson, Robert Eugene "Peasant Migration and the Russian Working Class:
Moscow at the End of the Nineteenth Century." *Slavic Review* 35 (1976):
652-64.

Johnson, Robert Eugene "Strikes in Moscow, 1880-1900." *Russian History*
5 (1978).

Kabanov, P., Erman, R., Kuznetsov, N., and Ushakov, A. *Ocherki istorii
rossiiskogo proletariata (1861-1917)* [An outline of the history of the
Russian proletariat (1861-1917)]. Moscow, 1963.

Kahan, Arcadius. "The 'Hereditary Workers' Hypothesis and the Development of a Factory Labor Force in 18th and 19th Century Russia." In *Education and Economic Development*, edited by C. A. Anderson and M. J.
Bowman. Chicago: Aldine, 1965.

Karzhanskii, N. S. *Moskovskii tkach Petr Alekseev* [The Moscow weaver
Peter Alekseev]. Moscow, 1954.

Bibliography

Katelin, A. "Brodiachaia Rus'" [Itinerant Russia]. *Severnyi vestnik* [Northern herald], 1894, no. 4, pp. 1-15.

Kazakevich, R. A. *Sotsial-demokraticheskie organizatsii Peterburga kontsa 80kh-nachala 90kh godov* [Social Democratic organizations of Petersburg at the end of the '80s and beginning of the '90s]. Leningrad, 1960.

Kazantsev, B. N. *Rabochie Moskvy i Moskovskoi gubernii v seredine XIX veka* [Workers of Moscow and Moscow province at the middle of the 19th century]. Moscow, 1976.

Keep, J. L. H. *The Rise of Social Democracy in Russia.* Oxford: Clarendon, 1963.

Kharitonova, Iu., and Shcherbakov, D. *Krest'ianskoe dvizhenie v Kaluzhskoi gubernii (1861-1917 gg.)* [The peasant movement in Kaluga province]. Kaluga, 1961.

Khromov, P. A. *Ekonomicheskoe razvitie Rossii v XIX-XX vekakh* [Economic development of Russia in the 19th and 20th centuries]. Moscow, 1950.

Kirianov, Iu. N., and Pronina, P. V., eds. *Oblik proletariata Rossii: Bibliografiia* [The outlook of the proletariat of Russia: A bibliography]. Moscow, 1967.

Koltsev, D. [B. A. Ginsburg]. "Rabochie v 1890-1904 gg." [Workers in 1894-1904]. In *Obshchestvennoe dvizhenie v Rossii v nachale XX veka* [The social movement in Russia at the beginning of the 20th century], edited by L. Martov, P. Maslov, G. Plekhanov, A. Potresov. Saint Petersburg, 1909.

Kondrat'ev, V. A., and Nevzorov, V. I., eds. *Iz istorii fabrik i zavodov Moskvy i Moskovskoi gubernii (konets XVIII-nachalo XX v.): Obzor dokumentov Tsentral'nogo Gosudarstvennogo Arkhiva goroda Moskvy* [From the history of factories and plants of Moscow and Moscow province: An outline of documents of the Central State Archive of the city of Moscow]. Moscow, 1968.

Kostomarov, G. D., ed. *Moskva v trekh revoliutsiiakh: Vospominaniia, ocherki, rasskazy* [Moscow in three revolutions: Recollections, essays, tales]. Moscow, 1959.

Kovalevskii, V. I., and Langovoi, N. P., eds. *Fabrichno-zavodskaia promyshlennost' i torgovlia Rossii* [Factory-and-works industry and trade in Russia]. 2d rev. ed. Saint Petersburg, 1896.

Koz'minykh-Lanin, I. M. *Semeinyi sostav fabrichno-zavodskikh rabochikh Moskovskoi gubernii* [Family composition of factory-and-plant workers of Moscow province]. Moscow, 1914.

Kruze, E. E. *Peterburgskie rabochie v 1912-1914 gg.* [Petersburg workers in 1912-1914]. Leningrad, 1961.

Kurkin, I. I. *Statistika dvizheniia naseleniia v Moskovskoi gubernii v 1883-1897 gg.* [Statistics on population movement in Moscow province in 1883-1897]. Sbornik statisticheskikh svedenii po Moskovskoi gubernii, Otdel sanitarnoi statistiki [Collection of statistical information on Moscow province, sanitary division], vol. 6, sec. 6. Moscow, 1902.

Landes, David S. *The Unbound Prometheus: Technological Change and Industrial Development in Western Europe from 1750 to the Present.* Cambridge: Cambridge University Press, 1969.

Lapitskaia, S. *Byt rabochikh Trekhgornoi manufaktury* [Everyday life of workers of the Trekhgornaia manufactory]. Moscow, 1935.

Laslett, Peter, ed. *Household and Family in Past Time.* Cambridge: Cambridge University Press, 1972.

Laverychev, V. Ia. *Krupnaia burzhuaziia v poreformennoi Rossii, 1861–1900* [The big bourgeoisie in postreform Russia]. Moscow, 1974.

Lenin, V. I. *The Development of Capitalism in Russia.* Moscow. Progress, 1960.

Lenin, V. I. "Days of Bloodshed in Moscow." *Collected Works,* vol. 7. Moscow: Foreign Languages Publishing House, 1962.

Levine, David. "The Demographic Implications of Rural Industrialization: A Family Reconstitution Study of Shepshed, Leicestershire, 1600-1850." *Social History,* no. 2 (1976): 177-96.

Listok Sankt-Peterburgskogo otdeleniia (Moskovskogo) komiteta o sel'skikh, ssudo-sberegatel'nykh i promyshlennykh tovarishchestvakh [Leaflet of the Saint Petersburg division of the Moscow committee on rural, savings-and-loan, and industrial associations]. Saint Petersburg, 1881-87.

Litvak, B. G. "Krest'ianskoe dvizhenie v Rossii v 1861-1869 gg." [The peasant movement in Russia in 1861-1869]. *Voprosy istorii,* November 1965, pp. 166-69.

Litvak, B. G. *Russkaia derevnia v reforme 1861 goda* [The Russian countryside in the reform of 1861]. Moscow, 1972.

Litvinov-Falinskii, V. P. *Fabrichnoe zakonodatel'stvo i fabrichnaia inspektsiia v Rossii* [Factory legislation and the factory inspectorate in Russia]. Saint Petersburg, 1900.

Livshits, R. S. *Razmeshchenie promyshlennosti v dorevoliutsionnoi Rossii* [The territorial distribution of industry in prerevolutionary Russia]. Moscow, 1955.

Lokhtin, Petr. *Bezzemel'nyi proletariat v Rossii* [The landless proletariat in Russia]. Moscow, 1905.

Lyashchenko, P. I. [Liashchenko]. *History of the National Economy of Russia.* Translated by L. M. Herman. New York: Macmillan, 1949.

McKay, John P. *Pioneers for Profit: Foreign Entrepreneurship and Russian Industrialization, 1885-1913.* Chicago: University of Chicago Press, 1970.

Markov, A. *Na Presne 30 let tomu nazad* [At Presnia 30 years ago]. Moscow, 1926.

Martynov, I. *Gosudarstvennyi russkii narodnyi khor imeni Piatnitskogo* [The Piatnitskii Russian state folk chorus]. 2d ed., rev. Moscow, 1953.

Meshalin, I. V. *Tekstil'naia promyshlennost' krest'ian Moskovskoi gubernii v XVIII i pervoi polovine XIX veka* [The textile industry of peasants in Moscow province in the 18th and the first half of the 19th centuries]. Moscow and Leningrad, 1950.

Ministerstvo Finansov, Departament Torgovli i Manufaktur [Ministry of

Finance, Department of Trade and Manufactures]. *Fabrichno-zavodskaia promyshlennost' i torgovlia Rossii* [Factory-and-plant industry and trade of Russia]. 2d ed. Saint Petersburg, 1896.

Ministerstvo Finansov, Departament Torgovli i Manufaktur [Ministry of Finance, Department of Trade and Manufactures] *Prodolzhitel'nost' rabochego dnia i zarabotnaia plata rabochikh* [The length of the working day and wages of workers]. Saint Petersburg, 1896.

Ministerstvo Finansov [Ministry of Finance]. *Spisok fabrik i zavodov Evropeiskoi Rossii za 1900–1903* [A list of factories and plants in European Russia]. Saint Petersburg, 1903.

Mitskevich, S. I., ed. *Na zare rabochego dvizheniia v Moskve: Vospominaniia uchastnikov Moskovskogo Rabochego Soiuza* [At the dawn of the workers' movement in Moscow: Recollections of participants in the Moscow Workers' Union]. Moscow, 1932.

Mitskevich, S. I. *Na grani dvukh epokh* [On the border of two epochs]. Moscow, 1937.

Mitskevich, S. I. *Revoliutsionnaia Moskva, 1888–1905* [Revolutionary Moscow, 1888–1905]. Moscow, 1940.

Mitskevich, S. I., and Miliutin, N. P., eds. *Literatura Moskovskogo Rabochego Soiuza* [Literature of the Moscow Workers' Union]. Moscow, 1930.

Moiseenko, P. A. *Vospominaniia starogo revoliutsionera* [Recollections of an old revolutionist]. 2d ed., rev. Moscow, 1966.

Moscow, Gorodskaia uprava, Statisticheskii komitet [Municipal administration, Statistical committee]. *Glavneishie predvaritel'nye dannye perepisi goroda Moskvy, 31 ianvaria 1902 g.* [Main preliminary data of the census of the city of Moscow, January 31, 1902]. Nos. 1–6. Moscow, 1902–7.

Moscow, Gorodskaia uprava, Statisticheskii otdel [Municipal administration, Statistical division]. *Smertnost' naseleniia goroda Moskvy, 1872–1889 gg.* [Mortality of the population of Moscow city, 1872–1889]. Moscow, 1891.

Moscow, Stolichnyi i gubernskii statisticheskii komitet [Metropolitan and provincial statistical committee]. *Statisticheskie svedeniia o zhiteliakh goroda Moskvy: Po perepisi 12 dekabria 1871 g.* [Statistical data on the occupants of the city of Moscow: According to the census of December 12, 1871]. Moscow, 1874.

Munting, R. "Outside Earnings in the Russian Peasant Farm: the Case of Tula Province, 1900 to 1917," *Journal of Peasant Studies* 3 (1976):428–46.

Nechkina, M. V., ed. *Iz istorii rabochego klassa i revoliutsionnogo dvizheniia (Pamiati akademika A. M. Pankratovoi): Sbornik statei* [From the history of the working class and the revolutionary movement: A collection of articles (In memory of academician A. M. Pankratova)]. Moscow, 1958.

"Neskol'ko dannykh o moskovskikh koechno-kamorochnykh kvartirakh" [Some data on Moscow flop-houses]. *Izvestiia Moskovskoi Gorodskoi Dumy* [Proceedings of the Moscow City Duma], April 1899, no. 1, pt. 2, pp. 1–21.

Nifontov, N. S. "Formirovanie klassov burzhuaznogo obshchestva v russkom gorode vtoroi poloviny XIX v." [Formation of the classes of bourgeois society in Russian cities in the second half of the 19th century]. *Istoricheskie zapiski* 54 (1955): 239-50.

Norman, Gerald. *All the Russias*. London, 1902.

"Obshchestvo vzaimopomoshchi rabochikh mekhanicheskikh proizvodstv v Moskve" [The aid society of workers in mechanical production in Moscow]. *Narodnoe khoziaistvo* [National economy], 1901, no. 6, pp. 162-65.

Orlov, P. A., comp. *Ukazatel' fabrik i zavodov Evropeiskoi Rossii s Tsarstvom Pol'skim i Vel. kn. Finliandskim: Materialy k fabrichno-zavodskoi statistike* [A directory of factories and plants in European Russia including the Kingdom of Poland and the Duchy of Finland: Materials for the statistics of factories and plants]. Saint Petersburg, 1881.

Orlov. P. A., and Buganov, S. G., comps. *Ukazatel' fabrik i zavodov Evropeiskoi Rossii. Materialy dlia fabrichno-zavodskoi statistiki (Po svedeniiam za 1890 god)* [A directory of factories and plants in European Russia. Materials for the statistics of factories and plants (According to information for 1890)]. Saint Petersburg, 1894.

Otchet postoiannoi Kommissii po delam potrebitel'nykh obshchestv za 1901-1905 gg. i svod statisticheskikh svedenii o deiatel'nosti potrebitel'nykh obshchestv v Rossii v 1900-1904 gg. [Report of the permanent commission on cooperative societies and summary of statistical evidence on the activities of cooperative societies in Russia]. Saint Petersburg, 1902-7.

Ovsiankin, V. A., ed. *Istoriia rabochego klassa Leningrada* [History of the working class of Leningrad]. 2 vols. Leningrad, 1962-63.

Owen, Thomas C. "The Moscow Merchants and the Public Press, 1858-1868." *Jahrbücher für Geschichte Osteuropas* 23 (1975):26-38.

Ozerov, I. Kh. *Obshchestva potrebitelei: Istoricheskii ocherk ikh razvitiia v Zapadnoi Evrope, Amerike i Rossii* [Consumer cooperatives: A historical sketch of their development in Western Europe, America, and Russia]. Saint Petersburg, 1900.

Ozerov, I. Kh. *Politika po rabochemu voprosu* [Policy on the worker question]. Saint Petersburg, 1906.

Pankratova, A. M. "Proletarizatsiia krest'ianstva i ee rol' v formirovanii promyshlennogo proletariata Rossii (60-90e gg. XIX v.)" [Proletarianization of the peasantry and its role in the formation of an industrial proletariat in Russia (1860s-1890s)]. *Istoricheskie zapiski* 54 (1955):194-220.

Pankratova, A. M. *Formirovanie proletariata v Rossii (XVII-XVIII vv.)* [Formation of the proletariat in Russia (17th-18th centuries)]. Moscow, 1963.

Pankratova, A. M., ed. *Istoriko-bytovye ekspeditsii 1949-1950: Materialy k voprosu rassloeniia krest'ianstva i formirovaniia proletariata v Rossii kontsa XIX-nachala XX veka* [Expeditions into the history of everyday life: Materials on the question of stratification of the peasantry and the formation of the proletariat in Russia at the end of the 19th century and beginning of the 20th century]. Trudy Gosudarstvennogo Istoricheskogo Muzeia, no. 23. Moscow, 1953.

Pavlov, F. P. *Za desiat' let praktiki* [Ten years in practice]. Moscow, 1901.

Pavlovskii, George. *Agricultural Russia on the Eve of the Revolution.* London, 1930.

Pazhitnov, K. A. *Polozhenie rabochego klassa v Rossii* [The condition of the working class in Russia]. 3d ed., rev. 3 vols. Leningrad, 1924.

Pazhitnov, K. A. "Rabochie arteli" [Worker artels]. *Arkhiv istorii truda v Rossii* [Archive of the history of labor in Russia] 15 (1924):54-74.

Pazhitnov, K. A. *Ocherki istorii tekstil'noi promyshlennosti dorevoliutsionnoi Rossii: Sherstianaia promyshlennost'* [An outline of the history of the textile industry in Russia: Woolen industry]. Moscow, 1955.

Pazhitnov, K. A. *Ocherki istorii tekstil'noi promyshlennosti dorevoliutsionnoi Rossii: Khlopchatobumazhnaia, l'no-pen'kovaia i shelkovaia promyshlennost'* [An outline of the history of the textile industry of prerevolutionary Russia: Cotton, linen, and silk industries]. Moscow, 1958.

Pekarskii, E. K. "Rabochii P. Alekseev (iz vospominanii)" [The worker P. Alekseev (recollections)]. *Byloe*, 1922, no. 19, pp. 80-86.

Perepis' Moskvy 1882 goda [Census of Moscow, 1882]. Nos. 1-3. Moscow, 1885-1886.

Perepis' Moskvy 1902 goda [Census of Moscow, 1902]. Vol. 1, pts. 1-3. Moscow, 1904-6.

Peshekhonov, A. V. "Krest'iane i rabochie v ikh vzaimnykh otnosheniiakh" [Peasants and workers in their mutual relations]. *Russkoe bogatstvo*, 1898, no. 8, pp. 173-95; 1898, no. 9. pp. 54-82.

Peskov, P. A. *Sanitarnoe issledovanie fabrik po obrabotke voloknistykh veshchestv v gorode Moskve* [A sanitary investigation of factories producing fibrous products in the city of Moscow], 2 pts., Trudy kommissii, uchrezhdennoi g. Moskovskim General-Gubernatorom, kn. V. A. Dolgorukovym, dlia osmotra fabrik i zavodov v Moskve [Proceedings of the commission, established by the Governor-General of Moscow, Prince V. A. Dolgorukov, to survey factories and plants in Moscow]. Moscow, 1882.

Petersen, Anita Bredahl. "The Development of Cooperative Credit in Rural Russia, 1871-1914." Ph.D. dissertation, Cornell University, 1973.

Phillips, Walter. "Technological Levels and Labor Resistance to Change in the Course of Industrialization." *Economic Development and Cultural Change* 11 (1963): 257-66.

Pintner, Walter McKenzie. *Russian Economic Policy under Nicholas I.* Ithaca, N.Y.: Cornell University Press, 1967.

Pipes, Richard. *Social Democracy and the St. Petersburg Labor Movement, 1885-1897.* Cambridge: Harvard University Press, 1963.

Pisani, Lawrence Frank. *The Italian in America.* New York: Exposition Press, 1957.

Plekhanov, G. V. *Selected Philosophical Works.* Vol. 1. Moscow: Foreign Languages Publishing House, 1961.

Plotnicov, Leonard. "Rural-Urban Communications in Contemporary Nigeria: The Persistence of Traditional Social Institutions." In *The Passing of Tribal Man in Africa*, edited by P. Gutkind. Leiden: Brill, 1970.

Pogozhev, A. V. *Uchet chislennosti i sostava rabochikh v Rossii* [The number and composition of workers in Russia]. Saint Petersburg, 1906.

Poida, D. P. "Krest'ianskoe dvizhenie v Rossii v 1881-1889 gg." [The peasant movement in Russia, 1881-1889]. *Voprosy istorii*, January-February 1963, pp. 119-20.

Polevoi, Iu. Z. *Iz istorii Moskovskoi organizatsii VKP(b), 1894-1904* [From the history of the Moscow organization of the Communist Party]. Moscow, 1947.

Polevoi, Iu. Z. *Zarozhdenie marksizma v Rossii* [The birth of Marxism in Russia]. Moscow, 1959.

Pollard, Sidney. "Factory Discipline in the Industrial Revolution." *Economic History Review*, 2nd ser. 16 (1963-64):254-71.

Polnoe sobranie zakonov Rossiiskoi imperii [Complete law code of the Russian empire]. Saint Petersburg, 1830-1916.

Polnyi svod zakonov o krest'ianakh (Izdanie neofitsial'noe) [A complete collection of laws on peasants (An unofficial publication)]. Saint Petersburg, 1908.

Popova, E., ed. *Rabochie o 1905 gode v Moskovskoi gubernii: Sbornik vospominanii* [Workers in 1905 in Moscow province: A collection of recollections]. Moscow, 1926.

Portal, Roger. "Industriels moscovites: le secteur cotonnier (1861-1914)." *Cahiers du monde russee et soviétique* 4 (1963):5-46.

Portal, Roger. "The Industrialization of Russia." In *Cambridge Economic History of Europe*, vol. 6, pt. 2, edited by H. J. Habbakuk and M. Postan. Cambridge: Cambridge University Press, 1965.

"Poslednie perepisi Peterburga i Moskvy" [The latest censuses of Saint Petersburg and Moscow]. *Izvestiia Moskovskoi Gorodskoi Dumy* [Proceedings of the Moscow City Duma], 1887, nos. 6-7, sec. 4, pp. 99-150.

Prokhorovskaia Trekhgornaia manufaktura [The Prokhorov Trekhgornaia manufactory]. Moscow, 1900.

Prokopovich, S. N. "K bibliografii stachechnogo dvizheniia v Rossii" [Toward a bibliography of the strike movement in Russia]. *Trudy Vol'nogo Ekonomicheskogo Obshchestva za 1903* [Proceedings of the Free Economic Society for 1903]. Saint Petersburg, 1903.

Prokopovich, S. N. *K rabochemu voprosu v Rossii* [The worker question in Russia]. Saint Petersburg, 1905.

Prokopovich, S. N. "Krest'ianstvo i poreformennaia fabrika" [The peasantry and the postreform factory]. In *Velikaia reforma* [The great reform], vol. 6, edited by A. K. Dzhivelegov, S. P. Mel'gunov, and V. I. Picheta. Moscow, 1911.

Proletariat Rossii na puti k oktiabriu 1917 goda: Oblik, bor'ba, gegemoniia: Materialy k nauchnoi sessii po istorii proletariata, posviashchennoi 50-letiiu Velikogo Oktiabria [The proletariat of Russia on the road to 1917: Outlook, struggle, hegemony: Materials from a scientific session on the history of the proletariat, commemorating the 50th anniversary of Great October]. Pts. 1-2. Odessa, 1967.

Pronina, G. V. "Iz istorii rabochego dvizheniia v Moskve i Moskovskoi gubernii v pervoi polovine 90kh godov XIX veka" [From the history of the workers' movement in Moscow and Moscow province in the first half of the 1890s]. *Uchenye zapiski Moskovskogo gosudarstvennogo pedagogicheskogo instituta im. Lenina* [Scholarly transactions of the Lenin state pedagogical institute in Moscow] 187 (1962):145-86.

Rabochee dvizhenie v Rossii v XIX veke: Sbornik dokumentov i materialov [The workers' movement in Russia in the 19th century: A collection of documents and materials]. Moscow and Leningrad, 1950-63. The editor in chief of volumes 1-3 was A. M. Pankratova; of volume 4, L. M. Ivanov.

Raeff, Marc. *Origins of the Russian Intelligentsia*. New York: Harcourt Brace Jovanovich, 1966.

Ransel, David, ed. *The Family in Imperial Russia*. Champaign and Urbana: University of Illinois Press, 1978.

Rashin, A. G. "Dinamika chislennosti i protsessy formirovaniia gorodskogo naseleniia Rossii v XIX-nachale XX vv." [Numerical growth and processes of formation of the urban population of Russia in the 19th and early 20th centuries]. *Istoricheskie zapiski* 34 (1950):32-82.

Rashin, A. G. *Naselenie Rossii za 100 let, 1811-1913* [The population of Russia over 100 years 1811-1913]. Moscow, 1956.

Rashin, A. G. *Formirovanie rabochego klassa Rossii* [Formation of the working class of Russia]. Moscow, 1958.

Redford, Arthur. *Labour Migration in England, 1800-1850*. 2d ed., rev. Manchester: Manchester University Press, 1964.

Reitlinger, N. A., ed. *Obzor polozheniia i deiatel'nosti potrebitel'nykh obshchestv v Rossii po dannym 1897 g.* [An outline of the position and activity of consumer societies in Russia according to data from 1897]. Saint Petersburg, 1899.

Rimlinger, Gaston V. "Autocracy and the Factory Order in Early Russian Industrialization." *Journal of Economic History* 20 (1960): 67-92.

Rimlinger, Gaston V. "The Management of Labor Protest in Tsarist Russia 1870-1905." *International Review of Social History* 5 (1960):226-48.

Rimlinger, Gaston V. "The Expansion of the Labor Market in Capitalist Russia." *Journal of Economic History* 21 (1961):208-15.

Robbins, Richard. *Famine in Russia, 1891-92*. New York: Columbia University Press, 1975.

Robinson, G. T. *Rural Russia under the Old Regime*. 1932. Reprint. Berkeley and Los Angeles: University of California Press, 1969.

Rosovsky, Henry. "The Serf Entrepreneur in Russia." *Explorations in Entrepreneurial History* 6 (1954): pp. 207-33.

Rozhkova, M. K. "Promyshlennost' Moskvy v pervoi chetverti XIX veka" [Industry of Moscow in the first quarter of the 19th century]. *Voprosy istorii*, November-December 1946, pp. 89-103.

Rozhkova, M. K. "Fabrichnaia promyshlennost' i promysly krest'ian v 60-70kh godakh XIX veka" [Factory industry and peasant crafts in the 1860s-1870s]. In *Problemy sotsial'no-ekonomicheskoi istorii Rossii* [Problems in the social-economic history of Russia] edited by L. M. Ivanov. Moscow, 1971, pp. 195-217.

Rozhkova, M. K., ed. *Ocherki ekonomicheskoi istorii Rossii pervoi poloviny XIX veka* [Essays in the economic history of Russia in the first half of the 19th century]. Moscow, 1959.

Ryndziunskii, P. G. *Krest'ianskaia promyshlennost' v poreformennoi Rossii* [Peasant industry in postreform Russia]. Moscow, 1966.

Sbornik materialov ob arteliakh v Rossii [A collection of materials on artels in Russia]. 3 vols. Saint Petersburg, 1873-75.

Sbornik statisticheskikh svedenii po Moskovskoi gubernii, Otdel sanitarnoi statistiki [Collection of statistical information for Moscow province, Division of sanitation statistics]. Vol. 3:

1. Sanitarnoe izsledovanie fabrichnykh zavedenii Klinskogo uezda [Sanitation study of factory enterprises in Klinskii county]. Compiled by F. F. Erisman. Moscow, 1881.
2. Kirpichnogoncharnoe proizvodstvo Moskovskogo uezda: Opyt sanitarno-promyshlennogo izsledovaniia [The brick-and-ceramic industry in Moscow county: An experiment in sanitary-industrial investigation]. Compiled by A. V. Pogozhev. Moscow, 1881.
3. Sanitarnoe izsledovanie fabrichnykh zavedenii Vereiskogo i Ruzskogo uezda [Sanitation study of factory enterprises in Vereiskii and Ruzskii counties]. Compiled by A. V. Pogozhev. Moscow, 1882.
4. The same, Moskovskii county. Pt. 1. Compiled by F. F. Erisman. Moscow, 1882.
5. The same, Moskovskii county. Pt. 2. Compiled by F. F. Erisman. Moscow, 1882.
6. The same, Mozhaiskii, Volokolamskii, and Zvenigorodskii counties. Compiled by A. V. Pogozhev. Moscow, 1882.
7. The same, Dmitrovskii county. Compiled by A. V. Pogozhev. Moscow, 1883.
8. The same, Podol'skii county. Compiled by E. M. Dement'ev. Moscow, 1883.
9. The same, Moskovskii county. Pt. 3. Compiled by F. F. Erisman. Moscow, 1883.
10. The same, Moskovskii county. Pt. 4. Compiled by F. F. Erisman. Moscow, 1884.
11. The same, Bogorodskii county. Pt. 1. Compiled by A. V. Pogozhev. Moscow, 1885.
12. The same, Moskovskii county. Pt. 5. Compiled by F. F. Erisman. Moscow, 1885.
13. The same, Kolomenskii county. Compiled by E. M. Dement'ev Moscow, 1885.
14. The same, Bogorodskii county. Pt. 2. Compiled by A. V. Pogozhev. Moscow, 1886.

15. The same, Serpukhovskii county. Pt. 1. Compiled by E. M. Dement'ev. Moscow, 1886.
16. The same, Bogorodskii county. Pt. 3. Compiled by A. V. Pogozhev, Moscow, 1888.
17. The same, Bogorodskii county. Pt. 4. Compiled by A. V. Pogozhev. Moscow, 1892.

Sbornik statisticheskikh svedenii po Moskovskoi gubernii, Otdel sanitarnoi statistiki [Collection of statistical information for Moscow province, Division of sanitation statistics]. Vol. 4, Pts. 1-2: Obshchaia svodka po sanitarnym izsledovaniiam fabrichnykh zavedenii Moskovskoi gubernii za 1879-1885 gg. [General summary of sanitation studies of factory enterprises in Moscow province]. Edited by F. F. Erisman and E. M. Dement'ev. Moscow, 1890-93.

Schneiderman, Jeremiah. "The Tsarist Government and the Labor Movement: The Zubatovshchina." Ph.D. dissertation, University of California, Berkeley, 1966.

Schneiderman. Jeremiah. *Sergei Zubatov and Revolutionary Marxism.* Ithaca, N.Y.: Cornell University Press, 1976.

Schofer, Lawrence. *The Formation of a Modern Labor Force: Upper Silesia, 1865-1914.* Berkeley and Los Angeles: University of California Press, 1974.

Schulze-Gaevernitz, Gerhart von. *Ocherki obshchestvennogo khoziaistva i ekonomicheskoi politiki Rossii* [Studies in Russia's social economy and economic policy]. (Translated from *Volkswirtschaftliche Studien aus Russland.* Leipzig, 1899.) Saint Petersburg, 1901.

Semanov, S. N. *Peterburgskie rabochie nakanune pervoi russkoi revoliutsii* [Petersburg workers on the eve of the first Russian revolution]. Moscow and Leningrad, 1966.

Semeniuk, G. F. "Polozhenie rabochego klassa v tekstil'noi promyshlennosti Moskovskoi gubernii v 90e gody XIX v." [The condition of the working class in the textile industry of Moscow province in the 1890s]. *Uchenye zapiski Moskovskogo oblastnogo pedagogicheskogo instituta im. N. K. Krupskoi* [Scholarly transactions of the N. K. Krupskaia Moscow regional pedagogical institute] 127 (1963): 141-74.

Semenov Tian'-Shanskii, V. P. *Rossiia: Polnoe geograficheskoe opisanie nashego otechestva* [Russia: A complete geographical description of our native land]. 19 vols. Saint Petersburg, 1899-1913.

Semevskii, V. I. *Krest'iane v tsarstvovanie imperatritsy Ekateriny II* [Peasants during the reign of Empress Catherine II]. Vol. 1. Saint Petersburg, 1903.

Shanin, Teodor. *The Awkward Class.* Oxford: Clarendon, 1972.

Shapiro, A. L., ed. *Sovetskaia istoriografiia klassovoi bor'by i revoliutsionnogo dvizheniia v Rossii* [Soviet historiography of class struggle and the revolutionary movement in Russia]. Leningrad, 1967.

Sher, V. V. *Istoriia professional'nogo dvizheniia rabochikh pechatnogo dela v Moskve* [A history of the trade-union movement of workers in the printing trades in Moscow]. Moscow, 1911.

Shestakov, P. M. *Rabochie na manufakture tovarishchestva "Emil' Tsindel'"* *v Moskve: Statisticheskoe issledovanie* [Workers at the factory of the Emil' Tsindel' company: A statistical investigation]. Moscow, 1900.

Skibnevskii, A. I. *Zhilishcha fabrichno-zavodskikh rabochikh Bogorodskogo uezda* [Living quarters of plant-and-factory workers of Bogorodskii county]. Sbornik statisticheskikh svedenii po Moskovskoi gubernii, Otdel sanitarnoi statistiki [Collection of statistical information for Moscow province, Sanitary section], vol. 8, no. 1, Moscow, 1901.

Sokolov, O. D. "Revoliutsionnaia propaganda sredi fabrichnykh i zavodskikh rabochikh v 70kh godakh XIX veka" [Revolutionary propaganda among plant and factory workers in the 1870s]. In *Iz istorii rabochego klassa i krest'ianstva SSSR* [From the history of the working class and the peasantry of the USSR], edited by M. I. Kim. Moscow, 1959.

Soloukhin, Vladimir. *A Walk in Rural Russia*. London: Hodder & Stoughton, 1966.

Statisticheskii atlas goroda Moskvy [Statistical atlas of the city of Moscow]. 2 vols. Moscow, 1890.

Statisticheskii ezhegodnik Moskovskogo gubernskogo zemstva [Statistical yearbook of the Moscow provincial zemstvo]. Annual (title varies), Moscow, 1886-1910.

Strumilin, S. G. *Ocherki ekonomicheskoi istorii Rossii i SSSR* [Essays in the economic history of Russia and the USSR]. Moscow, 1966.

Svavitskii, A., and Sher, V. *Ocherk polozheniia rabochikh pechatnogo dela v Moskve* [An outline of the condition of workers in the printing trades in Moscow]. Saint Petersburg, 1909.

Sviatlovskii, V. *Professional'noe dvizhenie v Rossii* [The trade-union movement in Russia]. Saint Petersburg, 1907.

Svod zakonov Rossiiskoi imperii [Law code of the Russian Empire]. Saint Petersburg, 1857-1916.

Tegoborski, M. L. de [Tengoborskii]. *Commentaries on the Productive Forces of Russia*. 2 vols. 1855-56. Reprint. New York and London: Johnson Reprint Co., 1972.

Thompson, E. P. *The Making of the English Working Class*. Harmondsworth: Penguin, 1968.

Tkachenko, P. S. *Moskovskoe studenchestvo v obshchestvenno-politicheskoi zhizni Rossii vtoroi poloviny XIX veka* [The Moscow student body in the social-political life of Russia in the second half of the 19th century]. Moscow, 1958.

Totomiants, V. F. "Kooperativnoe dvizhenie v Rossii" [The cooperative movement in Russia]. *Vestnik Evropy*, 1909, no. 11, pp. 81-98.

Totomiants, V. F. *Kooperatsiia v Rossii* [Cooperation in Russia]. Prague, 1922.

Tranter, N. L. *Population and Industrialization*. London: Black, 1973.

Treadgold, Donald W. *The Great Siberian Migration*. Princeton: Princeton University Press, 1957.

Trofimov, A. S. "Rabochee dvizhenie v Moskve i Moskovskoi gubernii vo vtoroi polovine 80kh godov" [The workers' movement in Moscow and Moscow province in the second half of the 1880s]. *Voprosy istorii*, September 1953, pp. 102–11.

Trofimov, A. S. *Rabochee dvizhenie v Rossii, 1861–1894 gg.* [The workers' movement in Russia]. Moscow, 1957.

Tsentral'nyi Statisticheskii Komitet [Central Statistical Committee]. *Pervaia vseobshchaia perepis' naseleniia Rossiiskoi imperii, 1897 g.* [The first general census of the population of the Russian empire]. 89 vols. Saint Petersburg, 1899–1905.

Tsentral'nyi Statisticheskii Komitet [Central Statistical Committee]. *Obshchii svod po imperii rezul'tatov razrabotki dannykh pervoi vseobshchei perepisi naseleniia, proizvedennoi 28 ianvaria 1897 g.* [General empire-wide summary of the results of the first general census of population, January 28, 1897]. Pts. 1–2. Saint Petersburg, 1905.

Tsetlin, L. S. "V Moskve pered II s'ezdom RSDRP" [In Moscow before the second congress of the RSDRP]. *Katorga i ssylka* 114–15 (1935):89–126.

Tugan-Baranovskii, M. I. *The Russian Factory in the 19th Century.* Translated by Arthur Levin and Claora S. Levin. Homewood, Ill.: Irwin, 1970.

Varzar, V. E. *Statisticheskie svedeniia o stachkakh na fabrikakh i zavodakh za desiatiletie 1895–1904 g.* [Statistical data on strikes at factories and plants in the decade 1895–1904]. Saint Petersburg, 1905.

Vasin, I. N. *Sotsial-demokraticheskoe dvizhenie v Moskve (1883–1901 gg.)* [The Social-Democratic movement in Moscow]. Moscow, 1955.

Verner, I. "Zhilishcha bedneishego naseleniia Moskvy" [Living quarters of paupers in Moscow]. *Izvestiia Moskovskoi Gorodskoi Dumy* [Proceedings of the Moscow City Duma], 1902, no. 19, pp. 1–27.

Vilenskaia, E. E. *Revoliutsionnoe podpol'e v Rossii (60-e gody XIX veka)* [The revolutionary underground in Russia (in the 1860s)]. Moscow, 1965.

Volkov, N. "Narodnicheskaia propaganda sredi moskovskikh rabochikh v 1881 g." [Populist propaganda among Moscow workers in 1881]. *Byloe*, St. Petersburg, 1906, no. 2, pp. 174–82.

Volobuev, P. V. "Nereshennye voprosy istorii rabochego klassa nakanune Velikoi Oktiabrskoi Sotsialisticheskoi Revoliutsii" [Unresolved questions in the history of the working class on the eve of the Great October Socialist Revolution]. In *Voprosy istoriografii rabochego klassa SSSR* [Questions in the historiography of the working class of the USSR], edited by M. I. Kim, pp. 69–73. Moscow, 1970.

Von Laue, Theodore. "Factory Inspection under the Witte System." *American Slavic and East European Review* 19 (1960):347–62.

Von Laue, Theodore. "Russian Peasants in the Factory." *Journal of Economic History* 23 (1961):61–80.

Von Laue, Theodore. *Sergei Witte and the Industrialization of Russia.* New York: Columbia University Press, 1963.

Von Laue, Theodore. "Russian Labor between Field and Factory." *California Slavic Studies* 3 (1964):33–66.

Vorozheikin, I. E. "Osnovnye etapy izucheniia istorii Sovetskogo rabochego klassa" [Fundamental stages in the study of the history of the Soviet working class]. *Voprosy istorii*, August 1968, pp. 153-63.

Walkin, Jacob. "The Attitude of the Tsarist Government toward the Labor Problem." *American Slavic and East European Review* 13 (1954):163-84.

Walkin, Jacob. *The Rise of Democracy in Pre-Revolutionary Russia: Political and Social Institutions under the Last Three Tsars*. New York: Praeger, 1962.

Wallerstein, Immanuel. *The Road to Independence: Ghana and the Ivory Coast*. Paris and the Hague: Mouton, 1964.

Weber, Adna. *The Growth of Cities in the Nineteenth Century*. 1899. Reprint. Ithaca, N.Y.: Cornell University Press, 1963.

Weber, Max. *The Protestant Ethic and the Spirit of Capitalism*. Translated by Talcott Parsons. New York: Scribner's, 1958.

Wildman, Allan. *The Making of a Workers' Revolution*. Chicago: University of Chicago Press, 1967.

Williams, Phyllis H. *South Italian Folkways in Europe and America*. 1938. Reprint. New York: Russell & Russell, 1969.

Wolf, Eric. *Peasant Wars of the 20th Century*. New York: Harper & Row, 1969.

Yaney, George L. "Social Stability in Prerevolutionary Russia: A Critical Note." *Slavic Review* 24 (1965):521-27.

Zagoskin, M. N. "Moskva i moskvichi" [Moscow and Muscovites]. In *Ocherki Moskovskoi zhizni* [Outlines of Moscow life], compiled by B. S. Zemenkov. Moscow, 1962.

Zaionchkovskii, P. A. *Otmena krepostnogo prava v Rossii* [The abolition of serfdom in Russia]. 3d ed., rev. Moscow, 1968.

Zaozerskaia, E. I. *Manufaktura pri Petre I* [The manufactory in the reign of Peter I]. Moscow and Leningrad, 1947.

Zelnik, Reginald. *Labor and Society in Tsarist Russia*. Stanford, Calif.: Stanford University Press, 1971.

Zelnik, Reginald E. "Populists and Workers: The First Encounter between Populist Students and Industrial Workers in St. Petersburg, 1871-74." *Soviet Studies* 24 (1972):251-69.

Zelnik, Reginald. "Soviet Materials on Industrial Workers and the Labor Question in the 1870's and 1880's." *Newsletter on European Labor and Working Class History* 2 (1972):13-15.

Zelnik, Reginald. "Russian Workers and the Revolutionary Movement." *Journal of Social History* 6 (1973):214-36.

Zelnik, Reginald. "Russian Bebels: An Introduction to the Memoirs of Semen Kanatchikov and Matvei Fisher." *Russian Review* 35 (1976):249-89, 417-47.

Zhbankov, D. N. *Bab'ia storona* [The women's side]. Kostroma, 1891.

Zherebiat'ev, I. F., comp. *Statisticheskie svedeniia o deiatel'nosti Obshchestv v Rossii za 1897 i 1898 gg. i sravneniia ikh s veliko-britanskimi koopera-*

tivnymi obshchestvami v 1898 g. [Statistical information on the activity of (consumer) societies in Russia in 1897 and 1898 and a comparison with British cooperative societies in 1898]. Saint Petersburg, 1900.

Zlotnikov, M. F. "K voprosu ob izuchenii istorii rabochego klassa i promy-shlennosti" [On the question of studying the history of the working class and industry]. *Katorga i ssylka*, no. 116 (1935), pp. 37-65.

Zlotnikov, M. F. "Ot manufaktury k fabrike" [From manufactory to fac-tory]. *Voprosy istorii*, November-December 1946, pp. 31-48.

Index

A

Abrikosov confectionary factory, 20
age at marriage, 57–59
age distribution: of printers, 48–49; of *sosloviia*, 46–48; of women, 172n13
agitation, 111, 113–14, 132; theory behind, 110
agrarian unrest. *See* unrest, agrarian
agriculture, 39, 66, 171n54. *See also* land holdings, land tenure
Alekseev, Petr, 100–101, 105, 117
archives, 69, 76, 77, 120–23, 170n42, 178n49, 182n49, 189n3n7n11; publications of, see *Rabochee dvizhenie, Krest'ianskoe dvizhenie*
artel' (pl. *arteli:* work crew), 91–92, 177n34, 178n55; employers' role in, 92; as living unit, 72, 92; as work crew, 72, 73, 76
artisans. *See* handcrafts
autocracy, role in industrialization, 11–12. *See also* legislation

B

Babushkin, I. V., 93
bachelorhood, 51, 57
bast matting industry, 70–71, 72
Bendix, Reinhard, 94
Bogorodskii county (of Moscow province), 25, 26, 34, 148
Boie, K. F., 109, 116, 118, 148
Bostanzhoglo tobacco factory, 20
Briansk province, 16
brickmaking industry, 81; hiring patterns of, 35–36, 72, 175n15; loca-

brickmaking industry (*continued*) tion of factories, 26; unrest in, 77–78, 126, 146, 148, 149; *zemliaki* in, 69, 178n56
Bronnitskii county (of Moscow province), 62
Brusnev, M. I., 105–6, 118, 148, 186n19
bunt, buntarstvo (riot, random violence), 125, 153, 159

C

Cabral, Amilcar, 157
capitalism, radicals' perception of, 102, 103
central industrial region, 16–17, 23–24, 31–34, 170n29
Central Workers' Circle (Moscow), 107–9
Central Workers' Circle (Saint Petersburg), 105
ceremonial ties, among *zemliaki,* 75
Chaikovskii circle, 100
chain migration, 74
cheating, in reckoning wages, 83
chemical industry, 20, 26
child labor, 68, 83
child rearing, 53, 66, 172n5
children of workers, 56, 62–65
china industry, 81
choral singing, as peasant tradition, 74
circles, propagandist. See *kruzhki*
city-born workers, 34, 44, 165n5
class consciousness, 5–7, 162, 193n7
"clusters" (nuclei) of *zemliaki,* 76–77